Contents

INTRODUCTION 7

WILD GAME: The Best Eatin' There Is 9

Wild Fowl 11
  Basic Fowl Recipes 12
  Duck 14
  Mourning Dove 25
  Bob-white Quail 33
  Wild Turkey 36
  Marsh Hen 38
  Goose 40
  Pheasant 42

Small Game 43
  Squirrel 43
  Rabbit 46

Furbearers 49
  Raccoon and Opossum 49
  Beaver 51

Large Game 52
  White-tailed Deer 52
  Bear 79

FRESH AND SALTWATER FOODS: The Other Best Eatin' There Is 81

Fresh and Saltwater Fish 82
  Basic Fish Recipes 85
  Freshwater Fish 92
  Catfish Stews 99
  Saltwater Fish 104

Shellfish 115
   Shrimp 115
   Rock Shrimp 127
   Blue Crab 128
   Stone Crab 138
   Northern Clam 139
   Eastern Oyster 142
   Calico Scallop 146
   Seafood Combinations 148

UNUSUAL, BUT STILL GOOD 155

   Snapping Turtle 156
   Bullfrog Legs 157
   Crawfish 159
   Eel 161
   Garfish 162
   Octopus 163
   Squid 164
   Whelk 165
   More Oddities n' Ends 167

WILD PLANTS: Woodland Harvest 171

   Wild Vegetables 172
   Wild Fruits 181
   Nuts 189

COOKIN' FOR THAT OUTDOOR FLAVOR 191

   Outdoor Grilling 192
   Iron Cookware 194
   Smoking 195
   Campfire Cooking 197

YOUR OWN WILD ORIGINALS 201

REFERENCE TABLES 211

REFERENCES 217

ACKNOWLEDGEMENTS 218

INDEX 219

Introduction

Cookbooks from the colonial period show how dependent our grandparents were on food taken from the wild. Lively stories of family dinner fare, especially on holidays or when entertaining guests, reveal another basic fact: Southeasterners love to eat good food, and wild food in particular.

In the 1700s the territory had plenty of wildlife. Many animals we hunt today were also hunted by our ancestors; ducks, doves, quail, wild turkeys, rabbits, squirrels and deer well-supplied the growing settlement towns.

Out of necessity, the colonists learned to use the exotic resources of their new homeland. Thus, Native American, European, Barbadoan and African cooking heritages merged, from which we inherited a highly specialized knowledge of game and seafood preparation.

An integral part of our history is the instruction in woodsmanship, boating, hunting and fishing that has been passed through the generations. A good sportsman or sportswoman not only knows how to stalk game and kill it swiftly, but also knows how to prepare it without waste for the finest of meals.

For those just learning game sports and cookery, this book offers an object lesson in one of the major principles of hunting and fishing and even gathering plants for food: **Use what you take.** Wanton waste is simply not acceptable to the responsible person who learns to respect living things through the challenge of his or her sport.

Also, this cookbook reaffirms the indescribable pleasure that many people feel when eating game or wild foods they have taken and prepared themselves. Not fattened on the farm, butchered at the slaughterhouse, or sold in cellophane packages at the supermarket, these foods are straight from their natural surroundings where they feed and live.

Considering the enormous quantity of cookbooks to be found in bookstores and the recipes packed into mass circulation magazines, one might wonder why we decided to compile another one. There is a reason. Regional cooking is fast approaching extinction when citizens of Montana can buy the same products in the same grocery chain as shoppers in Florida. Gardens have vanished from backyards and become concentrated in huge acreages belonging to international corporations that export all over the world. More people work in industries, live in urban areas, and have less time to hunt and fish for their food. The large majority of cookbooks are now published in big cities outside the Southeast. The recipes are geared toward the homogenized, uniform cuisine of too many Americans. We simply want to complement those books with a Southeastern book, using our native game, fish and plants, and our ways of cooking them.

Like the big-time cookbook editors, we employed a panel of experts to test our recipes. Unlike the big-timers, however, whose staff cooks experiment in a clinically sterile test kitchen, our panel of experts chop, stir, fry and taste on site — right in the swamp, the cabin, the tent, the pit and the home kitchen.

Our simple purpose in this collection is to continue the campfire, the oyster roast, the smoking of venison, the quail dinner, the folk remedy. We aren't really concerned here with calories or economy or even nutrition. We're not turning up our noses at grease or red meat or grits or white flour or cheap wine or fatback or pokeweed or possum. They're all a part of our heritage.

This book is for Southeasterners, a people not too uptight to try a "dash" of this and a "dollop" of that, but particular enough to know that sometimes only one brand name is the right one. It's for those who take the time for scouting the woods and wetlands to bring home quail or duck, for waiting hours on a deer or a turkey, for crabbing, shrimping, fishing. And it's also for those who don't have the means to hunt or fish, but do have access to the meat, and don't want to lose sight of it on the table.

— Nancy Coleman Wooten
— Julie Lumpkin

Wild Game

---

*The Best
Eatin' There Is*

Most people who contemplate preparing or eating wild game for the first time worry excessively about the "gamey" flavor. They go to great lengths to hide the wild taste, overcooking meats at high temperatures or masking it with a multitude of seasonings and stuffings. But they are denying the first principle in game cookery: If properly field dressed, *wild game should taste like wild game.*

Venison tastes like venison. Not chicken, beef or pork. Chicken is the favorite catch-all for the inevitable question, "What does it taste like?" For want of a better comparison, frog legs, snapping turtle, quail and rabbit all taste "a little like chicken." But face it, folks. There comes a time in the life of the eating epicure when you must accept that frog legs taste like frog legs. Quail like quail. And so on. To deny this is to deny the individual tastes and textures that attend a host of pleasurable eating experiences.

More often than not, the flavor most people attribute to a gamey taste is caused by meat spoilage which begins in the field and ends *before* the kitchen. Before you criticize the cook, checklist how the game was handled.

Dress it as soon as possible after the kill. The longer dressing is delayed, the more chance there is of losing or harming the flavor. Wash out blood and cut out the meat damaged by shot. Blood can taint the meat's flavor. Wrap the meat in a clean cloth or bag and keep it cool, because dirt, insects and heat can also ruin meat. Put the meat in refrigerator or freezer storage when you bring it home.

These are all matters of common sense. But if the hunter or game preparer ignores them, then the chances of another disappointing meal of wild game are multiplied. Preparing game meat for enjoyable eating is a total process from the point of kill to the table. Every good game cook knows that one depends on the other.

Consider the advice of wild game expert, Jim Byford of the University of Tennessee: "Don't be afraid to enjoy game! Don't try to hide its taste!" Too often the cook forgets that wild game should not receive the same treatment as domestic meats. The factors which influence texture, meatiness and fat content of domestic meat is entirely foreign to game meat.

The flavor of game will depend on such factors as whether the animal fed on other animals, plants or fish, whether its food was nutrient-rich or poor, and whether the season was mild or harsh, dry or wet. The animal's age will usually determine how tender or tough the meat is. Game animals use their muscles far more than domesticated; therefore, expect the meat to be lean and coarser in texture.

This is by no means a disadvantage, as long as you compensate for the lack of fat by adding a substitute. A vegetable oil like safflower or peanut oil can be brushed over the meat and used as a baste. Many game cooks rely on strips of bacon wrapped around or draped over the meat to lock in moisture and to enhance flavor.

The health benefits from eating game, leaner in fat content and denser in protein per pound, are noteworthy. Not only is it low in cholesterol, but it's nutritious, too. Certainly, eating meat straight from the wild is healthier and tastier, since it's been flavored by nature's seasonings rather than artificial chemicals.

Some basic additives that cooks use to enhance wild game are salt, pepper, beef or pork fat (for extra lean meats), onion, celery, vinegar and Worcestershire sauce. Also, to allow those seasonings to "blossom," cook the game at relatively low temperatures in a slow oven or over a grill.

Once you've learned the basics of cooking wild game, then you can get into preparing those more exotic recipes if you wish. Just remember: Never cook any food in a hurry. And the simple recipes are often the best.

Wild Fowl

Holiday feasts wouldn't be half as interesting without birds for the table. And a bird, for some strange reason, tastes twice as delicious when you call it down over an icy pond or scout it out of the woods yourself.

The following are considered game birds in the Southeast: duck, mourning dove, quail, wild turkey, marsh hen, pheasant, goose, ruffed grouse, brant, coot, gallinule, rail, Wilson snipe, woodcock, crow.

Dressing Fowl

Don't keep birds in your car trunk or vest pocket all day long. Put them in a cooler as soon as possible.

For large birds, draw (remove internal organs) while still in the field and put in a cooler. For small birds, such as quail, pluck before drawing, and try to clean them the day you kill them.

The sooner you clean your birds the better. The basic cleaning procedure is:

1. Pull out feathers from anus to breastbone.
2. Cut neck off close to body.
3. Cut through skin and muscle around anus and up to breastbone, being careful not to pierce the intestines or stomach.
4. Pull out all entrails, from windpipe to intestines.
5. If you want to save heart and lungs, leave them inside. If not, pull them out.
6. Pluck. It's easier if still warm.
7. Cut off wings and lower legs at joints. (You may want to pluck and save wings of turkey if you plan to serve it roasted whole.)
8. Pinfeathers and down can be singed off with matches or a camp stove. (This is better done outdoors, since it has an unpleasant odor.)
9. Rinse with cold water and wipe dry with paper towel.

For a large number of birds, you may find it worthwhile to use paraffin to remove feathers and down. Boil three cakes of paraffin in six quarts of water until dissolved. Remove from heat. Dip uncleaned birds in wax until coated. Cool and let harden. Peel off.

Skinning a bird is easier than plucking it, but many cooks say the skin holds in moisture and flavor and makes a more attractive roast.

To add moisture and lock in flavor, wrap skinned birds in bacon strips before cooking in a pot of sauce.

Breasting

There is very little meat on a dove except the breast, so often this is the only part that is kept. If so, the procedure is as follows:

1. Cool in ice chest until ready to dress.
2. Pull out feathers from anus to breastbone.
3. Put thumb between anus and breastbone. Push in and tear breast away.
4. Wash with cold water.

To store: Birds will keep in refrigerator for several days. Before cooking, some suggest soaking ducks in a cool place overnight in a quart of water with two tablespoons salt.

Don't season before freezing. Put cleaned and washed bird in polyethylene freezer bag. Force all air out with hand. Tie. Label and date. Frozen in single layers, birds are good for nine months. Thaw in refrigerator for 12 to 18 hours.

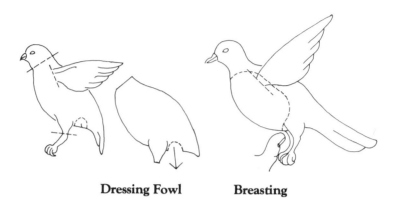

Dressing Fowl   **Breasting**

Trussing

1. With bird breast side up, lay cord across, around, and up through the drumsticks, crossing the two ends tightly over the closed cavity. Carry the cord over the legs, pulling the drumsticks together.

2. Turn the bird over. Pull the cord ends through the second joints of the folded wings, drawing them tightly together. Tie snugly and cut off ends.

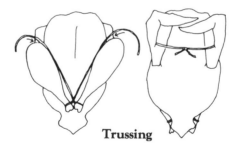

Trussing

Basic Fowl Recipes

Older birds are best in casseroles, pies, and stews, and never should be served cooked rare or medium. Younger birds are good for frying and barbecuing.

Quail, dove and marsh hen can be fried just like chicken. Salt and pepper, roll in flour, and fry in deep fat. Make gravy in drippings, and serve with hot biscuits.

OLD FASHIONED 'COUNTRY WAY' OF COOKING QUAIL OR DOVES

quail or doves	pepper
salt	rice

Parboil birds in enough water, seasoned with salt and pepper, to cover until they are tender, but not falling apart. Use the water the birds were cooked in to make rice. Serve birds on a bed of rice with a green salad and beans.

J. Oscar Sullivan

QUAIL OR DOVE CASSEROLE

1 doz. quail or doves (or 6 of each)	1 lg. raw onion, chopped
salt	2 stalks celery, chopped
pepper	½ c. rice
flour	1 No. 3 can tomatoes
grease for frying	

Salt, pepper and lightly flour birds. Brown in frying pan. After birds have browned, place in a baking pan, along with onion, celery and rice. Then add tomatoes and a cup of water to aid in the cooking of the rice. Salt and pepper to taste and cover with aluminum foil. Casserole should be cooked at 300 degrees until done.

Claudia Geddings

SMOTHERED GAME BIRDS

doves or quail (5/person)	2 envelopes AU JUS Gravy Mix
salt	bacon grease and/or lard
pepper	canned chicken broth
1 c. flour	yellow grits
1 c. corn meal	

First the Doves: Thaw doves from the freezer, using a small dishpan. If doves are plentiful (this is usually just the breasts), separate big from little into two groups. Save the thawed blood to enrich the gravy. Parboil the larger group briefly to make tender. Remove from water. Salt and pepper both groups, light on the salt, heavy with the pepper.

Mix a cup of flour with a cup of corn meal, add gravy mix to this. Roll or shake the birds into this mix. Using a big heavy deep iron frying pan, add enough bacon grease and/or lard to half cover birds when in the pan. When this is hot enough, add the birds, turning to cook both sides. Remove from pan; pour off grease, leaving sediment. Using flour and meal mixture, sprinkle over sediment. With the saved blood and canned chicken broth, make a gravy in the pan.

Return birds to the pan and gravy, add chicken broth, cover with a lid, and reduce heat to a gentle simmer. Cook about 30 more minutes. Serve with yellow grits and spiced peaches, using the gravy on the grits.

Now the Quail: Cook the quail exactly as you did the doves, but serve on big slices of diagonally cut French bread, toasted and buttered, with the gravy topping the birds on top of the toast.

Note: Livers, hearts and gizzards help make the gravy tasty, and the livers are especially easy to retrieve as you clean the birds.

Dana Crosland

BAKED RUFFED GROUSE, QUAIL OR PHEASANT

large birds	melted butter
Nature's Seasons (by Morton)	lemon juice
Lawry's seasoned salt	

Cut large birds in half. Season with Nature's Seasons and a pinch or two of seasoned salt. Place in aluminum or Pyrex pan and add butter. A few drops of lemon juice can be added to taste. Bake uncovered at 325 to 350 degrees for 30 to 45 minutes. When tender, switch oven to broil and brown for five to ten minutes to desired brown color.

Joe Hamilton

Duck

Dressed in waders, the duck hunter sets out his decoys before dawn on an overcast day and gets as comfortable as possible in the blind. His retriever occasionally whines about the intermittent drizzle, and cool winds make them both shiver. According to unwritten code, the hunter's blind and the land and water a couple hundred yards around it belong to him while he's there. And when he calls down a duck, he gets first crack at it before another guy shoots.

The only migratory waterfowl that nests regularly throughout the Southeast, the wood duck accounts for half of all waterfowl bagged in many states. This beautiful bird can be encouraged to nest on your land by building nesting boxes in conspicuous places in ponds. Instructions on constructing the boxes and planting for wood ducks can be obtained from your state wildlife department.

Three other common ducks, all known for their excellent flavor and all commonly taken, are the small, speedy green-winged teal; the familiar mallard; and the wary, prized pintail. Two other common dabbler ducks are the gadwall and the widgeon. Though seasons have been severely curtailed, the canvasback, called "king of waterfowl," and the black duck, "the Crown Prince," are highly prized by hunters, and are considered very tasty birds. Until its population was decimated by loss of habitat, the canvasback was considered one of the greatest delicacies in America.

ROASTED WILD DUCK

ducks	pepper
flour	1 onion per duck
salt	2 or 3 strips bacon per duck

Clean, wipe and dry the ducks. Sprinkle generously with flour, salt and pepper. Place whole peeled onion inside each duck and place in self-basting roaster. Fasten with toothpicks two or three strips of bacon across each bird. Cover bottom of roaster with water. Cover tightly and roast in oven at 350 degrees for one-and-a-half to two hours, depending on the number and size of ducks. Remove cover of roaster for last 15 to 20 minutes before taking from oven to allow skin to brown.

If desired, ducks may be stuffed with wild rice dressing made by boiling rice (wild) and seasoning with salt, pepper and chopped onion.

Marie DeWitt

ROASTED DUCK (RARE)

ducks	apples
unsweetened grapefruit juice	celery
dry sherry	margarine (optional)
green onions	

Marinate whole ducks in juice and sherry for two to four hours. Then stuff with chopped green onions, chopped apples, and sliced celery.

Heat oven to 500 degrees (hot as you can). Bake ducks for 15 minutes for rare or 20 to 25 minutes for crispy.

Baste once or twice with marinade liquid (and a little margarine, if desired). Then serve with mixed rice and vegetable of choice.

You can baste with barbecue sauce.

James P. Harrelson

BAKED DUCK

duck	2 ribs celery
salt	3 strips bacon
pepper	½ c. all-purpose flour
1 onion	

Salt and pepper duck inside and out and place in baking pan. Next, chop onion and celery, divide equally, place half in body cavity and remainder in baking pan. Strip bacon across top of duck. And three cups of water to pan. Place duck in pre-heated 350-degree oven and cook for two hours.

When duck has cooked, remove and wrap in aluminum foil to retain heat. Place cooked bacon back into pan and add flour. Stir until lumps are removed. Do not remove cooked celery and onions. Cook until flour turns almond color. Next add two cups of water and blend. Again, return to oven. More water may become necessary after gravy begins to cook. A medium thick gravy is desired. For a richer gravy, you may want to substitute milk in place of water.

Joyce D. Benson

ROAST DUCK

ducks	chopped apple
salt	3 or 4 bacon slices per duck

Season whole ducks lightly with salt. Stuff each duck with apple and wrap with bacon. If ducks are skinned, wrap entirely with bacon. Bake 350 degrees until tender (approximately one and one-half hours). Brown on broil until bacon covering is crisp. Allow to cool and remove all meat from bones. Chop bacon and add the cooked apple and all broth. Mix well. Can be served as a separate dish or over rice, preferably wild rice.

Joe Hamilton

EASY ROASTED WILD DUCK

1 duck per person (or however
    many you wish)
apples

onions
bacon

Clean ducks. Stuff loosely with sliced apples and onions. Place in Brown-n-Serve bag. Top each breast bone with a slice of bacon. Cook as directed in bag based on average weight of ducks. Cook one to one-and-a-half hours at 350 degrees.

Ginny Prevost

BRAISED WILD DUCK

1 duck, chopped
cooking oil
2 onions, diced
3 T. flour

¾ c. beer
½ c. chicken stock
⅛ t. thyme
⅛ t. basil

Brown meat in a little oil. Brown the onions. Add the flour. Stir in the beer, stock, thyme, basil. Add browned duck pieces. Cover and cook over low heat one hour or until duck is tender.

Gene Hayes

TENDER WILD DUCKS

ducks
bacon grease
butter
onion
celery
apple

bacon
salt
pepper
Uncle Ben's Wild Rice
Gravy (next page)

Thaw ducks the day before they are to be cooked. Take a syringe and inject a mixture of melted butter and bacon grease into ducks to make them juicy. Stuff small onion, celery, apple and bacon in the cavity of each duck. Salt and pepper and let sit overnight in refrigerator.

Put water in a large pot and bring to a boil. Place ducks in boiling water, cover pot, and lower heat. Cook ducks until leg joint moves easily. Young ducks may get tender in one to two hours, while older ducks may take four to five hours. As ducks get tender, remove from pot to baking dish. Remove apple, celery, onion and bacon from each duck's cavity.

Follow cooking instructions for Uncle Ben's Wild Rice on box except use duck stock rather than water to cook rice in. Save rest of stock for gravy (see next page). Stuff ducks with wild rice and baste with butter and bacon grease. Preheat oven to 500 degrees or broil. Put ducks in oven long enough to turn golden brown. Serve with vegetables and gravy.

Gravy

¼ c. Wesson oil	2 c. duck stock
1 or 2 chicken bouillon cubes	salt
¼ c. flour	pepper

Put oil in pot on high heat. While oil is heating, add bouillon cubes and flour. Stir until flour has mixed with oil and turned bubbly. *Do not burn.* Add stock slowly. Salt and pepper to taste. Lower heat and simmer five minutes. Stir so as not to stick to bottom of pan. Makes about two cups gravy.

Jimmy Miller

SMOKED DUCK

duck	Worcestershire sauce
1 qt. water	celery and/or other stuffing
4 T. Morton's sugar cure salt	red wine
dash of Tabasco	

Clean duck and soak overnight in a solution of water, salt, Tabasco, Worcestershire sauce. Remove duck, wash inside and out and stuff with celery, onions, apple, etc. Smoke 8 to 12 hours on top rack with a pan of red wine on bottom rack. (This can turn a "fishy" duck into a gourmet's delight.)

Robert L. Lumpkin

DUCK WITH GRAVY

6 ducks	¼ c. celery, chopped
salt	½ c. flour
pepper	1 c. dry white wine (or red if you
lemon juice	prefer)
¼ c. onions	½ c. cream

Place six ducks in roasting pan. Sprinkle with salt, pepper and lemon juice. Bake two and one-half hours at 300 degrees covered with a small amount of water in bottom. Saute' onions and celery. Pour in drippings from ducks. Add flour, wine and cream. Add gravy to ducks and reheat 15 to 30 minutes.

Sarah P. Lumpkin

WILD DUCK

6 ducks	2 cans cream of chicken soup
onion, chopped	1 soup can of wine
2 cans onion soup	rice

Salt ducks inside and out and fill with onion. Put in roaster, breast side down, with soups and wine. Cover and cook two hours at 300 degrees. Turn over and cook 15 minutes. Broil 15 minutes. Delicious gravy and wild duck! Serve with rice.

Mrs. C. Carrington Herbert

WILD DUCK WITH STUFFING

1 duck, 6-8 lb.
salt and pepper
Stuffing (see below)
2 bacon slices
1 onion, chopped

1 c. dry wine
1 t. butter
1 bell pepper, chopped
paprika

Salt and pepper inside of duck and add stuffing. Place bacon slices in bottom of Dutch oven and place duck over slices. Mix onion, wine, butter and bell pepper. Pour over duck. Cook covered for one hour and 15 minutes at 375 degrees. Uncover and sprinkle with paprika and cook 20 minutes to brown at 400 degrees.

Stuffing

1 lb. pork sausage
1 c. rice, cooked
¼ c. bread crumbs, fine
2 T. butter
2 eggs, beaten

1 celery rib, minced
1 clove garlic, minced
¾ t. dried thyme
¼ c. pecans, chopped

Mix all ingredients and cook in frying pan on low heat for 30 minutes.

Kathy T. Johnston

DUCKS IN ORANGE SAUCE

4 ducks
1 onion
2 stalks celery
2 oranges
½ t. salt per duck
⅛ t. pepper per duck
1 c. flour
6 c. bacon grease

1 apple, peeled and chopped
1 t. salt
¼ t. pepper
2 t. bacon grease
1 6-oz. can frozen orange juice,
   thawed
¼ c. water

Wash ducks in cold water. Dry and refrigerate. Chop onion and celery coarsely. Add peeled and sliced oranges. Refrigerate. Three hours before serving, sprinkle each duck with salt and pepper. Shake in bag with flour. Brown in bacon grease. Drain and cool. Stuff with onion, celery, oranges, apple, salt and pepper. Heat oven to 275 degrees. Place grease in roaster. Arrange ducks in roaster. Combine orange juice with water. Pour over ducks. Cover and bake three hours until done.

Gail B. Smith

BAKED DUCK AND VEGETABLES

2 ducks (8-10 doves or marsh hens
   may be substituted)
1 T. granulated garlic
2 T. Worcestershire sauce
2 T. soy sauce
1 t. parsley flakes
pepper

4 strips bacon
2 onions, sliced
2 carrots, chopped
2 stalks celery, chopped
½ c. fresh mushrooms, sliced
1 bell pepper, cut into strips
potato, salt, paprika (optional)

Cut slits into duck breasts and place in pan. Sprinkle with garlic, Worcestershire sauce, soy sauce, parsley and pepper. Place strips of bacon across ducks. Put onion, then other vegetables on top of ducks. Sprinkle with salt and paprika. Cover with aluminum foil and cook at 250 degrees for four hours or 300 degrees for three hours or until duck is tender. Potatoes may be added along with other vegetables if desired. Serves four.

Billy McCord

WILD DUCK WITH SAUSAGE AND RICE

2 wild ducks
1 lb. sausage (mild or hot), cut in
   half
1 med. onion, sliced
1 c. rice

1 t. salt
¼ t. pepper
¼ t. poultry seasoning
1 can chicken broth
2 slices bacon

Parboil ducks for five to ten minutes. Fry sausage. Sauté onions in sausage grease; add rice. Stir until each grain is coated. Place rice, onion and sausage in a roaster; sprinkle with salt, pepper, poultry seasoning; add chicken broth. Place ducks on top of mixture and cover with a slice of bacon. Cover and bake at 250 degrees for five hours. Serves six.

Rowena Dawson

BAGGY DUCK

duck
salt
pepper
1 stalk celery/duck
quarter of an onion/duck
quarter of an apple/duck

½ c. consommé
½ c. cooking burgundy
2 T. butter
2 T. bacon grease
orange sauce, if desired

Sprinkle duck's cavity with salt and pepper. Stuff with celery, onion and apple. Close cavity with pin. Salt and pepper outside of duck and place in individual baking bag. Pour over each duck a quarter cup of sauce made of consommé, burgundy, butter and bacon grease. Close bags, poke two slits in each, place on rack in roasting pan, and cook in 375-degree oven for one hour. An orange sauce can be prepared and served separately to be applied at the table for those who prefer it.

This is a recipe that I developed on the spur of the moment which turned out to be great.

Dr. Foster C. McCaleb, Jr.

DUCK A LA SOOKIE

This was my mother's roast duck recipe, which is fairly standard, but has always turned out beautifully. (My Dad called her "Sookie.") — Dr. Foster C. McCaleb, Jr.

duck
1 stalk celery
½ onion
½ Irish potato

2 strips bacon
1 c. water
1 c. Swanson's chicken broth
cornbread

Place duck on a rack in an iron skillet. Put inside body cavity celery, onion and potato. Lay bacon across the breast of the duck. Put water in the skillet. Bake covered for two hours in a 300-degree oven. Uncover and continue to bake for an additional 30 minutes until bird is brown. If frozen, duck must be thawed overnight. If dressing wanted, mix broth with cornbread.

Mrs. Foster C. McCaleb, Sr.

WILD DUCK

duck
soda water
salt
pepper
1 orange
1 onion

bacon strips
1 c. orange juice
1 c. red cooking wine
orange marmalade
wild rice and dressing

Wash the dressed duck. Wrap and let age a few days in the refrigerator. Wash again in soda water before preparing for cooking. Slice orange into four sections. Salt and pepper duck, then stuff with orange and onion. Place bacon across breast and put into baking dish, breast-side-up. Pour orange juice and wine over duck. Put cover on dish and bake at 300 degrees, two-and-a-half hours. Uncover, spoon orange marmalade on breast, and brown uncovered. Serve with wild rice and dressing.

Claudia Geddings

BARBECUED DUCK

2 ducks
Barbecue Sauce (see below)

Split and put ducks in baking pan. Baste with sauce every ten minutes or as often as convenient. Bake two and one-half hours at 300 degrees.

Barbecue Sauce
½ lb. butter
½ c. catsup
1½ t. lemon juice
1 T. Worcestershire sauce

1 sm. onion, chopped
½ t. Tabasco sauce
1 t. salt

Simmer five minutes.

Sarah P. Lumpkin

CHESAPEAKE BARBECUED DUCK

ducks
Barbecue Sauce (see below)

Split ducks in halves and flatten with side of cleaver. Place on rack in flat baking pan and bake at 375 degrees for one hour. Baste every ten minutes with barbecue sauce. Turn and cook other side one hour. Continue basting.

Barbecue Sauce

½ lb. butter	ground pepper to taste
½ c. catsup	1 t. salt
1 t. sugar	1 clove pressed garlic
1½ T. lemon juice	1 sm. onion, chopped
1 T. Worcestershire sauce	½ t. Tabasco sauce

Mix butter, catsup, sugar, lemon juice, Worcestershire sauce, ground pepper, salt, garlic, onion, Tabasco sauce. Simmer five minutes.

Joyce D. Benson

DUCK 'N CHICKEN

duck breast	garlic salt
chicken breast	pepper
equal parts lemon juice, cooking oil	1 onion, chopped
	drawn butter
1 t. soy sauce	

Filet breasts and marinate in half lemon juice, half cooking oil, plus one teaspoon soy sauce, garlic salt, pepper and onion for four to six hours.

Grill over a charcoal fire and arrange on plate, alternating duck, chicken, and serve with drawn butter.

Bill Chastain

DAWSON'S DUCK

3 or 4 ducks	½ c. Worcestershire sauce
Accent	bacon
¼ c. lemon juice	

Filet the breast of ducks. Sprinkle Accent on both sides. Let meat sit for 30 minutes. Put lemon juice and Worcestershire sauce in container, and then place ducks in it to marinate for an hour or longer. Turn at least once.

Wrap duck breasts with bacon and fasten with a toothpick. Cook on grill until done. For rare to medium, grill 20 minutes; for medium to well done 40 minutes. Turn at least once.

Calvin Dawson

DUCK BREASTS IN DURANGO SAUCE

duck breasts   **bacon strips**
Durango Sauce (see below)

Remove duck breasts by fileting. Using a pair of scissors and starting at the thin end of the breast in a circular motion, cut into a long strip about the size of your finger. Marinate in Durango sauce for 30 minutes. Meat should be completely covered by sauce. After duck has marinated, remove it. Using partially cooked bacon strips, roll duck into a patty with the bacon in between layers of duck. Skewer with toothpicks. Grill for minutes, like beef, depending on taste.

Durango Sauce

1 c. red wine   **1 T. Worcestershire sauce**
½ t. garlic salt   **1 T. monosodium glutamate**
1 stick margarine

Blend in a deep pan. Warm until butter melts. Do not overheat. Marinade must remain warm enough to keep butter melted, but not hot enough to cook meat. To double recipe, add as needed except for butter; one stick is plenty. Save and freeze sauce. It can be used again once.

Nancy Reese

FRIED DUCK IN GRAVY

duck   **flour**
whole onions   **bacon fat**
sage   **onions, finely diced**
vinegar

Cut duck in half. Parboil it with some onions, sage, and a 'shot' of vinegar until tender. Then take duck out and save juice. Roll duck in flour and fry in bacon fat until browned all over and set aside. Then fry some finely diced onions in the grease until golden and then brown some flour. When flour has browned, stir some of the juice the duck was cooked in to make your gravy, and simmer until ready to serve. The longer you wait, the better it will be.

Ivan "Boss Hog" Holden

PAN-FRIED WILD DUCK

duck breast   **flour**
salt   **bacon drippings**
pepper

Filet breast of duck and cut into bite-size pieces. Season with salt and pepper, roll in flour, and fry in bacon drippings.

As an option, make gravy and add crisp bacon bits.

Joe Hamilton

BRAISED DUCK

1 5-lb. duck	2 T. soy sauce
1 lb. can chestnuts in water	2 slices ginger root, minced
4 T. peanut oil	1 lg. ripe pear
1 c. beef broth	1 t. sugar
3 T. dry sherry	

Chop duck with bones into two-inch chunks. Wipe the duck pieces well with a damp cloth. Drain and rinse the chestnuts and reserve.

Heat oil in large frying pan: brown duck pieces quickly, a few at a time. Drain off most of the fat and return all duck to the pan. Add broth, sherry, soy sauce, and ginger root. Bring to a boil, cover, and lower heat. Simmer for one-half hour. Add chestnuts and simmer for ten minutes more, shaking pan to turn chestnuts. Peel and core the pear, slicing it into eight pieces. Dredge with sugar, add to duck, and simmer covered for four minutes, shaking the pan to cover pear and duck with juices. Makes three servings.

Maria Latto

WILD DUCK WITH MUSHROOMS

1 duck	1 bay leaf
1 onion, sliced	1 c. fresh mushrooms, sliced
¼ c. butter	2 T. flour
salt and pepper	⅛ t. powdered thyme
2 c. water	wild rice

Prepare and disjoint duck; brown with onion and butter. Add salt, pepper, water and bay leaf. Cook slowly one to one-and-a-half hours. Sauté mushrooms, flour and thyme. Add to duck and continue to cook 30 minutes. Serve bordered with wild rice.

Edith B. Jernigan

DUCK WITH DRESSING

1 duck	1 sm. onion
1 med. onion	pepper
salt	2 eggs
6-8 slices bread	

Put duck on to boil in enough water to cover. Add medium onion and salt to taste. When duck is tender, pour broth over bread. Let soak until bread softens. Add small finely chopped onion, more salt if needed, dash of pepper, eggs, and chopped deboned duck. Stir thoroughly. Pour into baking dish and cook at 350 degrees until done. (The mixture should be soft; if not, add a little water before baking.)

William A. Carson, Jr.

DUCK WITH MUSHROOM GRAVY

2 ducks, cut into serving pieces
1 sliced onion
½ c. margarine
salt and pepper
bay leaf

⅛ t. thyme
¼ c. sherry
cream of mushroom soup
rice

Brown meat and onions in margarine. Pour off drippings. After browning ducks and onions, add one cup water, season with salt and pepper, and add bay leaf and thyme. Cover and cook over moderate heat for an hour and a half. After that time, add sherry and soup and cook another 15 minutes. Serve with rice.

Gene Hayes

POACHER'S STEW

1 pkg. mushroom gravy
1 pkg. onion soup
3 c. water or gravy
1 qt. duck, cooled and cut up (left-over venison, doves, or any game or combination of game)

½ to 1 stick butter
corn starch
salt and pepper to taste (careful with salt as soups have salt)
1 pt. sour cream

Put soups in water and cook ten minutes. Thicken to a thick sauce. Add remainder of ingredients. Add sour cream just before serving. Do not boil after adding sour cream. Serves 12.

Sarah P. Lumpkin

DUCK BOG

1 duck
¾ lb. butt meat

rice
salt and pepper

Boil duck until meat starts to fall off the bones. Take out of the water and pick off all meat. Dice up butt meat and fry until crispy. Put duck and fried butt meat in pot. Add rice and some of the water the duck was cooked in. Salt and pepper to taste. Serve when rice is done. Serves a family of four.

Manning Shuler

Mourning Dove

The gregarious, highly mobile mourning dove is one of the most hunted game animals in this country. It is very adaptable and likes roadsides, open woods, suburbs, and farms.

DOVE SUPREME

6 doves	2 T. minced celery leaves
½ c. butter	salt
1 c. dry white wine	white pepper
¼ c. minced onion	½ t. tarragon

Brown doves in butter. Add wine, onion, celery leaves, salt and white pepper, and cover for simmering 20 minutes over low heat. Add the tarragon and simmer uncovered another 15 minutes.

Gene Hayes

DOVES

I usually cook about eight and never really measure, but for delicious tender ones, I'll try to pass it on:

1 med. onion, cut small	¼ c. oil
8 doves	salt and pepper to taste
1/3 c. (red or white) wine	

Put onion, oil and water to cover bottom of pan about three-fourths inch deep. Arrange birds with breast side up. Cook slowly about two and one half hours. Pour wine over birds and cook another 30 minutes or until birds are tender to touch. You can make gravy from juices, but we like them with or without gravy.

Vera Roukos

DOVES WITH GRAPES

doves	butter, salt, pepper and flour
1-1½ c. white seedless grapes, split	½ c. almond slivers
in half	1 piece of toast per bird
juice of 1 fresh lemon	

Rub doves inside and out with salt and pepper and coat with flour. Melt butter in a frying pan and brown doves to a turn. Reduce heat and add a cup or so of water and cook slowly until the birds are tender.

When birds are done, add grapes and cook for about 25 minutes or so.

Then take birds out and pour in almonds and lemon juice and cook a few minutes longer.

Serve each dove on a piece of toast with the grape sauce spooned over each.

Ben McC. Moise

BASIC GRILLED DOVES

doves
salt

pepper

Pluck doves, leaving the skin on. Sprinkle liberally with salt and pepper. Cook over hot coals just like barbecuing a chicken. Test with fork until they are tender enough to suit you. Use no sauce; the doves will be juicy and tasty without it.

Pat Robertson

GRILLED DOVES

2-3 doz. dressed doves
1 lb. sliced bacon
3 c. water
2 c. vinegar

1 c. cooking oil
1 lg. onion, chopped
1-2 T. salt
1-2 T. black pepper

Prepare marinade of water, vinegar, oil, onion, salt and pepper. Place doves in large pot and cover with marinade. Refrigerate three to four hours. Cut sliced bacon (across) in sizes to wrap each dove with part of a slice. Secure with toothpicks. Prepare charcoal grill (gray-hot coals). Arrange birds on grill eight to ten inches above coals or on indirect heat method. Close grill cover or cover with foil. Time: 15-20 minutes. Check two to three times for tenderness.

B.M. Blease

DOVE CASSEROLE

4 young doves
3 rashers fat bacon
butter
gravy

3 sm. green onions
2 oz. button mushrooms
1 glass claret or red wine
cayenne pepper, salt

Take doves trussed for boiling. Cover each with a strip of bacon, fry them in butter till nicely browned, drain them, and put in a casserole with just enough good gravy to barely cover. Add green onions and mushrooms, together with wine and seasoning of salt and cayenne pepper. Let the birds cook slowly for 45 minutes at the side of the fire; then, when cooked, serve in the same casserole.

Gene Hayes

WILD DOVES IN CASSEROLE

10-12 doves
½ green pepper, chopped fine
½ c. onion, chopped fine
8 T. butter/margarine
2 c. rice, yellow or wild (not white)
½ c. stuffed olives, chopped

1 c. canned or fresh mushrooms,
  chopped
paprika
salt
pepper
Worcestershire sauce
1 c. dry white wine

Dress and clean doves. Sauté onions and peppers in half of the butter. Add rice (cooked), olives, mushrooms and seasoning. Spread this mixture in bottom of baking dish. Place doves, breast-side-up on top of rice. Push them down into rice a ways. Roast at 450 degrees for ten minutes, then turn heat to 350 degrees and cook 30 minutes more. Baste at 10-minute intervals with rest of butter (melted) and white wine. If rice looks like it's about to dry out, add chicken stock.

Mrs. L.J. Slaughter

Side Dishes

A couple of recipes Ginny Prevost has found that go well with dove casserole are slaw and mushroom rice.

SLAW

cabbage
1/3 c. mayonnaise
1 T. vinegar
2 t. sugar

½ t. salt
½ t. celery seed
garlic powder (optional)

Shred cabbage in food processor or slice thin by hand. Mix rest of ingredients and coat cabbage with mixture.

Ginny Prevost

MUSHROOM RICE

1 c. uncooked rice
4 T. butter
1 4-oz. can mushrooms with
  juice

1 c. onion soup or/pkg.
  Lipton's onion with 10 oz.
  water

Brown rice in butter. Place rice in casserole. Add soup and mushrooms. Bake uncovered at 300 degrees for one hour.

Laura Morgan

OLD MARIA'S DOVES

3 onions
10 doves, including giblets
bacon grease
salt
1 t. peppercorns

1 bay leaf
1 T. Worcestershire sauce
1 c. white wine
2 T. burnt sugar

Stew giblets. Brown chopped onions slowly in bacon grease. Add doves (salted) and braise lightly. Add remaining ingredients and cook over low heat 45 minutes. Use two tablespoons burnt sugar (as for burnt sugar icing) and add broth from stewed giblets. Add to birds. Place in covered baking dish and bake at 350 degrees one and one-half hours. To serve, sieve gravy and thicken slightly.

This recipe was given to me by my neighbor, Mrs. Jean Parfitt.

Elaine Ferrell

MARY DRAPER'S DOVES

Everyone who has our doves says they are the most tender and "very best."

1 doz. doves
salt and pepper
¾ stick butter
1 T. Worcestershire sauce

1 c. water
2 rounded T. flour
Kitchen Bouquet

Pick and clean doves. Salt and pepper and place breast down in heavy iron frying pan. Put in butter, Worcestershire sauce and water. Cook covered over medium heat for 30 minutes and then turn to *low* heat for about one and one-half hours or until tender. Lift doves out and place breast up in Pyrex serving dish, then slip under broiler to brown slightly.

To make thickening for gravy, add a little water at a time to flour in a teacup, stirring until you have a smooth thin paste. Add thickening to liquid in frying pan to make gravy, using a *small amount* of Kitchen Bouquet, if necessary, to give color.

Georgia H. Hart

SIMMERED DOVES

doves
salt
pepper
1½ c. flour

cooking oil or bacon grease
2 T. cooking wine
grits or rice

Wash birds thoroughly. Sprinkle with salt and pepper. Put flour in a bag, then put birds in and shake vigorously, coating them well with flour. Use a heavy frying pan, putting in enough cooking oil or bacon grease to fry birds. Brown on both sides. Pour off oil or grease, leaving birds and drippings in pan. Add enough water to almost cover birds. Simmer for at least an hour or more until doves are tender. Watch often and add water as needed. Add wine about ten minutes before removing from heat. Serve with grits or rice.

Claudia Geddings

DOVES IN OLIVE OIL

doves
1 t. soda
olive oil
curry powder
dry mustard

celery salt
salt and pepper
2 T. Worcestershire sauce
2-3 T. lemon juice
rice

Soak doves in soda and water solution for two hours. Preheat oven to 250 degrees. Roll doves in olive oil. Sprinkle curry powder, dry mustard, celery salt, salt and pepper on doves. Place in cooking pan. Add water (one-half inch deep). Cover and cook for one-and-a-half hours. Put Worcestershire and lemon juice in and cook for 15 to 20 minutes. Serve with rice.

Gene Hayes

POTTED DOVES

doves
butter
bacon

Sauce: 1 c. catsup
1 onion, sliced
3 T. Worcestershire sauce
red pepper or Tabasco to taste

Brown doves in butter in heavy frying pan or Dutch oven. Cover with one-fourth slice of bacon each. Pour sauce over and cook at 300 degrees or low on stove-top two and one-half hours.

Sarah P. Lumpkin

D.J.'S DOVES

3 lg. potatoes
3 lg. onions
grease
salt

pepper
14 dove breasts
bacon slices

Slice potatoes in thin slices. Slice onions in thin slices. Use oblong baking dish. Grease bottom and arrange in alternate layers of potatoes and onions and season each layer lightly (two layers each). Season each dove breast and wrap with a half slice of bacon. Place on top of onions and potatoes.
Cover with aluminum foil. Cook in 325-degree oven until potatoes are done. Remove aluminum foil and put back in oven to brown bacon. Serve with garlic bread and slaw.

Danny Judy

SPORTSMAN'S DOVE DELIGHT

4 doves	¼ t. thyme
flour	½ c. water
2 t. parsley, chopped	½ c. white wine
3 T. butter or margarine	1 t. lemon juice
2 t. fresh onion, chopped	French bread
1 t. bay leaf	watercress, lemon and orange
1 t. salt and pepper	garnish

Split doves down back. Lightly cover with flour. Brown birds and parsley in butter in a heavy oven casserole; season with onion, bay leaf, thyme, salt and pepper. Gently stir in a smooth paste of flour, water and wine. Bring to a boil; cover and bake at 350 degrees for 30 minutes. Serve on toasted French bread.

Pour sauce over bird. Garnish with watercress, lemon or orange.

Thomas Simmons

DOVES IN ORANGE WINE SAUCE

8 doves, breasts only	¼ c. dry white wine
3 T. flour	½ c. water
3 T. melted butter	¼ c. brown sugar
1 c. orange juice	2 T. grated orange peel
salt and pepper to taste	

Brown doves in small amount of butter. Meanwhile, in saucepan, blend the three tablespoons butter with the flour. Add orange juice, wine and water. Cook, stirring, until mixture boils and thickens. Add brown sugar and orange peel. Salt to taste.

Pour sauce over browned doves. Cover and simmer gently about one and one-fourth hours or till doves are tender. Turn and baste occasionally. Add a little additional wine or water if gravy becomes too thick.

Carolyn Keck

DOVE STEW FOR THE R., G., B.M., S.D., & G.R.B.A.

1½ lb. salt pork
2 lb. hot lg. link country
   sausage
4 gal. water
5 lb. Idaho potatoes
5 lb. onions
6 lg. green bell peppers

3 T. black peppercorns
1 lb. fresh butter
1 lb. Pillsbury gravy flour
140-150 dove breasts
salt
rice
sour mash whiskey

In a five-gallon pot, fry salt pork finely diced, and sausage. Add water and Idaho potatoes, onions and bell peppers, all finely chopped. Put on high heat and, when it begins boiling, add peppercorns. Boil until the ingredients disappear, adding water to maintain the four-gallon level.

In a separate pan, melt fresh butter and add flour, stirring constantly until the butter is completely absorbed by the flour. Set aside.

When the ingredients in the main pot are no longer discernible, add fresh-killed, cleaned dove breasts, salt to taste, and cook until the doves breasts are tender. (Check frequently because this may not take as long as you think.) When the doves are tender, add the flour and butter paste, stirring constantly to prevent sticking. When the stew thickens sufficiently, serve over rice with sour mash whiskey on the side. Serves: a bunch of people.

Wade E. Holland, Jr.

DOVE-BROCCOLI CASSEROLE

8-10 dove breasts
2 pkg. frozen broccoli, chopped
1 can (10¾-oz.) cream of
   mushroom soup
2/3 c. mayonnaise
½ c. milk

½ c. shredded Cheddar cheese
1 T. lemon juice
1 t. curry powder
1 c. cracker crumbs
salt and pepper

Boil dove breasts and remove meat from bones. Cook broccoli by package directions and drain well. Place broccoli in lightly greased one-and-one-half quart casserole and cover with dove meat. Combine remaining ingredients except cracker crumbs, salt and pepper. Stir well and spoon mixture over dove and broccoli. Salt and pepper to taste and top with cracker crumbs. Bake at 350 degrees for 30 minutes. Serves six.

Billy McCord

DOVE JAMBALAYA

8-10 dove breasts (snipe or marsh
  hens may be substituted)
8 slices of bacon, fried and
  crumbled
1 sm. onion, chopped
2 stalks celery, chopped
1 sm. bell pepper, chopped

2 T. Worcestershire sauce
1 t. parsley flakes
1 T. granulated garlic
salt and pepper to taste
1 can cream of mushroom soup
1 c. cooked rice
(add other seasonings as desired)

Boil dove breasts and remove meat from bones. Fry bacon in frying pan, then remove bacon, leaving enough drippings to sauté onion, celery and bell pepper. Add dove meat and bacon crumbs to sautéed vegetables. Add Worcestershire sauce, parsley, garlic, salt and pepper as well as any other seasonings. Stir well. Add soup and a half soup can of water. Bring to boil. Cut down to low and simmer for 20 to 30 minutes. Serve over hot rice. Serves four.

Billy McCord

DOVE ON THE BED

(Dozen Dove Breasts on a Bed of Rice)

flour
oil
1 doz. dove breasts
¾ c. rice, uncooked
salt
pepper

3-oz. can of mushrooms
½ stick butter
1 T. grated onion (or half a garlic
  clove, minced)
2 beef bouillon cubes in 1¾ c.
  water

Flour and brown the breasts in a little oil. Mix all other ingredients in greased baking pan and spread evenly over bottom of pan. Arrange breasts in two rows and pour bouillon over breasts and pat with butter. Cover with tin foil. Bake at 350 degrees for one hour.

Bob Campbell

Bob-white Quail

The quail is considered the game bird of the South, but it can't thrive where there are no food plants close to adequate cover. Mr. Bob-white likes forests, brush, grass and cultivated land, and prefers it all within its 40-acre range.

Quail and gravy is a traditional Christmas breakfast in many parts of the South.

McGEE BARBECUE QUAIL (or chicken)

12 quail (or 6 chicken quarters)	½ c. olive oil
1 lg. bottle of Italian dressing	1 stick butter

Marinate the quail in Italian dressing for 24 hours. Remove the quail and retain the dressing.

Melt butter with olive oil over low heat and add this to the dressing.

Charcoal the quail slowly until done (approximately 30 to 45 minutes). Baste frequently with the dressing, butter and olive oil sauce. Four to six servings.

Jim Sorrow

DEEP-FRIED QUAIL

8 quail	egg
salt	flour
pepper	vegetable oil

Split quail and salt and pepper lightly. Dip quail into an egg wash. Remove and dust lightly with flour. If you are using an electric frying pan, heat to 340 degrees; use medium heat if in a skillet. The vegetable oil should just cover the birds. Cook until they are a crisp brown.

Joyce D. Benson

FRIED QUAIL

quail	butter
salt	basil
flour	fat

Clean quail thoroughly. Salt and flour each bird. Place a lump of butter and a few grains of basil in the cavity. Fry in deep fat, fast at first until birds are brown all over, then slower for about 20 minutes. Do not cover. Drain on paper towels. Serve hot.

Edith B. Jernigan

BAKED QUAIL

8 quail
1 stick margarine
seasoning salt
1 c. celery, chopped
1 lg. onion, chopped
1 c. mushrooms, diced

1 bell pepper, cut in strips
½ c. white wine
¼ c. lemon juice
¼ c. water
Wild Rice (see below)

Brown eight quail in margarine. Season with salt when brown. Remove from frying pan and sauté celery, onion, mushrooms and bell pepper in pan where birds were cooked. Place birds in casserole dish and pour sautéed vegetables over birds. Combine wine, lemon juice, water. Pour over birds. Cover with foil, and bake two hours at 325 degrees. Keep warm at 175 degrees until served. Serve with wild rice. Serves eight.

Wild Rice

1½ c. wild rice
4 10½-oz. cans beef broth
1 c. onion, chopped
1 stick margarine
1 c. bell pepper, chopped

1 c. mushrooms, sliced
1 c. celery, chopped
1 c. milk
salt
pepper

Rinse rice and cook in beef broth until liquid is absorbed. Sauté onion, bell pepper, mushrooms and celery in margarine. Combine rice, vegetables, milk, salt and pepper in casserole dish. Bake at 350 degrees for 25 to 30 minutes. Serve with baked quail. Serves eight.

Pat Turner

WILD QUAIL CASSEROLE

8 or 10 quail (breast or
    whole)
1 can water
1 can cream of mushroom
    soup

1 can cream of chicken soup
1 can cream of Cheddar cheese
    soup
1 sm. box Uncle Ben's Wild
    Rice

Preheat oven to 375 degrees.

Place quail in long casserole dish, sprinkle both packages of Uncle Ben's Wild Rice over quail. Pour cream of mushroom, water, cream of chicken, cream of Cheddar cheese over rice and quail. Do not stir.

Bake for one hour and 45 minutes covered with aluminum foil. Take foil off. Continue to bake for 30 minutes.

Luther W. Harmon, Jr.

QUAIL WITH MUSHROOMS AND ONIONS *Wonderful 3-6-03*

6 quail
salt
pepper
paprika
6 slices bacon, boiled for 5 minutes
½ c. lemon or lime juice

sweet butter and olive oil
1½-lb. fresh mushrooms
2 chopped onions
some chopped pimentos
wild rice

Pat quail dry with paper towels. Rub inside and out with mixture of salt, pepper and paprika. Fasten strip of bacon across breast of each quail.

Arrange birds in well-buttered baking pan and cover with lid or tin foil. Bake at around 350 or 400 degrees for about an hour, basting every now and then with the citrus juice and pan drippings.

Meanwhile, melt a little butter with a little olive oil and sauté the onions, mushrooms and pimentos until just tender. Salt and pepper to taste.

Pour mushrooms and onions in platter. Put quail, when done, on top and serve with wild rice.

Ben McC. Moise

PAN SIMMERED QUAIL

quail
flour
salt

pepper
butter

Lightly flour, salt and pepper each bird and brown on all sides, turning each four times, in a small amount of butter or oleo. Add enough water to cover birds about half-way with breast up. Put top on frying pan and slowly simmer about one-half hour. Serve birds in their own delicious gravy with rice or grits.

Mrs. C. Carrington Herbert

SOUTHERN FRIED QUAIL

quail
salt
pepper
flour

fat for frying
slices of lemon
sprigs of parsley

Dry-pick quail. Clean and wipe thoroughly. Salt and pepper and dredge with flour. Have a deep heavy frying pan with close-fitting lid, half full of hot fat. Put in quail. Cook for a few minutes over a hot fire, then cover skillet and reduce heat. Cook slowly until tender, turning the quail to the other side when golden brown. Serve on hot platter garnished with slices of lemon and sprigs of parsley.

Marie DeWitt

SMOTHERED QUAIL

6 quail	3 T. flour
salt	2 c. chicken broth
pepper	½ c. sherry
6 T. butter	cooked rice

Season quail with salt and pepper. Brown in a heavy skillet in butter. Remove quail to baking dish. Add flour to butter in skillet and stir well. Slowly add chicken broth and sherry. Salt and pepper to taste. Blend well and pour over quail. Cover baking dish and bake at 350 degrees for one hour or until done. Serve with cooked rice. Serves six.

Doves may be used instead of quail.

Mrs. J.T. McCabe

Wild Turkey

The wild turkey is as characteristically American as the eagle. King of game birds to the Indians, it was eaten at the Pilgrims' first Thanksgiving Dinner and John Smith's first Christmas Dinner with the Powhatans. During his exploratory travels through Carolina, Georgia and Florida, William Bartram complained about the early morning noise made by the many wild turkey cocks: "...The whole country is for an hour or more in a universal shout." To celebrate America winning the Revolution, the French took to eating turkey too - except they stuffed it with truffles.

SMOKED TURKEY

14-lb. turkey	vinegar
fresh hickory sticks	melted butter

This is not necessarily a recipe but my favorite method of cooking a turkey (either bought or wild).

I usually use a bird of about 14 pounds. I use the double-deck charcoal smoker. Prior to cooking, cut some fresh hickory sticks (some folks like them dried, but I prefer them green), and place them in a bucket of water for 15 to 20 minutes.

Let your turkey slow thaw in the refrigerator for at least 24 hours. Baste it with a mixture of vinegar and melted butter.

Heap charcoal into a cone in the pan and get it burning well. Place the water pan in the smoker and fill it almost full. Place the turkey on the rack over the water pan and simply cover the smoker with the hood and keep close check on the cooking range. Every two hours, check the water level and place two or three hickory sticks on the charcoal.

I have good success with a 14-pound bird cooking in approximately nine to ten hours.

Once cooked to a golden brown, the bird can be pulled apart, and succulent juices run freely.

Hams can be cooked in the same manner.

Larry C. Owen

FRIED WILD TURKEY

wild turkey　　　　　　　　　　　**flour**
salt　　　　　　　　　　　　　　　**hot fat**
pepper

Take breast, leg and thigh meat off bone, keeping as much skin on as possible, and keeping the meat in contiguous pieces as much as possible.

When boned, lay skin side down on a cutting board and cut as many half-inch thick 'steaks' as possible. Dust well with a sprinkling of salt and pepper and put aside for about 20 to 30 minutes, then lightly coat with flour.

Have a frying pan with hot fat at the ready and quickly fry each piece on both sides and drain.

Ben McC. Moise

FRIED WILD TURKEY BREAST

turkey breast　　　　　　　　　　**oil**
flour

Remove breast meat from turkey. Slice thin. Coat with flour and fry in small amount of oil. Season to taste. These will fry crisp and are delicious.

Tommy Lombard

WILD TURKEY

turkey　　　　　　　　　　　　　**pepper**
salt　　　　　　　　　　　　　　　**2 sticks butter**

Salt and pepper turkey. Place in a jacket made from cheesecloth (no substitute). Cut butter and place all over turkey under the cheesecloth. Put in covered roaster with water (approximately one pint). Bake slowly at 250 degrees until turkey is done.

Rowena Dawson

BAKED WILD TURKEY I

This dish has become the traditional Thanksgiving specialty since I began turkey hunting several years ago. To prevent freezer burn from spring to the following Thanksgiving, the bird is placed in a heavy-duty plastic bag and then into an appropriately sized cardboard box. Fill the bag with water until it fits the box. Fish often are frozen in the same manner to avoid freezer burn.

1 wild turkey　　　　　　　　　　**garlic powder or salt (optional)**
salt　　　　　　　　　　　　　　　**whole celery seeds**
pepper

Salt and pepper bird lightly. A pinch of garlic powder or salt may be added also. Cover entire bird, including body cavity, with whole celery seeds. Add two to four cups of water. Place in tightly covered pan and bake at 350 degrees until tender (approximately three hours). Since wild turkey has a tendency to be a bit dry, remove all meat in slices and pour broth over meat.

Joe Hamilton

BAKED WILD TURKEY II

wild turkey	salt
parsley (fresh if possible)	pepper
celery	butter
thyme	celery flakes
marjoram	1 t. parsley flakes
onion	1 t. dill seed

Stuffing (to be discarded): Fill chest with parsley, celery, thyme, marjoram, onion, salt and pepper.

Rub body with butter and then salt, celery flakes, one teaspoon marjoram, parsley flakes, dill weed. Use browning bag. Follow directions. Cook 30 minutes per pound at 325 degrees (more won't hurt).

Giblets: Put in water, celery, one teaspoon butter. Boil, then simmer till neck meat is tender (two or three hours).

Gene Hayes

BAKED WILD TURKEY III

wild turkey	pepper
salt	1 qt. water

You can either pluck or skin the turkey. I have done it both ways. Be sure when dressing the turkey to save the liver and gizzard for your gravy and dressing. Preheat oven at 500 degrees set on bake. Season the turkey with salt and pepper, just as you would with chicken. Put turkey in large pot or pan (deep pan). Add one quart of water and two tablespoons of salt to water. Cover turkey with aluminum foil, folding it under outside edge of pan or pot. Place lid on pan. Bake at 500 degrees for one hour. Cut oven off. Be sure not to open oven door for six hours once you begin cooking. After removing turkey five hours after cutting oven off, it is ready to be served. You may reheat before serving, if you wish.

Charles Stone

Marsh Hen

Hunting for the long, skinny marsh hen (clapper rail or *Rallus longirostris Waynei*) requires stamina and good eyesight. The thin, grayish-brown bird with a needle-like beak will scurry through the marshes, duck underwater, and even hold itself under by a weed to avoid hunters. Its slow, low flight has prompted a regulation against the use of a motor in the marsh. But those who cherish that delectable meat in brown gravy with onions will paddle and brave the cold autumn winds at high tide to bring home a clapper rail.

SMOTHERED MARSH HENS

8 skinned birds
2 c. chicken stock or 1 can chicken
  soup

6 T. browned flour
6 T. bacon grease
salt and pepper

Parboil birds in salt water just long enough to take out the blood and keep the shape. Drain and put in deep frying pan on top of stove. Mix the rest of ingredients and add to hens.

Cover and cook about one hour, then uncover and slip under the broiler flame for 15 minutes.

Barbara Jones

MARSH HENS IN GRAVY

10 marsh hens, halved
1 c. flour
salt and pepper to taste
½ c. vegetable oil

1 lg. onion, sliced
2-3 c. warm water
1 T. Kitchen Bouquet
rice

Flour, salt and pepper marsh hens. Place in heated heavy pot with vegetable oil. Brown on all sides, turning frequently to ensure even browning. Add sliced onion, warm water and Kitchen Bouquet. Cover and cook on low heat for one-and-a-half hours. Serve over rice.

Susan McIntyre

MARSH HEN I

4 marsh hens
vinegar
salt
pepper

flour
cooking oil or bacon grease
2 T. cooking wine

Cut hens into pieces. Soak in vinegar about four hours. Wash in water. Salt and pepper to taste. Dredge with flour. Place cooking oil or bacon grease in fry pan. Cook slowly on each side in covered pan until golden brown. Pour excess fat off, add one cup water, let simmer 30 minutes. Add wine and more water as needed.

Claudia Geddings

MARSH HEN II

marsh hens	flour
vinegar	2 beef bouillon cubes
fat	2 T. soy sauce
salt	6 to 8 Irish potatoes, peeled
pepper	4 to 5 whole onions, peeled

Dress out marsh hen by cutting off legs just above knees and wings at shoulder joint. Cut skin apart at abdomen and pull back over body. Cut neck off at backbone. Pull the innards out. Save and use the gizzard and liver. Cut breast off by diagonally cutting from neck joint across the rib line and cut the legs off across the back bone. Clean gizzard. Wash well and soak all meat in ice water with a dollop or two of vinegar for 30 minutes or an hour. Then throw meat in a pot with hot fat and salt and pepper and brown all around.

Add a little more fat to the pan and add enough flour to make a soft paste. Stir constantly until it is brown. Dissolve bouillon cubes in three cups of water, soy sauce, and pour in with the browned flour to make a gravy. Stir and mix well with a fork.

Put the marsh hens in a deep casserole. Add potatoes and onions, and pour in the gravy and cover. Cook in oven at 350 degrees for two hours.

Ben McC. Moise

Goose

Seasons are restricted or closed in many states where wildlife biologists are trying to relocate geese for resident flocks. Numbers of birds that winter in the Southeast have dropped severely in recent years. Serious goose hunters still travel to the East Coast's Delmarva Peninsula.

ROAST GOOSE

1 goose, picked, singed and cored	½ c. currants
mixture of salt, pepper, thyme, sage	¾ c. cornbread crumbs
and marjoram	1 lg. baking potato, cooked and
½ c. seeded raisins	mashed
2 apples, peeled, cored, finely	2 T. flour
chopped	1 stick butter

Rub goose thoroughly inside and out with the seasoning mixture. Mix together everything else for the stuffing, stuff in the goose, and truss it up.

Roast in oven for two and one-third to three hours and baste frequently with the pan juice.

Ben McC. Moise

GIBLET GRAVY

goose neck and giblets (heart, liver
   and gizzard)
½ c. goose pan drippings
3 to 4 T. onions, finely chopped
pinch of pepper

3 T. flour
sage
salt
pepper

Boil the giblets in water. When done, remove meat from neck and finely chop everything else. Save the water. Next heat the pan drippings from the goose until good and hot, then stir in onions. When translucent, add pepper and flour, and stir until light brown. Then add giblet water, and then the meat itself. Stir well. You may add a little sage, salt, pepper, etc. to taste.

Serve with wild rice and applesauce.

Ben McC. Moise

ROASTED GOOSE WITH WHEAT AND APRICOT STUFFING

1 10-lb. goose
½ c. butter
salt and pepper
1 recipe Cracked Wheat and
   Apricot Stuffing (see below)

1 onion, quartered
1½ c. beef broth
12 peach halves, canned
2 T. cognac
3 T. orange liqueur

Singe and wipe the goose. Rub inside of goose with 2 tablespoons softened butter. Season with salt and pepper and fill neck and body cavity with stuffing.

Fold neck skin over and secure with a small skewer. Sew up body cavity and truss bird. Prick skin all over with a fork. Spread with one tablespoon softened butter and butter a roasting pan with one tablespoon butter. Place bird in pan with onion. Roast in a preheated 400-degree oven for 30 minutes. Pour off fat, season with salt and pepper, and pour on port wine from soaked fruit in stuffing. Lower heat to 350 degrees and roast, basting four times, for one-and-a-half hours or until legs move freely in their sockets. Keep bird warm. Remove fat from roasting pan, pour in beef broth, and simmer for five minutes on top of stove, scraping the pan of all brown particles. Melt remaining four tablespoons butter and sauté well-drained peach halves until golden. Carve goose, arrange peach halves around it. Add cognac and liqueur to sauce and simmer for six minutes. Serve in a separate bowl. Makes six to eight servings.

Cracked Wheat and Apricot Stuffing

½ lb. dried apricots, pitted
1 c. tawny port wine
2 c. cracked wheat
¼ c. butter
2 med. onions, chopped
2½ celery stalks, finely diced

1 t. dried sage
salt and pepper
½ lb. dried prunes, pitted and
   halved
1/3 c. pine nuts
1 c. beef broth

Soak the apricots in the port overnight. Reserve port to baste bird. Soak the cracked wheat in four cups water for two hours. Drain well. Melt the butter and fry the onion and celery, add the well-drained cracked wheat, and sauté for six minutes. Season with sage and salt and pepper to taste. Mix in prunes, pine nuts, drained apricots, and broth. Simmer for 20 minutes. Makes enough stuffing to stuff body cavity and neck of a ten-pound bird.

Maria Latto

Pheasant

Pheasants don't exist in huntable numbers in much of the Southeast, but they are a prime target on shooting preserves and are occasionally brought home from hunts in the Midwest or the West.

SMOTHERED PHEASANT IN WINE

pheasant
seasoned flour
onions, peeled
thyme
marjoram

parsley, chopped
butter
celery stalks
½ c. condensed beef consommé
½ c. dry red wine

Disjoint pheasant. Shake pieces in bag of seasoned flour until thoroughly coated, then lay them in a deep casserole. Around the pieces place many peeled onions. Sprinkle pieces with generous pinch each of thyme, marjoram and chopped parsley. Dot liberally with butter. Cover pheasant and onions with stalks of celery, leaves and all.

Mix and pour around the edge consommé and wine. Cover casserole and bake at 450 degrees for about one-half hour. Reduce heat to 300 degrees and cook one and one-half hours more (I usually cook it two and one-half hours), basting once in a while. Add more wine if it seems to be getting dry.

Jane C. Compton

PHEASANT IN SOUR CREAM

1 pheasant, cut into serving pieces
1/3 c. flour
1 t. salt
1 T. sweet paprika
½ t. black pepper

3 T. butter
1 c. sour cream, at room
  temperature
1 c. light cream

Preheat the oven at 275 degrees. Rub the pheasant pieces in the flour mixed with salt, paprika and pepper. Reserve one tablespoon unused flour mixture. Heat the butter in a heavy skillet and brown the pheasant pieces in it on all sides. Place in a buttered casserole. Stir the reserved seasoned flour mixture into the skillet drippings. Blend in the sour cream and light cream. Pour mixture over the pheasant and bake three hours. Stir before serving. Makes three servings.

Mrs. Helen B. Lee

ROASTED PHEASANT AND SAUERKRAUT

2 pheasants
salt
pepper
1 lg. onion, halved
½ c. butter
2 apples, peeled, cored and diced
2 lg. onions, finely chopped

3 lb. sauerkraut, rinsed and drained
bouquet garni (12 juniper berries,
　½ bay leaf, 6 peppercorns, tied in
　cheese cloth)
1 bottle dry white wine
1 c. beef broth

Season pheasants with salt and pepper, insert one-half onion in each bird, and truss.

Melt one-fourth cup butter in a large Dutch oven and slowly stew the apple and chopped onion until soft but not brown, approximately ten to twelve minutes. Add the drained sauerkraut, the bouquet garni, salt, pepper, wine and enough water to cover. Bring to a boil, turn heat down, and simmer slowly, partially covered, stirring occasionally for two and one-half hours or until liquid has evaporated. When sauerkraut has cooked for one and one-half hours, spread the trussed pheasants with remaining one-fourth cup butter. Place in a buttered roasting pan, season with salt and pepper, and roast in a preheated 400-degree oven for 30 minutes. Lower the heat to 375 degrees and roast for one hour, basting two or three times. Remove pheasant from oven and let sit for ten minutes. Discard bouquet garni from sauerkraut. Put sauerkraut in a serving casserole. Cut pheasant into serving portions and bury in the sauerkraut. Deglaze roasting pan with beef broth and pour over sauerkraut. Put in a preheated 350-degree oven for 15 minutes. Makes six servings.

Maria Latto

Small Game

Two of the most popular small game mammals are the gray squirrel and the cottontail rabbit. The meat of both squirrels and rabbits is very tasty and has long been considered a highly preferred table food.

Squirrel

The gray squirrel that is so abundant in urban areas is the same species found in forested areas. Unlike many animals, gray squirrels have adapted well to urban life. However, replanting in pines and forestry practices associated with cutting mast-producing trees have diminished quality habitat for squirrels.

Many squirrel hunters find that using a .22 rifle to harvest squirrels is a true test of marksmanship. Because squirrels are plentiful, squirrel hunting is popular in training youngsters proper woodsmanship.

Dressing Squirrel

Small animals are easier to handle than large, since far less physical effort is required in preparing them for the table. Because the hide on a squirrel clings more tenaciously on the flesh than on rabbits, the "tail-cut" method or "stomp and pull" is recommended for dressing squirrels:

1. Get a good hold on the carcass by the hind legs, then make the first cut through the tailbone as shown, under the tail. Sever the tail from the body, but don't detach it from the hide.

2. Place the squirrel on its back on the ground, then step on the tail to anchor it with your foot and grip the hind legs. Then straighten up, pulling the hide free down to the squirrel's neck.

3. Swap to rear end and pull the hide off the hips and hind legs with your hands.

4. With remaining hide still hanging from the head, slit the carcass down the middle of the belly from back to front. If you can't remove all the entrails with your knife, then use your hand.

5. After the inside is cleaned out, cut off the head, and back and front feet, and discard the hide. Once you finish dressing it out, it's a good idea to trim off areas damaged by shot. Use cold water to wash off hair and dirt. This does not harm the meat if you pat dry quickly afterwards.

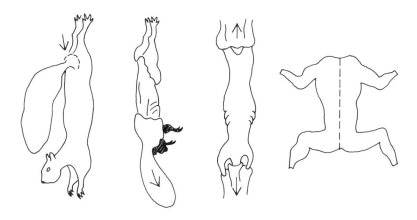

BROILED SQUIRREL

squirrel meat, cut into serving
  portions
melted bacon fat

lemon juice
salt and pepper

Squirrel meat is one that does not need any "treatment" before cooking. One simple way to cook it is to arrange the disjointed pieces on a broiling rack and baste with a mixture of melted bacon fat, lemon juice, salt and pepper. Cook 35-40 minutes.

Ben McC. Moise

BOBBY ASHLEY'S SQUIRREL AND PORK CHOPS

dressed squirrels
pork chops
onions
bacon fat

flour
salt and pepper to taste
cheese grits

Put the dressed squirrels, pork chops and onions in a pot and cover with water. Cook until tender, then remove the pork chop bones. In a skillet, take a little bacon fat and brown some flour in it. Add the juices from the meat pot, and let simmer until the gravy thickens, then mix the meat in with salt and pepper to taste. Serve over cheese grits. For cheese grits cook the grits down good - about an hour - then add chopped medium sharp cheese to it in the amount desired.

Bobby Ashley

SWEET AND SOUR CROCK POT SQUIRREL

6 squirrels, cut into serving size
¼ c. cider vinegar
¼ c. soy sauce
¼ c. brown sugar

¼ c. chili sauce
Variations on chili sauce:
½ c. taco sauce
½ t. chili powder

Salt and pepper squirrel pieces. Place in crock pot. Mix all ingredients in bowl and pour over meat. Cover and cook on low heat six to eight hours or until squirrels are tender. This recipe is also good for rabbits and fowl.

Hoyt McCaskill, Jr.

CAROLINA SQUIRREL STEW

1 gal. cold water
2 squirrels
2 t. salt
½ t. pepper
2 lg. onions, sliced
1½ c. fresh okra, sliced

3 c. tomatoes, peeled
2 c. fresh butterbeans
2 c. fresh carrots
5 potatoes, diced
4 c. fresh yellow corn

Bring water to a boil. Slowly add pieces of squirrel with bone left in. Be careful not to boil fast at any time. Add salt and pepper. Add onions, okra, tomatoes, butterbeans, carrots and potatoes. Add water occasionally and cook slowly for four hours. Then add corn and cook for one hour. Lower heat and stir occasionally to prevent scorching. Add two-and-a-half or three ounces of butter just before serving. Makes six servings.

Barbara Jones

SQUIRREL 'N RICE STEW

3 squirrels
2 onions, chopped
1 green pepper, chopped
2 medium potatoes, diced
¼ c. diced celery

4 T. chili powder
1 c. cooked rice
salt and pepper to taste
dash of hot sauce

Cover squirrels with water and cook until tender. Remove from water and cool; reserve broth. Remove meat from bones and put back into broth. Bring to a boil and add all other ingredients except rice. Cook for about 45 minutes or until vegetables are tender. Add cooked rice. Serve hot. Makes six servings.

Mrs. Addie Gunnels

Rabbit

Although cottontail rabbit populations have declined with the demise of the small farm, cottontails are still abundant. Because small game animals in general are very prolific, local populations usually respond quickly to proper habitat management.

Rabbit hunting in the South is centered around running rabbits with a pack of dogs, usually beagles. The frenzied excitement of a pack of beagles as they jump and chase the slick cottontail is a major part of the hunter's enjoyment.

Dressing Rabbit

The method below is recommended because it keeps most of the fur off the meat.

1. First remove the rabbit's head, either by twisting off or cutting it off with a knife.
2. Then trim off its feet at the joints.
3. Now pinch up the hide on its back and slip your knife through it as shown. Then cut upward and slice back through the skin.
4. Grasp the hide on either side of the cut and start pulling in opposite directions.
5. Continue pulling until you've peeled off all the hide. The legs will slip through easily, but you'll need to skin around the tail separately.
6. When the hide is completely removed, slit open the body cavity, starting from the chest and working to the tail.
7. Use your knife to clean out the pelvis, being careful not to puncture the intestinal tract.
8. Now dump out all the surplus parts, including the kidneys, wash with cold water and pat dry immediately.

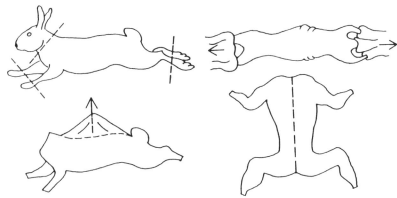

PAT ROBERTSON'S FRIED RABBIT OR SQUIRREL

rabbit or squirrel meat
   cut in serving portions

salt and pepper to taste
flour

Clean well and remove the fat. Salt and pepper to taste, roll in flour and fry in deep fat just like fried chicken. Make gravy in the drippings and serve with hot grits and hot biscuits. *Especially good at breakfast.*

Pat Robertson

GRILLED RABBIT OR SQUIRREL

Italian salad dressing
rabbit or squirrel meat, cut in portions

Marinate game in Italian dressing about one to three hours in refrigerator. Place on covered charcoal grill, baste frequently with excess salad dressing until done. *Procedure also favorably tried on marsh hen and doves.*

James M. Bishop

MARINATED RABBIT

2 rabbits, quartered
2 qt. boiling water
Marinate in mixture of 1 part
   vinegar to 3 parts dry red wine
1½ sticks sweet butter
5 T. olive oil
2 onions, chopped

2 T. flour
3 T. soy sauce
½ doz. whole cloves
1 whole sweet bay leaf
1 t. peppercorns
1½ t. salt
1 T. sugar

Kill two rabbits, skin, clean and quarter. Put the quarters in a bowl and pour about two quarts of boiling water over 'em, then drain and dry off on paper towels. Put the quarters back into the bowl and cover with a mixture of one part vinegar to three parts dry red wine. Use enough to cover well. Put the quarters in a refrigerator to marinate overnight. When ready to cook, take the quarters out of the marinade and dry them off on paper towels.

Heat a fry pan up to medium hot and melt a half a stick of sweet butter and add two tablespoons of olive oil. When hot, brown each piece of rabbit to a turn. When all the pieces are browned, wipe the pan clean and add one stick of sweet butter and three tablespoons of olive oil and bring up to heat again. Pour in two chopped onions and cook until they are just beginning to turn brown, and then sprinkle about two well-rounded tablespoons of flour over them and continue to cook until all is lightly browned.

Bring the marinade up to a boil and add the soy sauce, whole cloves, bay leaf, peppercorns, salt and sugar. Then pour in the browned onions and stir. Put in the quarters of rabbit and cook at a simmer for about two or three hours.

Ben McC. Moise

RABBIT STEFADO

See Venison Stefado on page 68.

RABBIT STEW

1 rabbit, dressed and cut into 4 parts	1 No. 2 can tomatoes
3 c. Irish potatoes, diced	3 T. sugar
3 T. onions, minced	¼ lb. butter or margarine
½ c. celery, chopped	¾ c. catsup
2 T. salt	2 T. Worcestershire sauce
½ t. pepper	1 c. corn, cream style

Put rabbit in deep boiler and cover with water. Cook slowly until meat is tender and ready to leave the bone. Remove meat from broth and set aside to cool. Next add potatoes, onions, celery, salt and pepper to broth and cook for 20 minutes. Add tomatoes, sugar and butter, cook 20 minutes more. Pull meat from bone and chop it to small bits. Add to broth and simmer for one hour. The last 15 minutes, add catsup, Worcestershire sauce and corn. Suggestion: If too thick, small amount of water may be added and seasonings varied to taste. Serve in soup bowl with crackers or Red Horse bread.

Mrs. Jerome Forrest

PAT ROBERTSON'S RABBIT AND/OR SQUIRREL STEW

rabbits and/or squirrels	salt and pepper to taste
potatoes, sliced	vinegar
onions, sliced	butter or bacon grease
1 or 2 cans of tomatoes	

Cook rabbits and/or squirrels in a pot of water until the meat is tender. Remove the meat and set aside to cool. While the meat cools, slice up some potatoes and onions in the broth and let them begin to cook down. When the meat is cool enough to handle, take the meat from the bones and add back to the stew pot. Put in a can or two of tomatoes and simmer it for a while. If you need more tomato flavor, add some tomato juice or catsup. Salt and pepper to taste. Stir in just enough vinegar to give the stew a tangy taste.

Serve when the potatoes and onions have cooked down some, but are still a very visible part of the stew. You can cut back on the amount of potatoes and omit the vinegar and serve this stew over rice. You may want to add a spoonful or two of bacon grease for flavoring, but I prefer to melt in a liberal amount of butter to give body and smooth texture to the pot.

Pat Robertson

Furbearers

Furbearers are mammals that are harvested primarily for sport or fur rather than for meat. Southeastern furbearers include fox, otter, mink, muskrat, bobcat, raccoon, opossum and beaver. Of these, raccoon, opossum and beaver are the most often eaten.

Raccoon & Opossum

Raccoons are hunted and trapped for meat, sport and fur, but the meat - although good tasting - is usually a by-product of the sport hunting and trapping. Raccoons were often eaten in the days when people depended on wild food more, particularly during the Depression. Today raccoon hunting is an increasingly popular sporting activity.

A primitive animal with a small brain, the opossum has survived because it is an opportunist, which is not picky about its food. A scavenger by inclination, the opossum is not highly desired for meat. Even so, opossums traditionally have been hunted and eaten by many people.

Dressing Raccoon and Opossum

The procedure for dressing raccoon and opossum is the same.

1. Cut through skin around raccoon or opossum's front and rear legs as indicated.
2. Then cut from one rear leg to and around the anus to the other rear leg.
3. Encircle the anus with another cut, skin-deep.
4. Using a small rope, hang the animal by one or both hind feet.
5. Separate the skin from the carcass with your knife for a small distance down the belly and down the back.
6. Cut the bone in the tail, and remove the tail along with the hide.
7. Grasp the hide with both hands and pull downward, separating the skin from the carcass.
8. Apply thumb pressure at the armpit areas in order to pull the front legs away from the hide.
9. Skin down to the back of the head and separate the head from the carcass.
10. Take the animal down and cut off the front and rear feet. Make a cut from the throat down to the anus, being careful not to puncture the intestinal tract.
11. Eviscerate, taking care to remove the anus with the intestines.
12. Wash out thoroughly with cold water.

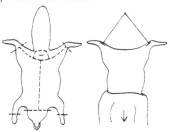

BILL HARRITT'S COON STEW

3-5 lb. coon meat, cubed
3 lb. Irish potatoes, diced
2 lb. onions, chopped

hot sauce to suit taste
2 8-oz. cans tomato paste
salt, pepper

Salt and pepper meat and boil until nearly done. Add potatoes, onions and hot sauce. Simmer for several hours. Add tomato paste just before stew is ready.

The late Dr. William Harritt was an avid outdoorsman and was well-known among the bow hunters on Bull Island. (Reprinted from Moise family cookbook, "Recipes of the Family Favorites".)

Ben McC. Moise

ROAST OPOSSUM

1 opossum
1 onion, chopped
1 T. fat (bacon if you like)
¼ t. Worcestershire sauce

1 c. bread crumbs
1 hard-boiled egg
1 t. salt
water

Rub opossum with salt and pepper. Brown onion in fat. Add opossum liver and cook until tender. Add bread crumbs, Worcestershire sauce, egg, salt and water. Mix thoroughly and stuff opossum. Truss like a fowl. Put in a roasting pan with bacon across back and pour one quart of water in pan. Roast uncovered in moderate oven (350 degrees) until tender. About two-and-a-half hours. Serve with potatoes - sweet potatoes are best.

Barbara Jones

HUNTER'S PILAU

½ lb. bacon
½ c. celery, finely chopped
1 c. onions, finely chopped
1 c. carrots, sliced into one-inch pieces
2 garlic cloves, mashed and finely chopped

2½-3 lb. boned rabbit, squirrel, coon or venison, cut into 1 inch cubes or pieces
2 T. cider vinegar
salt and pepper
2 c. water
1 c. quick rice
1 c. bell peppers, chopped
1 10½ oz. can beef broth (bouillon)

Fry the bacon in a large, heavy pot until it is fairly crisp and drain. Pour out all but a tablespoon or so of the bacon fat. Bring up to medium heat, add onions and celery and stir around gently until they turn a pale yellow. Then stir in the carrots and the garlic and cook for five or so minutes. After that, add the bacon, the meat, the vinegar, salt and pepper and about two cups of water. Cover and simmer (not boil) for about an hour. Then sprinkle the rice and chopped bell peppers over the top, adding a little more salt and pour in the bouillon. Bring to a rapid boil, cover and lower heat again to a simmer (just like for cooking rice) for about 15 or 20 minutes. *Makes a good stick-to-your-ribs meal!*

Ben McC. Moise

Beaver

Furred in a highly desired pelt, the beaver was trapped extensively by early trappers and by the early 1900s had disappeared from many areas. When the fashion for beaver hats ran its course in the nineteenth century, the demand for beaver pelts decreased and allowed a chance for beaver populations to return.

Even though beaver are trapped mainly for their fur, the meat is delicious when prepared properly and compares favorably to the flavor of good venison. According to Jim Byford of the University of Tennessee's Agricultural Extension, an average carcass weighs 15 to 25 pounds, providing a good quantity of meat that can be prepared in many ways like beef or venison.

Dressing Beaver

1. Cut off feet and tail at hairline with hand ax.
2. Separating the skin from the flesh, cut skin only from lower lip to anus. Do not cut through body cavity.
3. Cut skin away from body and legs with sharp knife or single-edge razor blade.
4. When belly is skinned, turn on belly and skin back, starting just above tail and working toward head.
5. After skinning, remove the glands which lie alongside the anus. Avoid contaminating the meat or the knife with the contents of these glands.
6. Cut off the head and remove the entrails with your knife, being sure not to puncture the intestinal tract.
7. Wash out cavity with cold water and immediately pat dry.

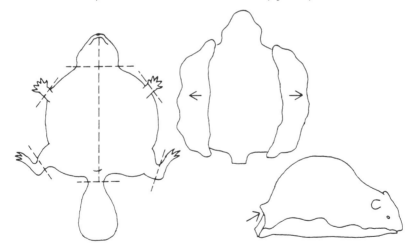

The beaver carcass should then be cut into pieces. Byford says the choicest parts are the loin and legs, which should be carefully washed in cold water, removing as much fat as possible. Tough pieces may be soaked in a suitable marinade, although this is unnecessary if cooked properly. As a general rule, treat it like a moderately tough cut of beef, but don't ruin the meat with excessive spices or seasonings. (For a successful marinade, try "Marinade for Tough Creatures" on page 77.)

BARBECUED BEAVER IN APPLE JUICE

meat from one beaver
apple juice - enough to marinate
  meat

salt and pepper
barbecue sauce

Clean and dress animal. Cut meat in two-inch by two-inch cubes. Soak cut-up meat in apple juice over night. Drain. Salt and pepper meat, then cover with barbecue sauce. Cook on grill for 30 to 45 minutes or until well done.

Derrell Shipes

BEAVER STEW

3 lb. boned beaver, cut in cubes
flour
vegetable oil or bacon fat
salt and pepper
1 or 2 bay leaves
1 dash Worcestershire sauce

water to cover
potatoes, diced
carrots, sliced
onions, chopped
turnips, diced
cabbage, cut in wedges

Remove all possible fat from beaver meat as cut in cubes. Flour cubes and brown on all sides in small amount of fat in a Dutch oven. Season with salt and pepper, add bay leaf, dash of Worcestershire sauce, and water to cover. Cover and simmer until nearly tender. (Time will vary according to age and condition of animal.) Add diced potatoes, carrots, onions and turnips, if desired. Cover and simmer until vegetables are tender, but still intact. Add cabbage, cut in wedges, and simmer again until cabbage is tender, about ten minutes. The gravy may be thickened, if necessary, with flour and water paste.

Barbara Bara

Large Game

Large game mammals in the Southeast are the black bear and white-tailed deer. This section will focus on deer, since these dominate the scene because of successful management.

White-tailed Deer

Many people remember when hardly any deer were to be seen. Although local deer populations were high when the colonists first came, extensive predation and the general lack of good deer habitat inhibited the growth of the deer herd. Herds remained relatively low until wildlife departments began deer restoration programs in the early fifties.

Hunting dogs and man drives are traditional throughout the Southeast. Still hunting and stalking have become more popular deer hunting methods in the last 20 years partly because many sportsmen believe that deer taken with one shot will provide more palatable venison.

Care of Deer Meat

Sometimes hunters spend so much time getting together their gear and making travel arrangements that they forget to plan for the care of their meat after the hunt.

Deer should be field dressed as soon as possible, preferably at the point of kill. Not only will your load be lightened if you carry a dressed deer back to your car or camp, but you'll retard the deterioration process that invariably taints meat if evisceration is delayed too long.

Most important, plan to provide quick cooler or freezer storage for the meat if temperatures are high. Many hunters prefer to eviscerate the deer in the field, then store the whole carcass in a local cooler or freezer while they return to their hunting. To locate the nearest commercial cooler-freezer, check where hunting licenses are sold in your area.

When carrying or dragging a deer, try to avoid getting dirt or leaves inside the carcass. If it's not too hot, you might want to wait till you return to your car or a suitable facility to dress it. That way you can ensure that your carcass stays clean. At certain times, hunters are asked to bring doe deer to check stations so that biologists can field dress these deer to get reproductive data. These are the only conditions where you should delay field dressing your deer.

Slinging the carcass in your vehicle not only bruises good meat, but shows an irreverence for wildlife that many find repugnant. The North American Indians respected the prowess of the game they depended on for survival so much that they recited a prayer over the animal's body, thanking the gods for their good fortune. Today this practice is still observed in part by those hunters who insist on treating their game with respect and skillful care.

Hunters should be careful when transporting deer, too. One of the worst things you can do to deer meat is to hang it over the hood of your vehicle or leave it exposed to the hot sun. Considering the amount of time and money invested in the hunt and the worth of the animal itself, ruining venison for any reason is unconscionable.

As long as you field dress your deer quickly, keep it cool, and place it in a cooler or freezer storage as soon as possible, you've taken the necessary precautions to ensure the venison's quality. Most experts agree that the flavor of venison will be greatly improved if it is aged in a cooler at a constant temperature of 36 to 40 degrees from three to ten days. Let it hang or rest on a rack so air can circulate around it.

Dressing Deer

The techniques for eviscerating a deer in the field or at a processing facility are similar. A processing facility providing a pulley arrangement for hanging deer and running water for clean-up is desirable. The following instructions are for field dressing a deer lying on the ground:

1. Do not cut the neck to bleed the deer, as all the blood will later be drained out when the deer is hung.

2. Run your fingers down the breast bone of the deer until you reach the first part of the soft upper belly. At this point just below the breast bone, insert the point of your knife.

3. Penetrate the skin completely, about one-quarter of an inch, but not so deeply as to cut the intestines. Make a small cut about one-half inch.

4. To extend the incision the whole length of the belly from pelvis to ribcage, place the knife, blade up, between your index and middle fingers and use these as a guide to make the cut while pulling the belly wall toward you. This should avoid cutting into any part of the intestinal tract which will contaminate the meat. (Be careful of your fingers!) The intestines will be exposed and fall out of the belly.

5. Put your hand into the cavity and over the liver. Pull down on the liver, which lies mostly on the right side of the deer. This will expose the diaphragm, a smooth muscle that separates the chest cavity from the abdominal cavity.

6. Cut the diaphragm where it is attached to the rib margins in a circular manner. Now place your hand in the chest cavity over the heart. Pull down firmly on the heart.

7. Reach as high as possible into the chest cavity toward the neck region and cut across the windpipe (trachea) and the gullet (esophagus), which lies behind the windpipe. Gradually cut all the attachments of the heart and pull down the chest contents.

8. Detach the heart and liver and put in a plastic bag if you plan to eat them. Cut or pull loose the attachments of the intestines from the deer.

9. The intestines will still be attached to the body by the rectal tube. It is very important that this tube should be completely and cleanly removed. Widely encircle the rectal tube opening or anus at the base of the tail with your knife deeply inserted to at least five inches. Encircle at least two or three times. (Many people prefer to use a short piece of cord to tie off the rectal tube.)

10. Insert your hand inside the deer and pull firmly on the rectal tube, carefully avoiding spilling its contents or that of the bladder on the meat. If the tube remains attached, gingerly cut around it from the inside to release it completely.

11. Roll the deer on its side to remove the viscera. Drain as much blood as possible from the cavity. Do this quickly, as blood congeals rapidly.

12. After removing the entrails, if possible, flush the body cavity thoroughly with clean water or wipe with paper towels to remove excess blood and other foreign matter like hair or debris.

13. Prop the cavity open with clean, green sticks, which will bend easily but will not snap.

14. If it is a cool day, hang the deer by its hind legs for about an hour or so to allow the meat to cool properly. If it is very hot outside, take the deer to your vehicle and bag it with a clean, damp cloth, such as cheesecloth, a bed sheet, or mattress cover.

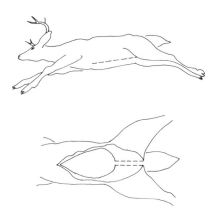

One final comment on field dressing a deer. Contrary to popular belief, it is not necessary to remove scent glands or testicles. Once the deer is dead, the glands do not contribute to the taste of the meat. Those who insist on cutting off the glands and testicles will only succeed in tainting the meat.

We cannot emphasize enough that proper treatment of the meat from field dressing to aging is in direct proportion to how much you'll enjoy - even relish - venison. Make your investment in the hunt count by caring for the game you take. It can guarantee you many good meals on the table, as shown by the chart below diagramming the different cuts of meat.

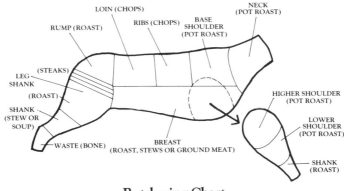

Butchering Chart

You can also use this chart as a guide if you're going to butcher the meat yourself. When skinning deer, avoid getting hair on the meat or pulling pieces of tissue off with the hide. Remember to cut off all ligaments, membranes and fat encasing the muscle tissue. Unlike domestic animals, deer fat does not enhance the flavor of the meat. Package venison in appropriate-sized servings using heavy plastic bags or good quality freezer paper. Each package should be labeled with the cut of meat and the date before freezing.

Starting from the front working backward, here's how to use the different cuts of deer meat:

1. **Neck and shoulders** - Good as roast or filet. Can grind into hamburger or cut up for stew.

2. **Loins** - The filet mignon on a deer. The most tender cuts which can be substituted for any fine beef steak, fried, grilled, broiled or charcoaled. Don't forget the tenderloin either - two thin strips, often overlooked, which lie on the inside of the backbone. Excellent. Can prepare like loins.

3. **Racks of ribs** - Barbecue or ground meat.

4. **Flanks** - Ground meat or stew meat. Mix beef fat to make venison burgers.

5. **Hams** - Next choice cut to loins. Good as roast or steaks, cubed.

BROILED VENISON

2 backstrap roasts or small rump or round roasts about 1 lb. each

Marinade:	**¼-½ c. green onions, chopped**
½ c. olive oil	**2 garlic cloves, chopped**
¼ c. dry white wine	**1 T. Grey Poupon mustard**

Combine all marinade ingredients. Coat steaks or small roasts in marinade and soak at room temperature for about one to two hours, turning occasionally. Place on a broiler rack and broil for about five to eight minutes on each side. Meat should be rare. Baste with marinade. Cut meat into thin slices across the grain.

This recipe is also good for the barbecue grill. Serve with cheese scalloped potatoes, steamed broccoli and rolls. Serves 4-6 and makes great sandwiches.

Laurie Fenwood

ROAST DEER WITH GRAVY

4 to 6 lb. deer roast	**1 can cream of onion soup**
salt	**1 can cream of mushroom soup**
pepper	**3 cans of water, more if needed**
garlic powder	**2 med. onions, quartered**
MSG	**3 or 4 med. potatoes, quartered**

Brown roast completely (either in skillet or under broiler) until it is crusty, but not burnt. Put roast into pan or Dutch oven large enough for meat to be at least half-submerged in gravy. Season both sides of meat with the salt, pepper, garlic powder and MSG. Pour soups over meat, add water, onions and potatoes, bring to a slow boil. Then cover and simmer for about two hours, longer if necessary, turning meat once. Meat should be tender and juicy. This recipe may be cooked in the oven. Just slow bake covered at 300 degrees for about three hours or longer, depending on size of roast.

Jeanette Heissenbuttle

HAWAIIAN VENISON ROAST

1 med. venison roast	**2 T. sugar**
1 c. red wine	**1 t. Tabasco sauce**
¼ c. soy sauce	**2 T. vegetable oil**
3 T. Worcestershire sauce	**dash garlic powder**
½ c. pineapple juice	**¼ t. ground ginger**
¼ c. water	

Combine all ingredients except venison in bowl. Mix well. Place meat in 13 by 9 inch pan or in marinating dish. Pour marinade over meat, covering meat entirely. Refrigerate at least four hours or overnight. (Increase marinating time for more flavor). After marinating, broil or cook over coals until desired doneness is achieved. *Good for wild fowl also.*

Wayne H. King

VENISON ROAST I

A) *Oven Roast*

1-5 lb. roast	1 t. mustard
1 t. Worcestershire sauce	2 t. lemon juice
1 t. catsup	2-5 slices bacon

Mix ingredients together to form a baste for your roast. Season roast to taste: salt, pepper, garlic salt, onion salt. Wrap roast in bacon, baste roast, wrap in foil. Cook in oven one to three hours depending on weight.

B) *Crock Pot Roast*

1-5 lb. roast	6-8 oz. red or white wine or beer
salt, pepper, garlic salt, onion salt to taste	

Season meat with salt, pepper, garlic salt and onion salt to taste. Add six to eight ounces of red or white wine or beer in a crock pot. Cook three to six hours, depending on weight.

C) *Crock Pot Stew Option*

1 can green beans	6 carrots, sliced length-wise
4-6 small red potatoes	3-6 small white onions

For last two hours of roast cooking time in (B) above, add green beans, red potatoes, carrots, sliced length-wise and white onions. Makes a great stew to serve over rice or just by itself. *What a meal!*

Hal Hall

VENISON ROAST II

2-4 lbs. roast	2 med. onions, diced
salt and pepper	2 cans golden mushroom soup
all-purpose seasoning	1 can water
flour	2 T. Worcestershire sauce
¼ c. bacon drippings	½ t. hot sauce
2 med. bell peppers, diced	1 sm. bay leaf

Trim and clean roast and drain on paper towels. Salt, pepper and sprinkle on small amount of all-purpose seasoning. Roll roast in flour, place in heavy fry pan with bacon drippings and brown slowly on all sides. Remove roast and place in heavy pot. Sauté diced onions and peppers in the bacon drippings until soft. Add mushroom soup, Worcestershire sauce, hot sauce and water to pan, stirring until dissolved. Pour these ingredients over roast in pot, add bay leaf and bring to boil. Cover and cook slowly about three hours or until tender. Serve with rice.

Glenn A. Hammond

VENISON ROAST III

3 lb. venison roast
1 T. bacon fat
salt and pepper to taste
2 T. red cooking wine

1 med. onion, chopped
1 bay leaf
2 T. water
fresh garlic to taste

Brown meat on all sides in a pressure cooker and sprinkle with salt and pepper. Pour wine over meat; add onion, bay leaf, water and garlic. Press garlic buds into slits in meat. Cook under pressure for 35 minutes. Allow pressure to cool before removing.

Claudia Geddings

VENISON ROAST IV

salt
6 lb. roast
peppered flour
1 T. steak sauce

1 c. catsup
1 t. Worcestershire sauce
hot sauce

Salt roast and roll in peppered flour. Brown on all sides. Remove and brown some flour for gravy, and to this add roast, steak sauce, catsup and Worcestershire sauce. Season to taste with hot sauce. Add water to cover half the roast. Pressure pot ten pounds for forty-five minutes or cook on low heat for two to three hours, or until done. *Delicious!*

Mrs. Alfred M. Avant

VENISON ROAST V

1 neck roast, 1 shoulder, or 1 deboned hindquarter
Nature's Seasons
2 packets Lipton's onion-
 mushroom soup mix
2 cans cream of mushroom soup
 and equal portions water

2 lg. cans mushroom stems and
 pieces or pack of fresh
 mushrooms
4 lg. onions
3 bell peppers
add Kitchen Bouquet for desired
 darkness
1 beef bouillon cube

Mix chopped onions, peppers and mushrooms with mushroom soup and onion-soup mixture. Season venison with Nature's Seasons and place in large baking pan. Pour soup mixture over venison and cover pan with aluminum foil. Bake for approximately four hours at 375 degrees.

Joe Hamilton

VENISON ROAST VI 3.25.11

venison roast
1 envelope onion soup
3 or 4 bacon slices

Place venison roast on heavy aluminum foil. Cover with one envelope onion soup. Place three or four slices of bacon on top. Seal foil and bake in 300 degree oven three hours or more.

Sarah P. Lumpkin

BILLY TOLAR'S DEER ROAST

4 lb. venison ham
salt and pepper
flour
Wesson oil

3 c. water
1 lb. onions, chopped
Worcestershire sauce to taste
1 t. French's mustard

Take a four-pound center cut of venison ham. Salt, pepper and flour it. Put Wesson oil in a large frying pan and bring up to heat. Brown the ham well all over and add three cups water, one pound chopped onions, salt, pepper and 'wooster' sauce to taste, and one teaspoon French's mustard. Cover and cook in oven at 350 degrees for two-and-a-half hours. Serve with rice or creamed potatoes. *A number one recipe!*

Billy Tolar

VENISON CHUCK ROAST

3 lb. venison chuck roast, 3 in.
   thick
4 T. instant tenderizer
2 T. black pepper
¼ c. butter

1 c. very hot water
1 bay leaf
1 med. onion, chopped
2 T. flour

Wash roast, trim off fat and wipe clean with damp cloth. Sprinkle both sides with tenderizer. Pierce to center with a fork from both sides, making holes about every half inch. Let roast stand for 30 minutes, then sprinkle with black pepper. Brown both sides of the roast in butter in iron skillet. Now place the meat in a roaster. Add pan drippings, water, bay leaf and chopped onion. Spread one tablespoon of flour over top of roast. Bake at 300 degrees for one hour and turn. Spread on the remaining flour and reduce temperature to 200 degrees. Bake until done, two hours or longer. Add flour and water to drippings in roast pan to make gravy.

Claudia Geddings

ROAST MARINADE OF VENISON

1 venison haunch, boned to fit pan
1-2 bottles of red wine, enough to
   cover meat
¼ c. vinegar

2 bay leaves
1 T. ground allspice
1 c. olive oil
salt and pepper to taste

Combine all ingredients except venison and simmer for one hour. Cool slightly. Pour marinade over haunch and marinate for one day, basting occasionally. Cook meat in roaster with marinade for one to one-and-a-half hours at 350 degrees. Remove from oven and leave to complete cooking in marinade as it cools. Slice meat and return to warm (not hot) marinade.

Gail B. Smith

BARBECUE DEER RIBS

rack of ribs
Nature's Seasons

Cut rack of ribs into hand-size pieces using a meat saw or hack saw. Rib bones fragment easily, therefore a hatchet or meat cleaver should never be used to divide ribs. Season ribs with Nature's Seasons which includes salt, pepper, parsley, onion and garlic. Tenderize ribs in a pressure cooker for 20 to 30 minutes. Apply your favorite barbecue sauce and charcoal or broil in oven. A thick sauce is desirable for charcoaling:

2 bottles (34 oz.) catsup
½ c. sugar
3 T. mustard
4-5 T. vinegar

2 squirts of lemon juice
add couple drops of hot sauce if
desired

Joe Hamilton

LOWCOUNTRY CHARCOALED VENISON

Use only the choice cuts of loin (backstrap) or individual muscle masses of the "ham" (hindquarters). If the loin is used, remove the thin cellophane-like membrane or fascia which partially covers this long muscle. Cut each loin in half, making two 8- to 10-inch portions. One will be uniform in thickness and the other tapered.

Individual muscle masses of the hindquarter can be separated to produce portions resembling those of loin, a process much easier if the meat is partially frozen. Remove the fascia from each portion as for the loin.

Season meat strips liberally with coarse ground black pepper, ground ginger, granulated or powdered garlic (not garlic salt), ground or whole celery seeds, rosemary and thyme. Force a wide-tined fork through the meat every quarter-inch along the entire length of each strip, all four sides, to tenderize and season it throughout.

Marinate venison overnight in the following: 2 cups safflower oil, 1½ cups apple cider vinegar, ¼ cup soy sauce and ¼ cup Worcestershire sauce.

Cook over very hot charcoal or on gas grill for four to six minutes per side. Cooking time will vary with type of grill and individual tastes. Baste cooked venison with marinade, carve into serving portions and enjoy.

Joe Hamilton

BAR-B-QUE VENISON

1 deer ham, neck or shoulder roast
2 med. onions
½ c. vinegar

½ stick butter
1 bottle barbecue sauce
plenty of salt and pepper

Lay a double thickness of heavy duty aluminum foil on a flat pan. Place roast in center of foil. Pour vinegar over top of roast. Lay sliced onion on top of this. Completely seal with aluminum foil, making sure that it is leak proof to hold in juice. Leave this on the flat pan to make sure you catch the juice in case of leakage. Place the pan in a 200 degree oven for four hours. Take roast out of foil from top. Pour bottle of barbecue sauce over roast and put back in the oven until the sauce dries out on top. Now it is ready to eat!

Robert McKettrick

BARBECUED VENISON

venison	vinegar
syringe of warm butter or liquid	salt
shortening	water
butter	

When barbecuing venison, take a syringe with warm butter or liquid shortening in it and inject it down to the bone. This makes the meat less dry, more succulent. Then heat butter, vinegar, salt, water and baste with this. If you're going to serve it on a plate, slice it. If you're going to do sandwiches, chip it. And don't try to cover up the taste of the meat with sauce.

Buck Tyler

BARBECUE SAUCE FOR VENISON

1 stick of butter or margarine	2 T. Worcestershire sauce
1 c. catsup	salt
½ c. vinegar	Tabasco sauce
½ c. prepared mustard	

Melt one stick of butter or margarine in sauce pan at low temperature. Add the catsup, vinegar, mustard, Worcestershire and salt to taste. Add Tabasco if you like your sauce hot. Once ingredients are blended, use as barbecue sauce.

Brock Conrad

DANNY FORD'S GRILLED VENISON LOIN

venison loin strips	pepper
Worcestershire sauce	bacon
garlic salt	

First - Ya gotta get a deer. Then you strip the loins out, then you gotta cut the loins into about one inch steaks. You get some Worcestershire sauce and garlic salt and pepper. Put the loin in a bowl and pour in about a half cup of Worcestershire sauce. Sprinkle heavy (or according to your taste buds) with the garlic salt and pepper. Wrap each individual piece in bacon, stick it on the grill for about 15 minutes - or even a smoker. The bacon won't get crispy but will help seal in the moisture of the loin. *You can't beat this with a stick!*

Danny Ford

BUTTERFLY VENISON LOIN

butterfly venison loins	1 t. soy sauce
bacon	garlic salt
½ c. cooking oil	pepper
½ c. lemon juice	1 onion, chopped

Strip loin from the bone. Normally you would cut one to one-and-one-half inch steaks off the loin, but here you cut your steaks off twice as thick as you want your steak to be (i.e. if you desire a one-inch thick steak, cut the loin two inches thick, etc.). Then cut the steak down the center to just short of cutting in half and open out. This produces the "butterfly." Then tightly wrap a piece of bacon around the outer edge of the "butterfly-ed" steak and secure with wooden toothpicks. Then you soak in a marinade of one-half cup cooking oil, one-half cup lemon juice, one teaspoon soy sauce, garlic salt, pepper and one chopped onion for four to six hours. Then grill over a charcoal fire.

Bill Chastain

TENDERLOIN ROAST

venison roast	1 onion soup mix
4 T. butter	½ c. dry vermouth
1 can cream of mushroom soup	

Brown roast in four tablespoons butter. Mix one can cream of mushroom soup, one onion soup mix, half a cup dry vermouth. Put roast in baking dish, pour mix over roast, cover and put in 325 degree oven about three hours.

Claudia Geddings

DEER TENDERLOIN WITH RED WINE SAUCE

One pan, quick and easy

8-16 slices tenderloins or backstrap about ½ inch thick	3 T. flour
½ lb. mushrooms, sliced	¾-1 c. red table wine (inexpensive, but dry)
¼ c. butter	1 c. beef stock, fresh or canned

Sauté the venison slices in a large frying pan using about one or two tablespoons of butter over medium heat for about 3 minutes per side or until lightly browned. Do not overcook. Remove venison from pan and reserve in a dish. Melt remaining butter in the pan and sauté the mushrooms until lightly browned. Sprinkle flour over mushrooms and butter and blend in. Add wine and beef stock and cook until mixture comes to a boil. Simmer about 8-10 minutes over low heat. Add venison slices and juices in dish to pan and cook until heated through. Serves 4-6.

To round out meal, serve with parmesan buttered noodles, crusty French bread, green salad and a full-bodied red wine or cold beer.

Laurie Fenwood

VENISON STEAKS

venison steaks (preferably sirloin,   salt
   tenderloin, round or rib)   pepper
flour

Roll in flour, salt and pepper and fry as you would country steak. The venison heart can also be sliced and fried in the same manner. *Very tasty.*

Mr. and Mrs. Joe B. Norris

VENISON PEPPER STEAK

*1½ lb. venison round steak, cut in   2 lg. fresh tomatoes, diced
   ⅛-in. strips   1 c. beef broth
1 T. paprika   ¼ c. water
2 t. garlic powder   2 T. cornstarch
2 T. butter   2 T. soy sauce
1 c. onions, sliced   3 c. hot cooked rice
2 green peppers, cut in strips

Sprinkle steak with paprika and set aside while preparing other ingredients. Melt butter and add garlic powder, steak, onions and green peppers. Continue cooking until vegetables are tender. Add tomatoes and broth; cover and simmer on low heat about 15 minutes. Blend water with cornstarch and soy sauce; stir into steak. Cook until thickened. Serve over rice.
   This really has a distinctive flavor if venison strips are marinated.

William Gary Freeman and Cindy Freeman

DEER STEAK

1-2 lb. deer meat, cut into steaks   pepper
1 can milk   salt to taste
flour   seasoned meat tenderizer

Place steak in pan, pour milk over, sprinkle with tenderizer. Let stand five minutes. Sprinkle salt and pepper to taste. Flour steak. Cook over medium heat until tender. Makes five servings.

Mrs. Alfred M. Avant

STUFFED VENISON STEAKS

2-3 lb. venison round steak
¼ t. meat tenderizer
2 c. dry bread crumbs
4 T. celery, chopped
¾ c. onion, chopped
½ t. salt
⅛ t. pepper

⅛ t. poultry seasoning
⅛ t. sage or to taste
2 T. butter, melted
water
2 cans tomato sauce (12 oz.)
2 T. taco sauce

Sprinkle steaks with tenderizer, pound with mallet and set aside. Melt butter in skillet and sauté celery and onion until tender. Place bread crumbs in a bowl with butter mixture, seasoning and enough water to make mixture sticky. Place two or three teaspoons of mixture on each steak, roll, and secure with toothpicks. Steaks should not be too large; serving size portions do better. Brown steaks thoroughly in a little oil. Mix tomato sauce and taco sauce according to taste and pour over browned meat (drain any oil left). Simmer slowly for one hour or bake at 350 degrees for one-and-a-quarter hours. Makes five to six servings.

Contributor Unknown

VENISON FRIED IN MUSTARD

venison ham, cubed
yellow mustard
soy sauce
black and red pepper

garlic salt
onion, sliced
flour

Bone and cube a venison ham. Marinate in mixture of regular yellow mustard, soy sauce, black and red pepper, garlic salt and sliced onion for two hours. Then roll in flour and drop in very hot, deep fry grease. The secret is having the grease deep enough where the cut browns all over before it hits the bottom of the pot. They should be done enough in three or four minutes.

Bill Chastain

VENISON POUPON

venison tenderloin
Poupon french style mustard

flour
cooking oil

Cut venison tenderloin or other tender pieces in half-inch thick pieces approximately two inches square. Dust pieces with flour, coat with mustard, and recoat with flour. Fry in deep, hot oil until golden.

David Allen

FRIED CUBED VENISON

8-10 lb. venison ham	salt
2 qt. water	pepper
2 T. vinegar	milk
½ c. salt	self-rising flour

Slice eight to ten pound venison ham in half-inch thick pieces and then 'hack' with edge of saucer on cutting board. Soak for six to eight hours in a salt brine and vinegar made of two quarts of water, two tablespoons vinegar, and half a cup of salt. Drain, rinse, rub with salt and pepper and soak in milk for two hours. Then dredge in self-rising flour and fry in fry pan with bacon grease on low heat until flour is browned on both sides. You can make a gravy out of the *pan drippings and serve on rice or grits along with cole slaw or a tossed salad.

"Bunk" Williams

*Just in case it's not common knowledge, the ratio for making pan drippings gravy is one tablespoon pan drippings (bacon grease), one tablespoon flour to one cup of water or 'pot-likker.' Bring grease to medium hot, sprinkle in and stir flour with a fork until good and brown and add water or 'pot-likker' and stir furiously with fork until bubbling hot. Season to taste with salt and pepper. *Fool proof!*

Ben McC. Moise

PAN FRIED VENISON

2 lb. venison, cut in serving pieces	1½ c. flour
vinegar	3 med. onions
milk	1½ c. water
unseasoned tenderizer	2 T. cooking wine
salt, black pepper and garlic to taste	

Wipe meat with vinegar-soaked cloth. Vinegar picks up hairs and clotted blood more easily. Cut two pounds of venison into serving pieces, removing all tough parts. Pound well and dip in milk. Sift unseasoned tenderizer over meat, then season with salt, black pepper and garlic to taste. Put pieces into a bag with flour. Shake vigorously. Slice three medium onions and brown in oiled fry pan. Remove cooked onions and add more oil or grease and fry venison until golden brown on both sides. Put onions on top of venison last few minutes cooking time. Remove venison to platter and make gravy by adding flour, salt and black pepper to drippings. Let brown lightly and add the water and cooking wine. Let simmer until thickened. Serve over rice or with grits. Serves four.

Claudia Geddings

BOBBY ASHLEY'S FRIED BREAKFAST VENISON

Take the eye of the round from the venison and slice it thin. Fry in a small amount of bacon grease and serve with eggs, grits and biscuits. *Better than bacon.*

Bobby Ashley

WEST TEXAS FRIED VENISON

2 lb. venison	1 celery stalk, sliced
¼ c. flour	3 med. onions, sliced
1 t. salt	1 T. Worcestershire sauce
fresh ground pepper to taste	2 c. canned tomatoes
3 T. bacon fat	noodles

Cut two pounds venison into serving size pieces. Mix flour, salt and fresh ground pepper to taste. Coat venison with flour mixture. Heat bacon fat in skillet and brown venison on both sides. Add the celery, cut up, and then the onions and brown. Add Worcestershire sauce, canned tomatoes and cook covered one to two hours or until tender. Cook (boil) noodles, drain and serve with venison.

Joyce D. Benson

VENISON MEATLOAF

1½ lb. ground venison	½ t. pepper
½ lb. pork sausage	¼ c. onion, chopped
2 eggs	1 T. Worcestershire sauce
½ c. milk	1½ c. bread crumbs
1 t. salt	

Heat oven to 350 degrees. Beat eggs, milk, salt, pepper and Worcestershire sauce. Stir in bread crumbs. Let stand for five minutes. Add ground meats and onions to above mixture. Grease nine by five by two inch baking dish. Pack in meatloaf mixture. Bake 60 minutes.

William Gary Freeman and Cindy Freeman

OWINGS' VENISON

2 lb. ground venison	2 c. fine bread crumbs
4 eggs	8 oz. sour cream
¼ c. Parmesan cheese	dry white wine
¼ t. salt and pepper	½ t. curry
½ t. oregano	¼ t. thyme
½ t. garlic powder	1 c. grated Mozzarella cheese
1 can cream of mushroom soup	

Mix venison, eggs, Parmesan cheese, salt and pepper, oregano and garlic powder and form into patties. Beat the remaining two eggs and prepare very fine bread crumbs. Dip patties into eggs, then bread crumbs. Fry patties in bacon grease or oil until browned on each side. To prepare sauce, combine the mushroom soup, sour cream, wine, curry and thyme. Place patties in baking dish and top each one with Mozzarella cheese. Pour sauce over top of each pattie and bake in oven for 45 minutes at 350 degrees.

Steve Owings

VENISON PARTY SAUSAGE

3 lb. ground venison
2 lb. ground beef
5 t. Morton's quick curing salt
1½ t. regular table salt
1 t. Italian seasoning

1 t. liquid smoke
2½ t. garlic salt
½ t. ground red pepper
½ t. ground black pepper

Mix all ingredients in a large bowl. Knead well, like you would bread. Refrigerate 24 hours. Mix again real good. Shape in rolls like sausage rolls. Makes about three or four rolls two inches by approximately 12 inches long. Place on rack in broiler pan or cookie sheet. Bake eight hours at 150 degrees. Let cool in oven. Will keep in refrigerator about five weeks or wrap well in wax paper and aluminum foil and freeze.

Gene Pluto

VENISON STROGANOFF I

1½ lb. venison
milk
unseasoned tenderizer
salt, pepper and garlic
1½ c. flour

4 med. onions, sliced
2 cans mushrooms
1½ c. water
2 T. red cooking wine

Cut venison into strips, removing all tough parts. Pound well and dip in milk. Sift unseasoned tenderizer over meat, then season with salt, black pepper and garlic to taste. Put pieces into a bag with the flour. Shake vigorously. Brown four medium onions, sliced thin, with mushrooms in lightly greased fry pan until light tan color. Remove to another pan. Brown seasoned venison strips on both sides quickly and drain. Put venison, onions, mushrooms and drippings in pressure cooker on rack. Add the water and wine, put pressure on and cook 15 minutes. Keep pressure low so it won't stick and burn. Serve with rice. Serves four.

Claudia Geddings

VENISON STROGANOFF II

1 lb. venison, cubed
flour
¼ c. butter
1 T. garlic powder
½ c. onion, chopped

1 T. salt
⅛ t. pepper
1¼ c. water
1 c. mushrooms
1 c. sour cream

Dredge venison cubes in flour and brown in butter over moderate heat with garlic powder. Add chopped onions, salt and pepper. Cook three to four minutes. Stir in water and simmer 30 minutes until tender. Add mushrooms and sour cream, and heat (but do not boil). Serve over rice or noodles. Makes four servings.

Contributor Unknown

VENISON CASSEROLE

1 lb. ground venison	½ c. uncooked rice
3 lg. onions, sliced	2 t. salt
1 lg. green pepper, chopped	½ t. chili powder
1 can (16 oz.) tomatoes	⅛ t. pepper

Heat oven to 350 degrees. In large skillet, cook and stir meat, onion and green pepper until meat is brown and vegetables are tender. Drain off fat. Stir in tomatoes, rice, salt, chili powder and pepper. Heat thoroughly. Pour into ungreased two-quart casserole. Cover and bake one hour.

W.A. Carson, Jr.

DEER-SAUSAGE CASSEROLE

1¾ lb. ground deer meat	¼ lb. uncooked elbow macaroni
¼ lb. mild pork sausage	¼ c. olive juice
garlic to your liking	½ c. ripe olives, sliced
onion, chopped (1 lg. or to taste)	2 lg. cans tomatoes (fresh in season)
dash pepper	1 sm. can white corn (fresh in
dash basil	season), drained
1 green pepper, chopped	½ lb. American cheese, grated (or
1-8 oz. can sliced mushrooms,	mild Cheddar)
drained	

Brown deer meat and sausage in large heavy skillet. Crumble meat, pour off excess fat. Add garlic, onion, pepper, sweet basil and remaining ingredients. Stir to combine. Place in 12 by 14 by three inch baking dish, cover generously with Parmesan cheese. Bake at 350 degrees for 45 minutes covered with foil. Uncover, cook until nice crust forms on top, approximately 15 minutes. Makes eight servings.

Barbara Jones

VENISON STEFADO

3-4 lb. boneless venison	2 bay leaves
3 garlic cloves, chopped	3 t. salt
3-4 lb. sm. whole onions, peeled	1 t. pepper
3 heaping T. tomato paste	¾ c. olive oil
2 c. dry sherry wine	

Cut venison in one-and-one-half inch cubes. Place in deep dish and marinate using the recipe below. Cover dish and refrigerate overnight, turning meat often. Drain meat.

Marinade

1½ c. vinegar	2 bay leaves
1 c. water	10 whole cloves
juice of two lemons	

In large Dutch oven, slowly brown meat and garlic slightly in hot olive oil. Arrange whole onions over meat. Dilute tomato paste in sherry and pour over onions and meat. Add spices and seasonings. Cover and simmer for two-and-a-half hours, or until meat is tender and liquid is reduced. Add water only if necessary. Serve over hot cooked rice or noodles. Makes six servings.

Two rabbits can be substituted instead of venison.

Maria Latto

VENISON RAGOUT

3 lb. venison sirloin, cut into ½ in.
  cubes
3 T. flour
1 t. salt
¼ t. black pepper
¼ c. olive oil

3 onions, quartered
2 c. dry red wine
2½ c. tomatoes
2 garlic cloves, crushed
1 t. ground ginger

Dredge the venison pieces in the flour mixed with the salt and pepper. Brown slowly in the oil in a large, heavy skillet. Transfer meat to a heavy casserole or Dutch oven. Sauté the onions in the fat remaining in the skillet. Add the wine, tomatoes, garlic and ginger. Bring to a boil, stirring, and pour into the casserole. Cover and let simmer four hours, or until the venison is very tender. Makes six servings.

Mrs. Helen B. Lee

WILD GAME RAGOUT

3 T. olive oil
3 lb. venison
3 lg. onions, chopped
5 garlic cloves, crushed
½ lb. bacon, chopped
½ or 1 t. curry powder (to your
  taste)

1 can tomato soup, undiluted
1½ qt. water
2 T. bourbon
¼ c. beer
1 T. salt
½ lb. fresh mushrooms, sliced

Place olive oil in electric skillet. Cut meat into cubes about one-and-a-half inches square; add to hot olive oil with the onions, garlic and bacon. Cook until all is richly browned, stirring frequently. Add all other ingredients except mushrooms. Cover and simmer for fifty minutes. Add mushrooms and simmer ten minutes longer. You do not need to marinate the game before using. In fact, it is better if you don't. Serve over rice. This dish reheats very well and can be prepared a day ahead of a dinner party. Makes eight servings.

Barbara Jones

VENISON PILAU I

4 lg. onions
3 bell peppers
2 lg. cans mushroom stems and
  pieces or pack of fresh
  mushrooms
2 cans cream of mushroom soup
2 packets Lipton's onion-mushroom
  soup mix
2-3 c. water

3-4 lb. well-trimmed venison
  chunks
Nature's Seasons
flour
rice (enough for 10 normal-size
  servings)
add Kitchen Bouquet for desired
  darkness
garlic powder, optional

Sauté onions, peppers and mushrooms in butter, then add mushroom soup, onion-mushroom soup mix and two to three cups water. Season meat chunks with Nature's Seasons, roll in flour, and brown in skillet. Place browned venison chunks in pressure cooker for 30 minutes. Chop venison into small pieces and add to soup. Mix in cooked rice. This dish may be spiced up a bit by the addition of garlic powder to taste.

Joe Hamilton

VENISON PILAU II

1½ or 2 lb. venison cut up, salted
   and cooked tender
2 cans onion soup
2 lg. onions, cut sm.

1 T. pepper or to taste
3 T. sage or to taste
1 stick margarine
2 c. long grain rice

Take venison out of water it was cooked in and put in large pot. Add soup, onions, pepper, sage, salt and margarine. Let boil and add long grain rice. When comes to a boil, turn stove down to medium for 15 minutes, then on low until done. Add a small amount of water if rice isn't done. Cook until done. Loosen up from bottom of pot several times, but don't stir. Will serve from eight to twelve.

Mrs. J.K. Johnson

OLD BAVARIAN DEER GOULASH

2 lb. deer meat, cubed
3 slices bacon
1 lg. onion, diced
1 T. fresh chopped parsley (or 1 t.
   dried)
1 sm. bay leaf

½ t. drained thyme
1 t. salt
2 c. water
2 T. flour
2 c. mushrooms, sliced
1 c. sour cream

Dice bacon and fry with onion until bacon is cooked and onion glassy. Add deer meat and herbs; brown. Add the water, simmer one to one-and-a-half hours until meat is tender. Mix flour with water to a paste, add to stew with mushrooms, cook ten minutes, then add sour cream and stir in one to two minutes. Serve with egg noodles, salad and red wine.

Best cooked a day ahead, omitting sour cream. Refrigerate overnight, reheat next day, add sour cream before serving.

S. Mary Revels

VENISON CHILI CON CARNE

3 lb. chopped venison
3 T. chili powder
1 T. black pepper
3 lg. onions, diced
1 lg. bell pepper, diced

3 T. Worcestershire sauce
½ T. salt
½ T. ea. oregano and thyme
   (optional)
2 cans kidney beans (optional)

Flour meat and brown in corn oil, pour off excess fat. Cook meat in Dutch oven or crock pot (45 minutes for Dutch oven, one-and-a-half hours for crock pot). Add other ingredients and cook until desired tenderness.

Hal Hall

TEXAS VENISON CHILI

2 lb. venison, ground
¼ c. oil
1 c. onions, chopped
2 t. garlic powder
1 lg. green pepper, chopped
3 T. chili powder

2 t. sugar
3½ c. whole tomatoes
1 c. tomato sauce
1 c. water
½ t. salt
2 c. cooked kidney beans

Brown venison in vegetable oil. Add onions, garlic powder and green pepper. Cook five minutes, stirring constantly. Add chili powder, sugar, tomatoes, tomato sauce, water and salt. Simmer one-and-a-half hours. If a thicker chili is desired, stir in one tablespoon flour mixed with two tablespoons water. Just before serving, add kidney beans. Makes six to eight servings.

Contributor Unknown

D.J.'s VENISON

4 lg. venison steaks
5 lg. onions
3 lg. potatoes
4 carrots
salt and pepper

2 10-oz. cans beef broth or 2 beef
    bouillon cubes and 2 c. water to
    make broth
Worcestershire sauce

Place steaks in large pot and cover with water. Slice two onions and put in pot with steaks. Bring to boil and cook on medium until meat is medium tender. Do not add salt. Cut potatoes and onions in one-quarter inch pieces and slice carrots. Cool and cut venison in bite-size pieces. In a four quart covered Pyrex dish, layer alternately venison, onions, potatoes and carrots. Season with salt and pepper. Pour in beef broth and add dash Worcestershire sauce. Cook at 425 degrees for one hour. Remove cover and reduce heat to boil off water until gravy thickens. Serve with garlic bread and wild rice.

Danny Judy

CAROLINA VERSION OF KENTUCKY BURGOO

1 or 2 chickens, ducks, or a turkey
  (anyway, 5 lbs. of fowl)
2 lbs. venison
1½ to 2 lbs. venison (or beef) bones
1 stalk celery
1 carrot, peeled
1 sm. onion, peeled
5 to 6 sprigs parsley
1 10-oz. can tomato puree
4 qts. water
1 red pepper pod
¼ c. salt
1 T. lemon juice
1 T. Worcestershire sauce

1 T. sugar
1½ t. black pepper
½ t. cayenne
6 onions, finely chopped
8 to 10 tomatoes, peeled and
  chopped
1 turnip, peeled and finely chopped
2 c. fresh butterbeans
2 c. celery, thinly sliced
2 c. cabbage, finely chopped
2 c. fresh okra, sliced
2 c. fresh corn (3 to 4 ears)
½ unpeeled lemon, seeded

Combine first 16 ingredients in large pot. Bring to a boil, then cover and simmer for four hours. Cool. Strain, reserving meat and stock; throw away vegetables. Remove bone, skin and gristle from meat; finely chop meat. Return to stock and refrigerate overnight.

The next day, skim fat off top. Add rest of ingredients; cover and simmer one hour. Uncover and simmer about two more hours, stirring frequently. Makes about one gallon of thick stew.

Nancy Coleman Wooten

KIM ASHLEY'S VENISON STEW

2 or 3 lb. venison roast with suet
2 cans of your favorite beer (one for
  the venison, one to drink)
2/3-1 c. onions, chopped
garlic salt to your liking and pepper

6 or 8 whole potatoes, peeled
1 box frozen limas
1 box frozen green beans or peas,
  corn, or a mixture of all

Throw it all in a crockpot and cook for eight to ten hours. It's even better if refrigerated overnight and eaten the next day.

Sorry about the haphazard measurements. I cook by the seat of my pants.

Kim Ashley

HE-MAN VENISON STEW

2 lb. tender venison, cubed	4 sm. carrots
2 T. fat	8 med. Irish potatoes, cubed
1 bay leaf	1 c. celery, diced
1½ t. salt	2 c. water or tomato juice
½ t. pepper	2 T. flour
1 c. water	2 T. butter
6 sm. onions	

Melt fat in bottom of open pressure cooker. Add meat and brown on all sides. Add bay leaf, salt and pepper, and cup of water; cover and cook 20 minutes. Remove from heat; release pressure. Remove cover and add onions, carrots, potatoes, celery and tomato juice. Cover and cook ten minutes or longer. Cream flour and butter together. Stir into stew until thickened.

Marie DeWitt

BOBBY ASHLEY'S BROWN GRAVY VENISON STEW

venison	1 can onion soup
salt and pepper	onions
flour	Kitchen Bouquet

Use any cuts of venison you have available. Cuts from the loin, hindquarter and part of the front shoulder can be fried. Odd cuts from the ribs and small parts of the shoulder should be cooked in the pressure cooker at ten pounds of pressure. Salt and pepper the tender pieces. Roll in flour and fry in deep fat. Remove the bones from the meat in the pressure cooker and put this meat, the broth and the fried meat into a pot. Add canned onion soup to beef stock and slice up some fresh onions into the stew. Let it simmer down until the fried meat portions are tender. If there is too much liquid, thicken it with a little flour and add a touch of Kitchen Bouquet. Serve over rice with a side dish of tossed salad.

Bobby Ashley

VENISON STEW I

10 lb. venison	2 lg. cans tomatoes
3-4 lb. pork	1½ lg. bottles catsup
4 lb. potatoes	2 c. mustard
4 lb. onions	1 c. vinegar
1-2 lb. fatback	1 bottle Worcestershire sauce
1 lb. butter or oleo	salt and pepper to taste

Parboil venison 15 to 20 minutes. Pour off all water. Rinse venison in warm water. Pour off. Dice potatoes, onions and fatback. Cover venison and pork with water. Simmer-boil until tender one to one-and-a-half hours. Remove when done. Keep broth. Remove all bones and pull meat apart. Return meat to broth pot. Add potatoes, onions, fatback and butter. Bring to slow boil. Stir often. After potatoes and onions are done, add other ingredients and small amount of water if desired. Salt and pepper to taste and cook until done to taste. Stir often.

Lonny Slade

VENISON STEW II

Clean meat thoroughly and put in a big pot to boil. Add salt, pepper and a medium sliced onion. This flavors as it boils. When tender, cool and remove all bones; cut meat into small pieces.

Add meat back to some of the juices it was cooked in (about 3 cups) being careful not to pour in any bone fragments that may have been in the bottom of the pot. Add 1 lb. pork sausage (bulk, not links) to each 1½ lb. venison. Crumble it into venison and juices. Add 2 medium chopped onions, several large cubed Irish potatoes and more salt and pepper if needed. Cook until potatoes are done.

Serve on hot cooked rice or alone in a bowl as soup.

Shirley W. Robinson

VENISON STEW WITH WINE

2 lbs. stew meat, cut into 1″ cubes	1½ c. canned beef stock
1 lg. onion, sliced	2 sprigs parsley, chopped
1 c. red wine	¼ t. thyme
1 lg. bay leaf	¼ t. rosemary
1 clove garlic, chopped	⅛-¼ t. ground cloves
½ t. salt	Suggested vegetables:
½ t. freshly ground black pepper	4 lg. potatoes, cut in cubes
2 T. olive oil or vegetable oil	6 med. carrots, cut in sticks

In a large stewpot over medium heat, sauté onions and garlic until limp and yellow. Add venison cubes and brown on all sides. Add stock, wine and all seasonings. Add water to bring level of broth in the pot up to stew level. Cover and simmer until meat is tender, about 1½ to 2 hours. About 30 minutes before serving, add vegetables and cook until they are tender. Taste and correct seasoning with salt and pepper.

Thicken gravy, if desired, with cornstarch, ½ t. per cup of broth, mixed with a little cold water. Boil and stir after addition. Serve with biscuits or cornbread. Serves 4.

Laurie Fenwood

POPPA PIERCE'S VENISON HASH

Not to be used for your choice venison cuts such as roasts or steaks

venison (not choice cuts)	Worcestershire sauce
2 med. onions, diced	bacon
salt and pepper	

Place meat in large pot. Cover with water and boil until meat separates from bone. Remove from pot and "shred" meat finely as opposed to "tearing" or "cutting." Place in nine by twelve inch pan. Dice two medium onions over meat. Salt and pepper meat to taste. Then douse with Worcestershire sauce. Stir all together, and spread meat mixture evenly across bottom of pan. Cover with single layer of bacon slices. Place in oven and bake 350 to 375 degrees until bacon is done, being careful not to let bacon become overly crisp. (If meat mixture is still warm from boiling at this stage, it may be broiled instead of baked to cook bacon slices.) When done, remove from oven and slice bacon into venison mixture.

Poppa P. used to serve this with grits and hot biscuits. We like it equally as well accompanied with a salad and dinner rolls.

D. Pierce

VENISON HASH

venison (not choice cuts)
onions, diced
sage

shot of vinegar
salt and pepper
barbecue sauce (optional)

Have venison cut off the bone (like stew beef). Put in pressure cooker with a little water, and put under pressure with diced onions, sage, and shot of vinegar, salt and pepper until done. Remove the venison from the pressure cooker and hash the meat up. Put in a roaster and add some Crisco (enough to coat all the meat) and slide in oven at 350 degrees until the Crisco has melted. Then add in some diced up onions and salt and pepper to taste. Cook until all the onions are done. If you want to, add your favorite barbecue sauce and let bubble for a while.

Ivan "Boss Hawg" Holden

DANISH DEER PATÉ

1 lb. deer liver
¾ lb. pork fat
1 onion, quartered
4 flat anchovies
2 T. butter
2 T. flour

2 c. milk
2 lg. eggs
salt to taste
¾ t. freshly ground black pepper
½ t. allspice
¼ t. ground cloves

Preheat oven to 350 degrees. Grind the liver, pork fat, onion and anchovies two times. Melt the butter in a sauce pan and, using a wire whisk, stir in the flour. Add the milk, stirring rapidly with the whisk. Cook, stirring until sauce is thickened and smooth. Cool slightly and add the sauce to the liver mixture. Beat with a wooden spoon and add the eggs, one at a time, beating well after each addition. Beat in the remaining ingredients and pour mixture into a loaf pan. Set the loaf pan in a shallow pan of water and bring the water to a boil on top of the stove. Place in the oven and bake one-and-a-half hours. Cool. Serve sliced. Serves eight.

Mrs. Helen B. Lee

PAT'S VENISON SALAD

venison meat from neck
celery
onion
green pepper

pickles
salt, garlic salt to taste
black pepper to taste
Hellman's mayonnaise

Boil venison meat until very tender with salt, garlic salt and black pepper. When tender, drain and cool. Chop fine, add chopped celery, green pepper, onion, pickle and lots of mayonnaise. (Meat seems to absorb the mayonnaise.) I do not show amounts to use because I fix according to the crowd. This is better served the next day with Ritz crackers.

Patricia Pope

VENISON FONDUE

venison
Worcestershire sauce
soy sauce

onions, chopped
mushrooms, fresh

Cut venison into bite-sized chunks. Marinate for several days in Worcestershire sauce, soy sauce, lots of onions and mushrooms. Refrigerate and stir several times a day. Cook mushrooms, onions and meat together on fondue fork in pot filled with peanut oil.

Billy DuRant

STIR-FRIED VENISON (A wok dish)

1 lb. round or rump roast (trim any gristle or connective tissue and cut into ¼″ slices across the grain)

1 T. cornstarch
1 T. sherry
½ T. sugar
1 beaten egg

2 t. salt (optional)
1 t. fresh ginger, minced
½ c. canned beef or chicken stock
1 lb. vegetables (see below)

Vegetables I use, cut into bite-sized pieces:

1 lg. clove garlic, minced
1 med. onion, thinly sliced
2-3 green onions cut into ½″
    sections

½-1 c. bite-sized broccoli
½ c. snow peas, trimmed
2 celery stalks, sliced
½ c. fresh mushrooms, sliced

(Other additions or substitutions include sliced water chestnuts, bamboo shoots, cauliflower florets, carrots sliced into thin "coins" and green peppers.)

Heat ½ T. oil in a large wok, add half the meat slices and stir-fry until browned. Remove to the serving dish using a slotted spatula. Stir-fry the rest of the venison and remove the dish. Add garlic and onion and stir-fry until tender. Add broccoli, ginger and celery and stir-fry one to two minutes. Add snow peas, mushrooms and green onions; stir-fry one minute and add stock. Stir and simmer over medium heat until vegetables are almost done. Add venison to heat through and blend flavors.

Vegetables should be crisp and tender and venison should not be gray, but a little pink.

Laurie Fenwood

ROUND-O-RACK (SMOKED MARINATED VENISON)

The following recipe makes a very tangy and mildly hot, smoked snack which can be kept for days in the frig and sliced as needed. A smoker is required. The recipe's name acknowledges Mr. Thomas C. Hulsey of Round-O, South Carolina, who has been the host of many a fine hunt and subsequent source of venison through the years.

1 sm. venison ham
a garlic clove
1 bottle Teriyaki Barbecue
  Marinade
¼ bottle Worcestershire sauce
5 splashes Tabasco sauce
1 t. dry horseradish
1 T. minced garlic

1 T. minced onion
1 t. rosemary
1 t. marjoram
1 t. salt (or onion or garlic salt)
1 t. black pepper (or red pepper,
  depending on taste)
1 bottle cheap dry white wine

Marinate venison in bottom of broiler pan or similar size pan large enough to hold meat and marinade. Poke and score venison with knife to let marinade seep deep into meat. Rub venison with garlic clove, leaving leftover clove in pan. Add Teriyaki, Worcestershire, Tabasco, horseradish, herbs and spices. Put enough wine in (usually half a bottle or so) to partially cover meat. Let set, covered with foil, at least overnight, but preferably one day or more. Turn meat as often as you can remember. Remove and pepper meat to taste before smoking. Smoke according to your smoker's direction until done (undercooking is a bigger problem than overcooking). Use leftover marinade in smoker's marinade pan. I prefer smoking with one-third hickory, one-third oak and one-third fruit tree (plum). Add a few sprigs of rosemary, marjoram or sage to the coals for an extra touch.

Greg R. Alexander

VENISON JERKY

lean venison strips
salt and pepper

Cut lean venison strips about one-quarter inch to three-eighths an inch thick and six inches long. Rub well with salt and pepper and hang on a rack in a cool, dry place and let the meat dry until stiff. Then smoke with hickory chips in a smoker and store in a jar.

This always used to be in the pantry and was our "candy" in the old days. (For more information on smoking, see page 195.)

J. Oscar Sullivan

MARINADE FOR TOUGH CREATURES

½ c. pineapple juice
½ c. red wine
1 bay leaf
½ t. whole peppercorns
½ t. marjoram

½ t. parsley
½ t. thyme
1 or 2 garlic cloves, peeled, mashed,
  and finely chopped

Mix all ingredients, then pour over game and marinate overnight. You can also add soy sauce, paprika, chopped onion, Tabasco, olive-oil - most anything!

Ben McC. Moise

TONY CHACHERE'S ALL-PURPOSE WILD GAME MARINADE

1 c. water
2 T. vinegar
1 lemon, sliced
½ doz. peppercorns, crushed
2-3 carrot slices
1 stick green celery, chopped

1 t. bay leaf
2-3 parsley sprigs
2-3 whole cloves, crushed
1 T. seasoning salt
2 garlic cloves
2 T. oil

Mix all ingredients and marinate overnight - the longer the better. After marinating, game may be roasted, barbecued, stewed or prepared in any other of your favorite ways.

Jim and Marty Sorrow

MARINADE FOR VENISON STEAK OR ROAST

¼ c. soy sauce
¼ c. Teriyaki sauce
2 T. Worcestershire sauce

1 t. garlic powder
1 t. salt
½ c. oil

Let meat sit in mixture overnight. Great for grilling!

William Gary Freeman and Cindy Freeman

SAUTÉED MUSHROOMS WITH VEGETABLES

¾ lb. mushrooms
3-4 spring onions
3 celery stalks
1 lg. bell pepper or 2 sm. ones

slightly less than T. salt
T. pepper
¼ lb. (1 stick) butter or margarine

Slice up mushrooms or use store-bought kind in jars. Clean and chop onions up to where the tops become all green. Slice up celery stalks, chop in green bell peppers rather fine, throwing insides away. Use a large iron frying pan that you can cover with a lid. After preparing ingredients, put two-thirds a stick of butter into pan; when hot, add everything! Cook about five minutes, stirring with a fork. Add a little less than a tablespoon of salt and a level tablespoon of pepper, both sprinkled all over. Put the other one third of butter stick on top in middle. Cover pan with lid, but not tight. Reduce to low heat and let simmer for another five minutes. Lift it out of pan spoon. The left-over butter can help the meat make gravy. Serves three.

Goes with any meat, especially red meat.

Dana Crosland

Bear

ROAST BEAR

1 bear meat roast	2 bay leaves
1 lg. onion, chopped	¼ t. rosemary
1 garlic clove, chopped	1 celery stalk
1 c. Wesson oil	Worcestershire sauce
1 t. dry mustard	celery salt
½ c. catsup	vinegar

Peel all fat from the meat and dry it. Place it in a pot, and after mixing all the rest of the ingredients together, pour them all over the roast. Let it marinate the meat for eighteen to twenty-four hours. Remove meat from herb mixture, scraping all clinging ingredients. Rub with salt and pepper and sear well in a little fat. Pour on enough hot water to cover a quarter of the roast. Add marinating mixture of oil and herbs and cover the pot. Simmer very gently, allowing 45 minutes cooking time to the pound. Keep the water up, and turn the meat to keep it moist. Before serving remove roast and thicken gravy.

Served with saffron rice, stewed tomatoes and green salad, this is a dish to smack the lips over.

Faye Harris

BEAR PAW

bear paws	bacon fat
onions	bread crumbs
whole peppercorns	meat marinade
minced garlic	

Bear meat, being rather dark and tough, is only suitable for cooking after removing all fat and marinating for a long time. Four parts of the bear that are considered somewhat of a rare delicacy are its paws (the hind paws especially), which when skinned, parboiled, marinated, stewed and fried, produce a meal with a destructively "different" taste, an undertaking not without some difficulty.

First, scald the paws to remove skin and hair. Then simmer in several changes of water for about an hour to an hour-and-a-half. Put the paws in a large bowl and cover with a marinade for several days or so. (See "Marinade for Tough Creatures" on page 77.) Then stew the paws with your trimmings, onions, whole peppercorns and minced garlic for about five or six hours.

After that, rinse, pat dry, and then chill the paws. When they are firm, slice the paws lengthwise into four pieces and brush them with just melted (but not hot) bacon fat. When the bacon fat forms a coat over the pieces, roll them in bread crumbs and broil for about 25 to 30 minutes. Serve with red-currant jelly.

Just about any recipe for venison or wild hog can be used for bear meat. The saddle and the hind quarters are considered the choicest parts. Chicken is a hell of a lot simpler.

Ben McC. Moise

Fresh
and
Saltwater
Foods

The Other
Best Eatin' There Is

Fresh and Saltwater Fish

Fish meat is reasonably priced, tasty and lean, high in protein and other nutrients, and lower in calories than beef, pork, chicken or canned tuna. No wonder that in recent years fish has become one of our most sought-after food items. But, it's still a mystery food to many consumers. Why? Probably for the same reasons that wild game is misunderstood: People unwittingly let the meat spoil, mishandle it from point of catch to table, or don't know the best cooking methods.

Like game meat, every effort should be made to keep fish fresh. As soon as you catch a fish, you should place it in a cooler on ice. When ice is unavailable, wrap your catch in wet newspaper or a cloth and leave it in the shade. Gut and bleed the fish before you put it on ice if you have time.

If the fish are still hitting, be sure to clean your catch as soon after fishing as possible. Don't let the fish flop around on the dock or in the bottom of the boat. Just as flinging a deer carcass carelessly into the back of a truck bruises the meat, so will continuous jumping bruise the fish's delicate flesh and speed degeneration.

Whether caught or bought, fish deteriorate rapidly. The longer the fish is out of water, ungutted and un-iced, the sooner the bacteria will begin tainting the flesh, producing that all too familiar "fishy" odor. Fresh fish simply do not smell!

For the best taste and nutrition, freshly caught fish should be cooked within twenty-four hours. Three days is the longest cooking can be safely delayed. Both caught and bought fish should be refrigerated immediately and left refrigerated until you are ready to cook.

Freezing your catch should also be done immediately. Unless you're certain the fish is fresh off the boat, don't freeze bought fish, since it may have been already frozen in transit to the market. To freeze, douse the fish in water first, then wrap it tightly in moisture-proof freezer bags or aluminum foil *while still wet*. The wetter the fish while freezing, the longer it lasts.

When thawing frozen fish, just place it in the refrigerator to thaw overnight. If the time is short, place it still wrapped in a bowl under *gently* running cold water. Never thaw fish at room temperature.

Here's how to eye and buy whole fish:

SKIN: Look for iridescent skin and distinct, colorful markings. The longer the fish is out of water, the more the colors fade and the skin loses its shiny appearance.

EYES: These should be bulging and bright. This is a good sign of the fish's age. If the eyes are sunken and clouded, then the fish is probably old.

GILLS: One of the best signs of freshness is the color of the gills. When fresh from the water, the gills are vivid red. As the fish ages, they become duller until they are muddy brown.

FLESH: Flesh should be firm and springy to the touch. If your finger leaves an indentation when you press, then the fish is older than desirable.

SMELL: The fish should have a fresh, mild scent, not a strong "fishy" odor. Saltwater fish will smell of the sea.

When choosing portioned fish, such as fillets or steaks, look for firm, moist flesh, with no discoloration or dry edges. The flesh should be firmly attached to the bones and again should not possess a strong odor.

82

How to Clean Fish

A fish scaler and a sharp knife are essential tools for cleaning fish. Clean on a flat surface with water nearby. A fish cleaning sink, such as those at docks or under vacation homes is perfect, but if that's not available, just spread newspapers on a table with a bucket of water for rinsing.

1. If you are not a "head-on" fish eater, you will want to remove the head first. Place the fish, stomach-down, on the newspaper and grip the spine firmly with your hand. Slice the head off just behind the gills.

2. Then lay it on its side, hold it firmly by the tail and scrape the scales, using a brushing motion that goes from tail back to head. If the fish is too small or tends to slip out of your grasp, merely hold the tail down firmly with a fork. After scaling one side of the fish, repeat on the other side.

3. Now cut the belly from between the gills down to the anal opening. Look for the roe (eggs) in two long sacs and cut away carefully, being sure not to damage the sacs. Wash them and reserve for another meal. Now remove all the innards, including the kidneys, which are bright red strips running along the spine.

4. Wash the fish thoroughly under running water. Make sure all the blood spots are removed and that none of the entrails are attached to the cavity.

5. Wipe the fish dry, cover with foil or plastic wrap, and refrigerate immediately.

How to Fillet

1. Place the fish on newspaper or on a cutting board. Make a cut right behind the gills, going diagonally down to the belly. Avoid cutting too deeply and puncturing the belly.

2. Turn the fish with its back toward you and make a cut just about an inch deep, slicing along the fish from head down to tail, feeling the bones with the knife.

3. Hold the knife at a slight angle and begin to cut down along the center bone, using a slicing and sliding motion. With your other hand, pull back the flesh so you can see what you're doing. When done, the entire side of the fish should lift off, though the fillet will still be attached to the tail. Do not separate them yet.

4. With the fillet still attached, turn the fish over onto the other side and repeat the process. Leaving the first fillet attached provides a firmer base for slicing the second fillet.

5. Cut away the fillets at the tail. You should have two pieces of meat, skin attached, with little meat attached to the skeleton. Proceed to skin the fillets by first laying the fillet flat. Place the skin down on the table, hold the tail firmly with your fingernail, and begin to cut from tail end by holding the knife firmly between skin and flesh at an angle.

6. Using a slight sawing motion, separate the skin from the flesh. As you progress, grip the skin firmly while the knife slices between skin and flesh. If the fish is properly skinned, the fillet should be clean looking and the skin should be clean of all meat.

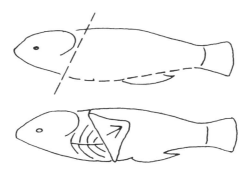

How to Cook Fish

How to cook fish is not determined by whether it's from fresh water or saltwater, but by the individual fish's particular properties. To substitute saltwater for freshwater fish in a recipe, remember these points:

1. Fish is *lean, moderately fatty, or fatty. If it is* **lean,** *it will take nicely to buttery sauces or other liquids. It may be cooked using any method of cooking, but when broiling or baking, it must be basted with extra butter or oil to prevent it from drying out.*

2. **Moderately fatty** *fish is particularly well-suited for broiling or baking, since it requires very little extra lubricating butter or oil to keep it moist. It takes nicely to mayonnaise-based sauces and vegetables.*

3. *If you prefer a milder taste when cooking* **fatty** *fish, use citrus juices or vinegar.*

Although the fat content of individual fish varies according to season, locale or maturity, fish can be generally classified according to the categories above. For example, freshwater bass, crappie and yellow perch are lean, catfish are moderately fatty, and trout are fatty. Saltwater croaker, bass, snapper and shark are lean. Jack crevalle, striped bass, swordfish and sea trout are moderately fatty, while bluefish, mackerel, mullet and shad are fatty.

One of the biggest mistakes people make when cooking fish is overcooking it. Raw fish is translucent. When done it turns milky-white in color or opaque; the flesh will flake easily and separate from the bones. When cooking fish, then, remember to control time and temperature according to the thickness of the fish.

1) *Measure the thickness of the fish by standing a ruler straight up against the thickest part.*

2) *Allow about ten minutes per inch-thickness of fish.*

3) *If fish fillets are baked with or covered with sauces, allow an additional four to five minutes more per inch at the thickest part.*

4) *If frozen fish is cooked without defrosting it first, allow twenty minutes per inch-thickness of fish.*

5) *Cook all fish at the proper temperatures and as quickly as possible.*

There are almost as many ways to prepare fish as there are varieties of fish. Versatile, quick-cooking and easy to prepare, fish adapt well to the hurried pace of today's lifestyle. Preparing a simple fish dinner can let the cook relax while on vacation, too. Although most folks are happy to fry, bake or broil their fish, some variations on the theme could change your whole outlook.

Fish can also be steamed, poached, boiled, smoked, grilled and stewed. Use the fish bones and head for soup and chowder stock, and leave the head on while cooking a whole fish to retain the juices for succulent and moist meat. However you choose to cook fish, just remember that the fresher the fish is, the better it tastes.

84

Basic Fish Recipes

FISH THE EASY WAY

Transfer pan-size fish from the water to the ready coals of a small campfire, no scaling, no cleaning, no preparation at all. If the fish is still alive, in 15 seconds, he won't be. In a very short time, he will need turning and using a twig and his tail, do so; in an equally short time, he will be done. Remove and let cool enough to handle.

To eat, use your pocket knife and on any flat, clean, hard surface, cut the fish behind the head to the gill opening, do the same under his neck area (to the gill opening). The head is now free and can be wiggled, and the fish's entire insides can be pulled out still attached to the head. This can be thrown to the cooters or saved for catfish bait.

Now open up the fish, exposing the white meat and eat "down" to the skin which is also thrown away. *It tastes just exactly like any other cooked fish. Good!*

This recipe may be too primitive for the usual person and if you think it improper, forget it. The Pacific Island people did this years ago. I think it would be good in a survival section. Anyway, it does taste good.

Dana Crosland

GRILLED FISH

Baste raw fish fillet with Italian salad dressing; place on covered grill and continue to baste frequently until done. *Procedure favorably tried on grouper, porgy, snapper, mackerel, barracuda, wahoo and cobia.*

James M. Bishop

BARBECUE FISH

**any number of fish, 1 to 2 lb./
  person best**
6-8 oz. bacon or fatback, sliced
2-4 oz. vinegar or lemon juice

2 T. mustard
salt
black pepper

Clean fish thoroughly. They need not be scaled. Fry out bacon. Save grease. Salt and pepper fish, inside and out. Mix bacon grease, mustard, vinegar (or lemon juice) together for basting mixture. Set aside. Have bed of charcoal or hickory-oak wood coals ready (gray ash). Use metal grill if available or *green* branches (hickory best) to prop fish over or around hot coals about six to eight inches distant. Brush fish with basting mixture and turn two to three times, four to five minutes per side. Serve with corn hoe-cake or "cement" (stiff) grits. Salad, if desired, or heart of cabbage palmetto slicedthin. Sprinkle with vinegar, salt and pepper.

Charlie Laffitte

MARINATED FISH 1-12-02

¼ c. soy sauce
¼ c. Madeira wine OR dry sherry
¼ c. olive oil
2 cloves garlic, chopped
1 T. fresh ginger, minced OR 1 t. powdered ginger

juice of one orange
2 T. orange rind (orange part only)
2 lb. fresh tuna or other fish steaks or fillets

Combine soy sauce, Madeira, olive oil, garlic, ginger, orange juice and zest in a shallow dish or pan. Add fish and marinate for two hours. Place over hot coals and cook 2 to 3 minutes on each side or until just done. Makes 4 servings.

Chef Fran Freeberg

SMOKED FISH

1 qt. water
4 T. salt
dash of soy, Worcestershire and Tabasco sauce

liquid oil
lemon pepper
salt and pepper
powdered garlic and paprika

Soak fish overnight in a brine solution of one quart water, four tablespoons of salt and a dash each of soy, Worcestershire and Tabasco sauce. Drain fish on rack for one to two hours. Coat with liquid oil. Sprinkle heavily with lemon pepper, lightly with salt, pepper, powdered garlic and paprika. Smoke eight to twelve hours.

Dr. Robert L. Lumpkin

BASIC PAN FRIED FISH

2 lb. fresh fillets, steaks or pan-dressed fish
salt and pepper
1 egg

1 T. milk or water
1 c. dry bread crumbs, cracker meal or flour

Cut fillets into serving-size portions. Sprinkle both sides with salt and pepper. Beat egg slightly and blend in milk or water. Dip portions in the egg mixture, then roll them in crumbs. Place fish in a heavy frying pan with about one-quarter inch melted fat, hot, but not smoking. Fry at moderate heat until fish is brown on one side. Turn carefully and brown the other side. Cooking time is about ten minutes, depending on the thickness of the fish. Drain on absorbent paper and serve with lemon wedges or sauce. Makes four to six servings.

Variations: Salt and pepper fillets and dust lightly with flour. Place about one-third stick of butter in pan and place over moderate heat. Cook fillets over moderate heat until brown on both sides. Remove from pan. Add remaining stick of butter until lightly browned and squeeze juice of one lemon into butter. Pour the butter mixture over the warm fillets and sprinkle with chopped parsley.

Donna Florio

When you fry fish in the house, one way to keep the whole place from smelling "fishy" is to stick a thin slice of onion inside each fish before you fry it.

Ivan "Boss Hog" Holden

86

FRIED FISH

whole or filleted fish
salt and pepper
sm. jar of mustard
Worcestershire

cornmeal
green onions, chopped
onion rings, thinly sliced

Season fish inside and out thoroughly with salt and pepper. Dip in mixture of mustard diluted with enough Worcestershire to make a thin paste. Shake in cornmeal seasoned with salt, red and black pepper. Fry in very hot grease until done, but *do not overcook*. As the fish is done, drain and cover with chopped onion and onion rings. Continue with layers of fish and onions. No onion or mustard flavor should be prominent. *These fish will be the best you ever tasted.*

Mrs. J.T. McCabe (Barbara)

FRIED FISH STICKS

fish cut in 1 in. width to 3-4 in.
   long strips
salt and pepper

buttermilk
corn meal

Cut in about one inch wide and three to four-inch long strips. Salt and pepper to taste. Dip strips of fish in buttermilk. Shake in corn meal. Fry fast in hot grease until golden brown.

Gene Pluto

Side Dish

SQUASHPUPPIES

squash
1-2 eggs, depending on amount of
   squash

onion, chopped
cornmeal/flour mixture
salt and pepper or other seasonings

Cook as many squash as you desire. Add the eggs, chop onion into the mixture, then add enough cornmeal/flour mixture to thicken the squash. Season to taste. Cook in deep hot oil as you would hushpuppies. These will not be as round as hushpuppies, but make a delicious dish to eat with fish or anything.

Norma Owens

FRIED FISH (WITHOUT THE FRYING PAN)

fresh fish or fish fillets
flour

1 stick margarine
salt and pepper

Wash fish, sprinkle with salt and pepper, coat with flour. Melt margarine in large baking dish or broiler pan. Place coated fish in pan and bake on each side for about 15 to 20 minutes at 350 degrees. *Tastes like crispy fried fish without the grease.*

Irene Richards Bennett

TEMPURA FISH

With few exceptions, frying seafood (or wild game) involves about the same procedure, regardless of the species. In general, fish should be cooked as quickly as possible without burning the oil. This requires constant attention to raising or lowering the heat as fish is added and removed. Fish should be cut into pieces no more than about one inch thick. This allows a good surface area to volume ratio, which permits relatively quick cooking and proper seasoning penetration.

1 c. all-purpose flour	**1 egg**
1 c. water	**salt and pepper to taste**

Combine all ingredients, mix thoroughly. Dip fish into batter, drain slightly, and fry.

Or for a mustard and vinegar dip, mix approximately equal portions of prepared yellow mustard and vinegar (resultant concoction should be about like thin pancake batter). Dip fish or game into mustard sauce, drain slightly, dust in seasoned all-purpose flour and fry.

Above procedure favorably tried on fish, frog's legs and softshell crabs.

James M. Bishop

BASIC BAKED FISH

3-4 lb. fish, dressed for baking	**¼ c. melted butter**
salt and pepper	

Place fish in a well-greased baking dish and brush with melted butter. Sprinkle with salt and pepper. Bake at 350 degrees for 40 to 60 minutes, depending on thickness of fish. Fish will be done when the thickest part flakes easily when tested with a fork. Baste once or twice with drippings or melted butter. Garnish and serve with lemon wedges. Makes four servings.

Variations: Fish may be sprinkled liberally with lemon juice or wine prior to baking. You may add stuffing and leave the head on for a dramatic presentation. Add any of your favorite herbs and spices for a flavor that is your own. Fish may be garnished with a delicate sauce to add elegance and interest.

Donna Florio

BAKED FISH I

fish steaks or fillets	**green onions**
sherry	**carrots**
lemon or lime juice	**potatoes, quartered**
Worcestershire, dash	**Worcestershire sauce**
1 can onion soup	**salt and pepper**
margarine	

Use fish steaks or fillets. Cut into serving-size pieces and marinate fish for one hour in sherry, lemon or lime juice and a dash of Worcestershire. Place on rack in broiling pan and pour in onion soup (surround, but don't cover the fish). With the soup add a pat of margarine, green onions, carrots and Worcestershire sauce and salt and pepper to taste. Broil or bake until done.

James P. "Preacher" Harrelson

BAKED FISH II

largemouth bass or any large fish
  with flaky meat
4 onions
4 green peppers

tomato sauce
seasonings like salt, pepper, bay leaf,
  small amount of oregano

Clean fish and leave whole. Place in baking dish, salt and pepper. Parboil onions and peppers in rings about eight minutes, then drain. Place onions and peppers on fish, cover with tomato sauce with herbs mixed in. Bake at 375 degrees for one or two hours, depending on size of fish. Tomato sauce also good on rice.

Jacqueline Squires

FISH BAKE

3½ lb. fish fillets
2 cans frozen cream shrimp soup or
  Campbell's shrimp soup

½ c. wine or sherry
Progresso bread crumbs

Sprinkle fillets with crumbs and dot with butter. Roll fillets, pour sauce over them, then hold together with toothpicks. Lay fish in flat casserole. Pour soup and wine mixture over fish. Bake at 350 degrees for 40 to 50 minutes.

Margaret Maynardie

FISH 'N DRESSING

1-2 c. flaked fish
1-2 t. pimentos, chopped
2 c. cornbread and bread crumbs
salt and pepper to taste
2 T. onion, finely chopped

2 T. green peppers, finely chopped
2 T. celery, finely chopped
1 t. Worcestershire sauce
1 egg
milk

Mix all ingredients, adding enough milk to moisten the mixture well. Place in a well-greased baking dish and bake at 350 degrees for 15 to 20 minutes. Makes six servings.

Mrs. Addie Gunnells

BASIC BROILED FISH

2 lb. fresh fillets or steaks	¼ c. melted butter
1 lemon	salt and pepper

Cover broiler pan with aluminum foil. Brush foil with oil or shortening. Baste fillets with melted butter and juice from lemon. Sprinkle both sides with salt and pepper. Place fish on broiler pan. Broil about four inches from source of heat for eight to fourteen minutes, depending on thickness of fish. Fish will be done when it flakes easily when tested with a fork. Baste once during broiling, but do not turn. Makes four to six servings.

Variations: Fish may be sprinkled with an assortment of herbs and spices prior to broiling. Oregano, rosemary, garlic, paprika and green onion are particularly suited to fish. Sautéed vegetables may be placed on top of the fish before serving. Fish may be basted with wine rather than lemon juice; tomato sauce with onion, garlic and spices; or Hollandaise, Brown-butter sauce with lemon, Mornay sauce; or dill sauce made with mayonnaise, sour cream, dill weed, sugar and seasonings to taste.

Donna Florio

TROPICAL BROILED FISH

6 6-oz. fish fillets	½ t. black pepper
4 sprigs fresh basil	½ t. ground red pepper
2 sprigs fresh coriander or parsley	1 t. paprika
3 cloves garlic, peeled	1 t. salt
1 slice (1¼-in. thick) fresh ginger	3 T. olive oil or salad oil
1 shallot, peeled	

Place fillets on a foil-lined baking sheet, skin side down. Place other ingredients in a food processor or small bowl. Process or stir vigorously until combined into a thin paste. Lightly spread seasoning over fillets. Broil at 550 degrees until done, about eight to ten minutes for a ¾-inch thick fillet. Makes six servings.

Serve with tropical fruit slices such as mango, pineapple, papaya or kiwi fruit, and garnish with raspberries or strawberries.

Fish may also be grilled, four to five minutes per side until done.

Joyce Kim

HEAVENLY BROILED FISH

2 lb. skinless fish fillets, fresh or frozen	3 T. mayonnaise or salad dressing
	3 T. chopped green onion with tops
2 T. lemon juice	¼ t. salt
½ c. grated Parmesan cheese	Dash liquid hot pepper sauce
¼ c. margarine or butter, softened	

Thaw fish if frozen. Place fillets in a single layer on a well-greased baking pan, approximately 15 x 10 x ½ inches. Brush fillets with lemon juice. Let it stand for ten minutes. Combine remaining ingredients. Broil four inches from source of heat for approximately six to eight minutes. Remove from oven. Spread cheese mixture evenly over fish and continue to broil two to three minutes or until lightly brown and fish flakes easily when tested with a fork. Makes six servings.

Doris Akers

FISH STEW

1 fish/person
fatback
1 med. onion/fish, sliced
salt and pepper
2 sm. cans tomato sauce OR
  1 sm. can tomato paste

½ bottle of catsup
½ stick of butter
pinch of baking soda
½ c. flour

Select one fish per person. Small pan fish like bream, catfish or redbreast with firm meat are good. (Bass and crappie are not the best). Brown fatback one inch to one-and-a-half inch square and one-quarter inch thick in deep pot. Remove fatback to paper towel. Add onion to grease. Cook, but do not brown. Place layer of fish and layer of onion in pot. Salt and pepper each layer. Then add tomato sauce or tomato paste and the catsup. Add water to cover well. When this comes to a boil, boil for 20 minutes. Do not stir.

Add half a stick of butter or margarine and a pinch of soda. Add half a cup flour to thicken. Mix flour together with some of hot stew in cup before adding back into big pot of stew. Serve in soup bowls or deep lard tray with rice or slice of thick bread in the bottom. Carefully dip one fish per serving and pour stew over this. Add red pepper or Tabasco to taste.

Arthur McCall

ONE-FISH FISH STEW

10-15 lb. fish
2 lg. cans whole tomatoes
5-6 lb. red Irish potatoes
6 lb. onions
½ lb. bacon
2 sticks butter

1 lg. can tomato paste
Tabasco to taste
2 T. Worcestershire
1 t. Accent
1 lemon

Boil fish approximately one hour. Remove bones, mash up fish completely. In broth put onions (cut in small pieces), cook on slow boil 30 minutes. Add cubed potatoes, cook another 30 minutes, add mashed up tomatoes and tomato paste. All this should cook another 40 to 60 minutes. Add fish.

Fry out bacon crisp and crumble. Pour grease and bacon in pot. Add to taste Tabasco (Texas Pete), Worcestershire, butter, salt and pepper. Last add Accent for each gallon stew. Cook on low about one hour, during which time stir constantly, or it sure as hell will stick. The time of cooking from start to finish - about four hours. The longer it simmers, the better.

Romie Forrest

FISH AND CHEESE SOUP

1 lb. fresh fish fillet	¼ t. salt
¼ c. onion, finely chopped	dash paprika
¼ c. carrot, diced	3 c. milk
¼ c. celery, diced	1 13-oz. can chicken broth
2 T. butter	2 oz. American cheese
¼ c. flour	¼ c. celery

Thaw fish. (*I have used bass from our pond, boiled it, and taken it from the bones or I have just filleted the bass.*) Cook onion, carrot, celery in butter until tender. Blend in flour, salt, paprika. Add milk and broth. Cook until thickened. Add fish. Return to boiling. Reduce heat and cook, stirring until fish flakes easily, five to eight minutes. If I have cooked fish as I mentioned earlier, I only drop it into heat. Stir in cheese until melted.

Alice W. Gentry

FISH MARINADE SAUCE

½ c. Kikkoman's soy sauce	¼ c. lemon juice
½ c. Worcestershire sauce	1 t. salt
¼ c. melted butter	1 t. pepper

Mix all ingredients in a small bowl. Pour sauce over fish five minutes before broiling. *Also may be used as steak marinade. Place steak in a flat pan, add sauce and marinate for three to four hours. Then broil.*

Thomas Simmons

Freshwater Fish

BROILED BLUEGILL

bluegill bream	Italian salad dressing
melted butter	salt
lemon juice	

Cover the bottom of a baking dish with melted butter or oleo, and place bluegills side by side. Squeeze lemon juice (the real stuff) over each fish. Baste each fish liberally with Italian salad dressing. Broil until the top side turns brown, usually about four minutes, then turn, baste and brown the other side. Salt lightly and serve.

Claudia Geddings

FRIED CRAPPIE FILLETS

24 to 32 crappie fillets	2 t. salt
1 lb. corn meal	1 t. pepper
¼ c. plain flour	1 c. milk

Place corn meal, flour, salt and pepper in a heavy paper bag and shake to mix. Dip fillets in milk to moisten both sides. Drop fillets into paper bag and shake until they are lightly coated. Place into hot shortening (480 degrees for electric fryers) and remove when fillets are a rich golden brown and flesh is flaky, milky-white. Serve with hush puppies, slaw, sweet pickles and plenty of iced tea or beer.

John Davis

BROILED SHAD

2 lb. shad fillets, fresh or frozen	2 t. prepared mustard
¼ c. butter or margarine, melted	1 t. salt
2 T. horseradish	¼ t. pepper
2 T. lemon juice	paprika

Thaw fillets if frozen. Cut into serving-size portions. Combine butter or margarine, horseradish, lemon juice, mustard, salt and pepper. Place fish, skin side up, on a well-greased broiler pan. Brush with sauce. Broil about three inches from source of heat for four to five minutes. Turn carefully and brush with sauce. Broil four to five minutes longer or until fish flakes easily when tested with a fork. Sprinkle with paprika. Makes six servings.

Maria Latto

SHAD FILLETS WITH CLAMS AND OLIVES

1½ lb. shad fillets, fresh or frozen	14 med. stuffed olives, sliced
2 T. melted butter or margarine	2 T. lemon juice
1 t. salt	1 t. parsley, chopped
dash white pepper	1 t. oregano
½ c. clams, drained, cooked, minced	

Thaw fish if frozen. Cut fillets into six serving portions. Arrange fish in well-greased, shallow, two-quart casserole. Brush fish with butter or margarine; sprinkle with salt and pepper. Cover with aluminum foil, crimping it securely to edges of casserole. Bake in hot oven 400 degrees for 20 minutes. While fish is baking, combine remaining ingredients. Uncover fish; spoon clam mixture over fish. Again cover casserole with foil; return to oven and bake ten minutes longer or until fish flakes easily when tested with a fork. Makes six servings.

Maria Latto

BONELESS BAKED SHAD

1 shad	2 T. melted buter
large square cheesecloth	salt and pepper
1 onion, chopped	pinch of thyme
2 qt. water	5-6 bacon strips
2 T. vinegar	

Place the shad in a large square of cheesecloth, sprinkle with onion. Lower the shad into a greased roaster with the water and vinegar. Gently boil the shad about 20 minutes. Lift the ends of the cloth and remove the shad. Place shad on a large piece of tin foil. Add salt, pepper, thyme and rub with butter. Place bacon strips across shad. Wrap tightly, place in roaster. Bake shad at 250 degrees for six hours. This causes the bones to disintegrate. If roe available, add the last 30 minutes of cooking. Shad can be placed under broiler for browning. Serves six.

Mrs. John Todd, Jr.

SHAD ROE

1 shad roe	½ stick margarine
6 eggs	salt and pepper

Cover shad roe with water, bring to boil, then turn heat to low. Stir until separated. Let cook approximately 45 minutes. When water is cooked out, add eggs, half a stick of margarine, and salt and pepper to taste. Serve hot.

Contributor unknown

SPECIAL HERBED SHAD ROE

2 sets of shad roe	melted sweet butter
4 c. white wine	½ t. ea. chives, parsley, chervil,
2 T. tarragon vinegar	rosemary
salt and white pepper	2 t. shallots, chopped
olive oil	5 T. sherry

Two sets of shad roe that have been cleaned of all blood, veins and outer membranes. Leave the thin inner membrane intact. Immerse them in ice cold, salty water for five or ten minutes or so and then drain them. Line them up in a pan and pour in four cups of white wine and about two tablespoons of tarragon vinegar and some salt and white pepper. Bring to a boil and then reduce the heat and simmer for about 15 minutes.

Then remove the roes and drain them. Lightly coat each roe with olive oil and place them in a shallow casserole. Prepare a mixture of one stick of melted sweet butter and a half teaspoon each of the herbs. Also add two well-rounded teaspoons of finely chopped shallots. Pour this over the roes to evenly cover and add about five tablespoons of sherry. Braise them at about 350 degrees for around ten minutes.

Ben McC. Moise

HICKORY SMOKED STRIPED BASS

2 lb. fresh striped bass
½ c. oil
½ c. sesame seeds
1 T. liquid smoke
1/3 c. cognac

1/3 c. lemon juice
3 T. soy sauce
1 t. salt
1 garlic clove, crushed

Cut fish into serving-size portions and place in single layer in shallow baking dish. Combine remaining ingredients. Pour sauce over fish and let stand for 30 minutes, turning once. Remove fish, reserving sauce for basting. Place fish in well-oiled, hinged wire mesh rack. Cook approximately four inches from moderately hot coals for eight minutes. Baste with sauce. Turn and cook for five to seven minutes longer or until fish flakes easily when tested with a fork. Makes six servings.

Maria Latto

FANCY STRIPED BASS GRILL

2 lb. fresh or frozen striped bass
    steaks, cut into serving pieces
½ c. melted butter
2 T. crushed dill
1/3 c. dry sherry
1/3 c. lemon juice

1 t. salt
1 garlic clove, minced
parsley sprigs
lemon slices
2 T. melted butter
3 T. soy sauce

Place fish in a deep plater. In a bowl combine butter, dill, sherry, lemon juice, soy sauce, salt and garlic. Pour over fish. Let stand for 30 minutes, turning once. Remove fish, pour sauce into a cup. Place fish in a greased, hinged basket broiler. Cook four inches from coals for eight minutes. Baste with sauce. Turn; cook for seven to ten minutes longer until fish flakes easily with a fork. Remove fish to a platter. Spread with melted butter, garnish with parsley and lemon slices. Serves six.

Marie DeWitt

BAKED STUFFED ROCK FISH

Clean rock fish, dredge with salt and pepper.

Savory Mushroom Stuffing

¾ c. mushrooms, finely chopped
  and fried in butter
few drops onion juice
1 c. bread crumbs
¾ t. salt
⅛ t. celery salt
⅛ t. red pepper

few grains nutmeg
few grains black pepper
1 t. chopped parsley
½ t. chopped chives
2 T. melted butter
½ c. stock or water

Mix above in order given, makes two cups. Place stuffing in fish, use skewers to hold fish together. Place on flat shallow pan. Cover fish with strips of bacon. Bake at 500 degrees for ten or fifteen minutes until brown. Reduce heat and bake ten minutes to pound or until tender.

Capers Sauce

½ c. butter
3 T. flour
1½ c. hot water

½ t. salt
⅛ t. pepper
1 t. lemon juice

Melt half of butter, add flour with seasoning. Pour on water gradually. Boil five minutes. Add lemon juice and remaining butter in small bits. Add capers drained from their liquor. Serve with baked rock fish.

Marie DeWitt

CARP IN PAPRIKA SAUCE

2 lb. carp fillets, cut into serving
  portions
juice of one lemon
¼ c. butter
½ c. onion, coarsely chopped

1½ t. paprika
2 green peppers, diced
3 small tomatoes, peeled and
  diced
fresh dill for garnish

Sprinkle fish with lemon juice. Let it stand for 20 minutes. Dry fish well. In a small saucepan, melt butter and sauté onions. Sprinkle with paprika. Add the green peppers and tomatoes and bring to a boil. Place the pieces of fish on the bottom of an oval, shallow, buttered casserole. Pour the sauce over. Bake for 20 to 25 minutes in a 350 degree preheated oven, basting the fish occasionally. Sprinkle with dill before serving. Makes six servings.

Maria Latto

PIKE AND WILD RICE

2 lb. pike fillets, fresh or frozen
1 t. salt
¼ t. pepper
3 slices bacon, diced
1 c. fresh mushrooms, chopped
    (about ¼ lb.)
¼ c. minced onion

¼ c. minced celery
2 c. cooked wild rice
½ t. salt
2 T. melted margarine or butter
Mushroom-Walnut Sauce (see
    below)

Thaw fillets if frozen. Cut fillets into serving-size portions. Season fillets with one teaspoon salt and a quarter teaspoon pepper. In a skillet, cook bacon until lightly browned. Add mushrooms, onion and celery; cook until tender. Stir in cooked rice and salt. Place pike fillets in a well-greased baking pan. Place approximately half a cup rice mixture on top of each fillet. Drizzle the two tablespoons melted margarine over rice. Cover. Bake in moderate oven 350 degrees for about 20 minutes or until fish flakes easily when tested with a fork. Serve with Mushroom-Walnut Sauce. Makes six servings.

Mushroom-Walnut Sauce

3 T. margarine or butter
1 T. minced onion
1 c. mushrooms, sliced (about
    ½ lb.)
3 T. flour

½ t. dry mustard
½ t. salt
¼ t. thyme
2 c. half and half
¼ c. toasted walnuts

In a saucepan melt three tablespoons margarine. Add onion and mushrooms, and cook until tender. Stir in flour, mustard, salt and thyme. Gradually stir in half and half. Cook over medium heat until thickened, stirring constantly. Stir in nuts. Serve sauce over fish and wild rice. Makes approximately two-and-a-half cups sauce.

Maria Latto

SAUTÉED TROUT WITH LEMON SAUCE

large trout, about 9 in. or larger
    (best to leave head on while
    cooking)
fresh lemon juice

margarine
flour
salt and pepper

Season trout with salt and pepper. Squeeze half fresh lemon inside and outside trout. Coat trout with flour, shaking off excess flour. Melt enough margarine in skillet to cover bottom. Place trout in skillet and cook over medium heat. Turn trout over when browned (turn one time only) and brown other side. Place in preheated oven at 400 degrees and cook for approximately 12 minutes, or until trout is completely white inside. Remove trout from pan and place on platter. Squeeze half a fresh lemon into butter remaining in skillet. Cook this mixture of butter and lemon juice over medium heat until sauce begins to bubble (about 30 seconds). Pour this sauce over trout. Serve immediately.

David Long

FRIED RAINBOW, BROWN OR BROOK TROUT

1 lb. of freshwater trout	margarine
2 eggs, well beaten	oregano
Italian bread crumbs	paprika

Using fillets or pieces of whole fish, soak in beaten eggs. Roll and cover fish with the bread crumbs and lay in baking dish. Place a small, thin pat of margarine on each piece. Garnish with oregano and paprika. Bake at 350 degrees for 45 minutes. The fish will turn a light brown and have a crunchy outer coating.

William M. Hyler

CAMPFIRE TROUT

To keep trout cool while fishing, pack in creel with moist grass. Clean them promptly. Avoid carrying them in plastic bags, as they will get too warm. Fry or boil trout up to 12 inches; bake or broil and fillet larger trout.

To boil trout, put a flat pan of water on fire and bring to a boil. Water should be just deep enough to cover fish and may be seasoned lightly with salt, pepper, lemon and parsley flakes if available. Place fish in boiling water for a few minutes until flesh on both sides of backbone can be easily removed.

For frying trout, margarine or butter or cooking oil is better than bacon grease, which is too strong. When boning, cut the meat lengthwise and, if prepared correctly, it should fall away from the bones readily. Wrap cold fried trout in wax paper for a delicious lunch.

Nancy Coleman Wooten

HOW TO SKIN A CATFISH

Wash catfish thoroughly. Cut out the fins if you have not already. Take a sharp knife and cut, just lightly enough to cut skin, around the catfish's head. Using pliers, grab the fish's skin and slowly start pulling the skin back toward you. If the skin tears before you finish, just grab another piece and continue pulling until the skin is off the fish's tail.

Cut off the head. Skin head and save if you wanna' make catfish stew. Gut the catfish. Wash meat thoroughly. Cut catfish into slices, salt and pepper, dust in meal, and pan fry in hot grease. Delicious with grits.

If you prefer, you may skin a frozen catfish. Remove the catfish about thirty minutes or more from freezer. Run warm water over the catfish for a few minutes before attempting to skin. Then follow same instructions as above.

Patricia G. Way

CATFISH DELIGHT

catfish	onion, choppped
salt and pepper	Irish potatoes, sliced thin
Worcestershire	butter

If catfish are large, fillet them; if small, cook whole. Salt and pepper each piece. Place in baking dish. Sprinkle with Worcestershire sauce. Sprinkle with chopped onion. Top with butter and Irish potatoes, sliced very thin. Cover entire dish and seal with aluminum foil and bake at 350 degrees for 45 minutes. Serve while hot.

Jean Geddings

Catfish Stews

Catfish stew recipes are obviously special to our contributors. You may notice they are generally arranged in ascending order from small-size stews to large stews for a crowd.

CATFISH STEW I
An old, old recipe

10 lb. (dressed) catfish	1½ doz. eggs
5 lb. onions	2 tall cans Carnation milk
2 lb. bacon	salt and pepper to taste
6 med. Irish potatoes, sliced	

Remove fins and tails from fish while dressing them. Boil fish in enough water to cover them thoroughly and add salt to taste. Boil fish until tender, remove from fire, cool. Remove the bones from fish and return the meat to the water the fish were boiled in. Do not continue to boil.

While the fish are boiling, prepare the Irish potatoes, boil them until tender and mash. Hard boil the eggs and cut into small slices. Cut bacon into small pieces, fry crisp. Remove the bacon from the grease. Cut onions into small pieces and put them to the bacon grease. Cook thoroughly, but do not allow to brown or burn. Stir often. When the onions are done, add some to the fish meat, and bring to a boil. While onions and fish meat are boiling, add eggs. Add potatoes, salt and pepper to taste.

Stir often to keep potatoes from sticking to the bottom of the pot. Boil long enough to get good and hot. Just before serving, add Carnation milk. Keep stew hot, but do not boil. *Other fresh fish may be substituted for catfish, but catfish better.*

Contributor unknown

CATFISH STEW II

catfish	butter
slab bacon, chopped	salt and pepper
onions, chopped	fresh corn cut off cob (optional)
potatoes, chopped	tomato sauce (for red stew)
boiled eggs, mashed	milk (for white stew)

Boil down the fish in water until meat just leaves the bones. Don't cook too long as the bones will crumble and be harder to pick. Pick all meat off and set aside, reserving liquid also. In large skillet, chop up slab bacon in small pieces and fry til crisp. Add chopped onions and cook until beginning to brown. Put all this in the stew pot with reserved liquid and catfish, and add chopped potatoes, boiled eggs that have been mashed up, butter, salt and pepper to season. Can also put in fresh corn cut off the cob. At the end of cooking time, add either tomato sauce or milk, depending on whether you like red stew or white stew.

Another good way to fix the stew is by starting out frying the chopped bacon in your Dutch oven. Then layer chunks of raw fish on top of that, following with a layer of chopped potatoes, then a layer of chopped onions. Relayer with fish, potatoes and onions to the top and then season and add water to cover and simmer over slow fire several hours. This version will have the bones still in the stew.

Mr. and Mrs. Joe B. Norris

SANTEE CATFISH STEW

3 slices salt pork
2 c. water
5 med. sized catfish
1 onion

3 potatoes, diced
1 can of tomatoes
1 t. Worcestershire sauce

Brown salt pork. Add two cups water, boil fish and onions in water for thirty minutes. Remove bones and return to water. Add other ingredients and simmer one hour.

Mrs. Alfred M. Avant

CONGAREE SWAMP WHITE CATFISH STEW

1 lb. rough catfish or ½ lb.
   dressed/person
10 lb. dressed catfish cut in thirds
2 lb. butt meat or dry fatback, sliced
3 lb. onions, diced

3 lb. potatoes, diced
rice
salt
pepper
hot sauce

Use one pound rough catfish or half a pound dressed catfish per person. Ten pounds dressed catfish cut in thirds; head, middle, tail. Fry two pounds of sliced butt meat or dry fatback. When done, take out of the pan, drain, and add three pounds diced onions, three pounds diced potatoes. Fry until brown and set aside with the meat. Then begin layering the catfish in the pot. Put the heads on the bottom layer, next the middle cut, and last the tail cut.

Wash rice and save the water. Pour two cups of the water used to wash rice in with the catfish. Season with salt, pepper and hot sauce. Then add browned onions, potatoes, butt meat. Cover and cook for around 20 minutes. Serve over rice.

Billy Tolar

1-2-3 CATFISH STEW

½ lb. streak of lean (unsmoked),
   sliced
1 lb. onions, diced
2 lb. potatoes, diced
2 cans Campbell's condensed
   tomato soup

2 cans tomatoes
3 lb. lg. dressed catfish
dash of Texas Pete
salt and pepper
½ can Carnation condensed milk

Fry out streak of lean until nice and brown and grease is all cooked out and remove. Fry onions in grease until brown. Add potatoes and fry until they are brown. Add tomatoes and tomato soup and cook for about 15 minutes and add fish. When the fish is cooked until it falls off bones, take all the bones out with tongs. Add a dash of Texas Pete, salt and pepper. Let cool a little and add Carnation milk. Serves six to eight. *This is an old family recipe.*

"Bunk" Williams

GARRETT'S CATFISH STEW

1 5-lb. catfish
1 12-oz. bottle tomato catsup
4 large potatoes, chopped
2 large onions, chopped
3 bell peppers, chopped

4 sticks celery, chopped
4-6 ears of tender baby corn
hot sauce, salt and pepper to taste
1½ qt. water

Cook catfish until bones fall from meat. Let all other ingredients — catsup, water, potatoes, onions, celery, bell peppers, corn, hot sauce, salt and pepper — cook while you pick the bones from catfish. Add catfish to other ingredients and cook at 350 degrees for one hour. Serves eight or nine.

Mrs. Annie S. Garrett

CATFISH STEW III

½ lb. bacon
6 egg-size onions
1 bottle catsup
2 cans tomato soup
5 cans water
2 T. Worcestershire sauce

2 t. salt
1 t. black pepper
red pepper to taste
4-6 lb. boneless catfish meat
¼ lb. butter or margarine

Fry bacon in stew pot, then remove the bacon and leave grease. Dice onions and sauté in bacon grease until light brown. Add water, catsup, soup, Worcestershire sauce, salt, pepper and fried bacon. Bring to boil. Add fish and boil slowly for half hour, uncovered. Foam which forms on top should be continually skimmed off. Add butter and cook ten minutes more. Serve plain or over rice. Serves 12.

M.G. White, III

"BO's" RIVERBANK CATFISH STEW

6 lb. dressed catfish (fish larger
　　than 2 lb. preferred)
6 lb. Idaho potatoes, diced
3 lb. med. white or yellow onions,
　　chopped

¼ lb. fatback, sliced thin
2 15-oz. cans tomato soup
1 8-oz. glass whole milk
salt and pepper
Tabasco sauce

Boil fish until done (about 20 minutes). Drain, remove bones, and save all broth. Fry fatback until crisp, remove and drain on paper towel. Add potatoes and onions to fatback grease and sauté (stir fry) until potatoes and onions are done. Add fish, broth and crumbled fatback to potatoes and onions. Reduce heat, add tomato soup and simmer 15 minutes. Add milk and simmer ten minutes. Season to taste with salt, pepper and Tabasco sauce. *Recipe serves 12 persons at home, or six persons on the riverbank.*

This recipe was one which had been handed down father to son by Mr. H.T. "Bo" Hughes. Unfortunately, Bo died tragically in a boating accident. This recipe and his love of the outdoors are two of the many legacies which he left to his friends and family. We never cook this stew without giving thanks to God for creating the woods, waters, wildlife and sportsmen like Bo Hughes.

Phil Lucas

D.J.'s CATFISH STEW

6 lb. catfish
5 lb. onions (variable)
5 lb. potatoes (variable)
1½ lb. side meat (smoked or plain)
6 eggs (optional)
2 #2 cans tomatoes (whole)

2 cans tomato paste or catsup
salt to taste
pepper to taste
hot sauce to taste
1 T. sausage seasoning

Boil fish until flaky and remove flesh from bones. Save stock. Slice side meat into half-inch squares and place in frying pan. Cook until all fat is removed. Slice onions and dice into medium pieces. Using the fat from side meat, sauté until glassy. Hard boil eggs and separate whites from yolks. Dice whites into small pieces. Peel potatoes and dice in half-inch squares, boil until tender. Dice whole tomatoes. Use a large pot and combine: catfish, onions, side meat, egg whites, potatoes, tomatoes, tomato paste or catsup, salt, pepper, hot sauce and sausage seasoning. Use stock from catfish or add water to desired consistency. Bring to a boil and let simmer for one-and-a-half hours or until done. Stir regularly.

Some cooks use fish stock for liquid, others discard and use fresh water. When selecting fish for stew, use only white meat. If fish has streaks of yellow, trim and discard. When seasoning stew, don't add all of hot sauce and pepper at one time. You can always add to, but you can't take out! Serve with rice and hush puppies.

Danny Judy

CATFISH STEW IV

5 lb. catfish fillets
3 lb. whole kernel corn
5 lb. potatoes
5 lb. onions

2 lb. butter
milk
salt and pepper
hot sauce

Mince potatoes and onions; cook separately until done. Cook fish until it turns white and falls apart. Cook corn until done. Combine ingredients and add desired amount of milk. Add butter and bring combination to slow boil; add salt, pepper and hot sauce for flavor. Let simmer and serve. May be served with bread and/or crackers. May be refrigerated or frozen to thaw at a later date. Serves 15 to 20.

L.E. Gable

CATFISH STEW V

10 lb. catfish
3 lb. white potatoes
2 lb. onions
1 lb. butt meat
1 can tomatoes
1 bottle catsup
1 can tomato sauce
1 block butter

1 can tomato paste
½ bottle Worcestershire
½ bottle hot sauce
black pepper
salt
garlic
red pepper

Dice butt meat and cook until slightly brown. Remove from pan, leave grease. Cook potatoes and onions separately in grease until slightly brown. Cook catfish in pot until soft enough to remove from bones; place fillet of catfish, butt meat, onions and potatoes in pot with hot water; add tomatoes, catsup, tomato sauce, tomato paste, butter, hot sauce, Worcestershire sauce, pepper, salt and garlic to taste. Cook and simmer approximately one hour, gauging water to produce desired consistency. Serves 24.

Senator Rembert C. Dennis

RED CATFISH STEW

25 lb. dressed catfish
3 lb. onions, diced
5 lb. potatoes, diced
1½ lb. link pork sausage

4 jars spaghetti sauce with meat and
    mushrooms
4 cans tomato paste
salt and pepper to taste

"Cook sausage off," add potatoes and onions and brown 'em in the sausage grease. Add whole catfish and cover to within three-fourths of top of pot with water. When catfish cooks off bone, take the bones out. Then add tomato paste and spaghetti sauce and let cook on medium to medium-low heat for one-and-a-half to two hours, "and that's about it!"

Bill Peaks

LADDIE BOONE'S CATFISH STEW (for 50 people)

25 lb. dressed catfish, use ½ lb./
    person as a rule of thumb
12½ lb. onions, chopped (Use one-
    half as much onions and potatoes
    as you do the catfish.)
12½ lb. potatoes, chopped

5 lb. dry, salted butt meat,
    preferably off the hog's head
1½ gal. catsup
4 10½ oz. cans tomato soup
4 10½ oz. cans cream of mushroom
    soup

Finely dice and fry butt meat out until it is good and brown. Remove from grease and drain. Then fry half of the onions in the grease and drain. Boil the catfish in enough water to cover, season water with a little salt and pepper. When the catfish is done and falling off the bones, remove them from the water and scrape all the meat off the bone. While you are scraping the meat off the bones, put the rest of the onions and all of the potatoes in the water the fish was cooked in and cook until well done. Then add everything left to the pot (the catfish, browned butt meat, catsup and soup). Adjust seasoning to taste and simmer for an hour or so, stirring occasionally to keep from scorching.

Laddie Boone

Saltwater Fish

BAKED SEA BASS WITH SPINACH AND BREAD STUFFING

3 or 4 lb. dressed sea bass, fresh or
   frozen
2½ t. salt
1½ c. celery, thinly sliced
¼ c. green onions, sliced
½ c. butter or margarine, melted

4 c. soft bread cubes (½-in.)
4 c. fresh spinach leaves, washed,
   well-drained
1 T. lemon juice
¼ t. pepper

Thaw fish if frozen. Clean, wash and dry fish. Sprinkle inside and outside with one-and-a-half teaspoons salt. Cook celery and onion in six tablespoons butter or margarine until celery is tender. Stir in bread cubes and spinach leaves. Cook and stir until spinach is tender. Add lemon juice, remaining one teaspoon salt, and pepper; toss lightly. Stuff fish loosely. Close opening with small skewers. Place fish in well-greased baking pan. Brush with remaining butter or margarine. Bake in a moderate oven, 350 degrees for 40 to 60 minutes or until fish flakes easily when tested with a fork. Makes six to eight servings.

Maria Latto

SEA BASS FILLETS

1½ lb. sea bass fillets, fresh or
   frozen
½ c. lemon or lime juice
¾ c. flour

1½ t. salt
½ c. sesame seeds
olive oil

Thaw fish if frozen. Cut into six portions. Place fish in shallow baking dish. Pour lemon or lime juice over fillets and let stand for one hour. Turn once. Combine flour and salt. Roll fillets in flour mixture; dip in lemon or lime juice again and roll in sesame seeds. Fry fillets in olive oil until nicely browned on one side; turn carefully; brown on the other side. Fish is done when it flakes easily when tested with a fork. Cooking time is from eight to ten minutes, depending upon thickness of fish. Makes six servings. Serve with lemon butter.

Maria Latto

FRIED WHITING WITH VEGETABLES

2 lb. whiting fillets, fresh or frozen
½ t. salt
½ t. garlic salt
¼ t. pepper
1 c. all-purpose flour
¼ c. margarine or butter
¼ c. cooking oil
2 T. margarine or butter

¼ c. chopped onion
2 T. chopped green pepper
1 garlic clove, crushed
1 can (1 lb.) tomatoes, undrained,
 cut up
¼ t. leaf thyme
3 slices (1 oz. ea.) cheese, cut in half

Thaw fish if frozen. Divide into serving-size portions. Sprinkle with salt, garlic salt and pepper. Roll fish in flour. Heat margarine and cooking oil in frying pan until hot, but not smoking. Place fish in pan and fry for four to five minutes or until fish is browned and flakes easily when tested with a fork. In a saucepan melt two tablespoons margarine. Add onion, green pepper, and garlic and cook until tender. Add tomatoes and thyme. Heat sauce. Pour sauce into baking dish, 12 by 8 by 2 inches. Place fish on top of sauce. Arrange cheese on top of fish. Bake fish in a moderate oven, 350 degrees for eight to ten minutes or until cheese melts. Makes six servings.

Maria Latto

FLOUNDER IN WINE SAUCE

2 lb. flounder fillets, fresh or frozen
1½ t. salt
dash pepper
3 tomatoes, sliced
½ t. salt
2 T. flour

2 T. butter or margarine, melted
½ c. skim milk
1/3 c. dry white wine
½ t. crushed basil
chopped parsley

Thaw flounder fillets, if frozen. Skin fillets. Sprinkle fillets on both sides with salt and pepper. Place fillets in a single layer in a greased baking dish, 12 by 8 by 2 inches. Arrange tomatoes over top of fillets. Sprinkle with salt and pepper. Blend flour into butter. Add milk gradually and cook until thick and smooth, stirring constantly. Remove from heat and stir in wine and basil. Pour sauce over top of tomatoes. Bake in a moderate oven, 350 degrees for 25 to 30 minutes or until fish flakes easily when tested with a fork. Sprinkle with parsley. Makes six servings.

Maria Latto

FLOUNDER WITH CRAB STUFFING

6 pan-dressed flounder, fresh or
   frozen (¾ lb. ea.)
Crab Stuffing (see below)
¾ c. butter or margarine, melted

1/3 c. lemon juice
2 t. salt
paprika

Thaw frozen fish. Clean, wash and dry fish. To make a pocket for the stuffing, lay the fish flat on a cutting board, light side down. With a sharp knife, cut down the center of the fish along the back bone from the tail to about one-inch from the head end. Turn the knife flat and cut the flesh along both sides of the backbone and to the tail, allowing the knife to run over the rib bones.

Crab Stuffing

1 lb. crab meat, fresh or frozen or
   3 cans (6½ or 7 oz. ea.) crab meat
½ c. chopped onion
1/3 c. chopped celery
1/3 c. green pepper, chopped
2 garlic cloves, finely chopped

1/3 c. melted fat or oil
2 c. soft bread cubes
3 eggs, beaten
1 T. chopped parsley
2 t. salt
½ t. pepper

Thaw frozen crab meat. Drain. Remove any remaining shell or cartilage from crab meat. Cook onion, celery, green pepper and garlic in fat until tender. Combine bread cubes, eggs, parsley, salt, pepper, cooked vegetables and crab meat; mix thoroughly.

Stuff fish loosely. Combine butter, lemon juice and salt. Cut six pieces of heavy-duty aluminum foil 18 by 18 inches each. Grease lightly. Place two tablespoons sauce on foil. Place fish in sauce. Bring the foil up over the fish and close all edges with tight double folds. Makes six packages. Place packages on a grill about six inches from moderately hot coals. Cook for 25 to 30 minutes or until fish flakes easily when tested with a fork. Serves six.

Maria Latto

SMOTHERED FLOUNDER

approximately 1 lb. flounder,
  grouper or other fish fillets
2 c. shrimp, peeled and deveined
1 c. fresh mushrooms, sliced
1 med. onion, chopped
1 med. tomato, sliced

1 sm. eggplant, sliced
½ c. shredded Cheddar cheese
1 c. White Sauce (see below)
salt, pepper, paprika, parsley flakes,
  garlic salt

Place flounder, skin side down, in pan and spread shrimp over the fish. Salt and pepper as desired. Sprinkle onions, mushrooms and cheese over fish and shrimp. Place tomato and eggplant slices on top. Pour white sauce over top. Garnish with paprika, parsley and garlic salt. Bake at 400 degrees for 20 to 30 minutes or until fish flakes easily. Serves four.

White Sauce

2 T. margarine
2 T. flour
dash pepper

1 c. milk
¼ t. salt

Melt margarine, blend in flour, salt and pepper. Add milk. Cook and stir over medium heat until sauce thickens and bubbles. Continue to cook for two minutes longer. Makes one cup.

Billy McCord

FLOUNDER CASSEROLE

1 lb. of skinless flounder
1 t. lemon juice
1 can cream of shrimp soup

1 stick oleo
35-40 Townhouse cookies
dash of salt and pepper

Flake flounder over bottom of two-and-a-half quart casserole. Sprinkle lemon juice over flounder. Pour shrimp soup over this. Melt oleo and pour over soup. Sprinkle lightly with salt and pepper. Crumble cookies over top. Bake in preheated oven 45 minutes at 350 degrees.

Mrs. Alfred M. Avant

FLOUNDER STEW

2 lb. fillet of flounder
4-6 slices bacon, cut up
¾ c. onions, chopped
1 bottle catsup
1 can tomato paste

water
salt to taste
pepper to taste
hot sauce to taste

In Dutch oven: Fry bacon until crisp, sauté onions until clear in bacon grease. Drain off oil. Add catsup and tomato paste. Add three or four bottles of water (catsup bottles) to catsup and tomato paste mixture. Bring to a boil. Add seasonings and fish to mixture. Bring to a boil, let simmer about two hours. As mixture cooks, fish will flake off into small sections.

Mrs. Stanley Vick

PORGY WITH CHEESE FILLING

3 lb. pan-dressed porgy, fresh or frozen	1 T. grated lemon rind
Cheese Filling (see below)	2 t. salt
½ c. margarine or butter, melted	¼ t. pepper
¼ c. lemon juice	paprika

Thaw fish if frozen. Clean fish thoroughly and dry. Place cheese filling in cavity of each fish. Place fish in a well-greased, hinged, wire grill. Combine margarine, lemon juice, lemon rind, salt and pepper. Mix thoroughly. Baste fish with sauce. Sprinkle with paprika. Cook approximately five inches from moderately hot coals for eight to ten minutes. Turn fish and baste with sauce. Sprinkle with paprika. Cook for eight to ten minutes longer or until fish flakes easily when tested with a fork. Makes six servings.

Cheese Filling

1 pkg. (3 oz.) cream cheese, softened	1 T. grated lemon rind
¼ c. cucumber, peeled and chopped	1 T. chopped fresh dill
2 T. diced lemon, peeled	½ t. dill seed

Combine all ingredients. Mix thoroughly. Makes approximately two-thirds cup stuffing.

Maria Latto

PORGY STEW WITH BACON-CORNBREAD DUMPLINGS

2 lb. porgy fillets, fresh or frozen	2 cans (10¾ oz. ea.) condensed cream of celery soup
1½ c. sliced onion	1 c. milk
¼ c. margarine or butter, melted	1 t. salt
1 pkg. (10 oz.) frozen mixed vegetables, partially defrosted	½ t. thyme leaves
1 can (4 oz.) sliced mushrooms, undrained	4 bacon slices, diced
	1 pkg. (8 oz.) corn muffin mix

Thaw fish if frozen. Skin fillets and cut into one-inch pieces. Cook onion in margarine until tender in a six-quart Dutch oven with heat-proof handles. Add frozen vegetables, mushrooms, soup, milk, salt and thyme. Heat and stir until hot. Fold in fish. Cover and bake in a hot oven 400 degrees for 15 minutes or until hot and bubbly. Fry bacon until crisp; drain on absorbent paper. Prepare muffin mix as directed on package label, reducing liquid by half. Stir in crisp bacon and drop six to eight mounds of batter onto hot fish mixture. Return to oven and continue to bake for 20 minutes or until dumplings are done and fish flakes easily when tested with a fork. Makes six servings.

Maria Latto

ELEGANT HOLIDAY POMPANO

2 lb. pompano fillets, fresh or
  frozen
1 t. salt
⅛ t. pepper
1 can (10¾ oz.) condensed cream of
  shrimp soup
¾ c. dairy sour cream
⅛ t. nutmeg
1½ c. cooked rice

¼ c. almonds, toasted, blanched,
  slivered
¼ c. chopped parsley
¼ t. salt
⅛ t. pepper
¼ c. almonds, toasted, blanched,
  slivered
paprika

Thaw fish if frozen. Skin fillets and cut into serving-size portions. Sprinkle with one teaspoon salt and one-eighth teaspoon pepper. Combine soup, sour cream and nutmeg. Reserve three-fourths cup of soup mixture for topping. Combine remaining soup mixture, rice, one-fourth cup almonds, parsley, one-fourth teaspoon salt and one-eighth teaspoon pepper. Spread rice mixture over bottom of a well-greased baking dish, 12 by 8 by 2 inches. Arrange fish over rice. Sprinkle with remaining one-fourth cup almonds and paprika. Bake in a moderate oven, 350 degrees for 35 to 40 minutes or until fish flakes easily when tested with a fork. Top with reserved soup mixture and serve. Makes six servings.

The pompano is one of the most delicious fish. It has firm, white meat that is delicately fatty. Broiling either in the oven or open fire with a butter baste is ideal. Olive oil may be used in place of butter. All flounder and sole recipes may be used.

Maria Latto

HEAVENLY SNAPPER

2 lb. snapper fillets, fresh or frozen
2 T. lemon juice
½ c. Parmesan cheese, grated
¼ c. margarine or butter, softened

3 T. mayonnaise or salad dressing
3 T. green onion, chopped
¼ t. salt
⅛ t. liquid hot pepper sauce

Thaw fish if frozen. Skin fillets and cut into serving-size portions. Place fish on a well-greased broiler pan, approximately 13 by 10 inches. Baste fish with lemon juice and let stand for ten minutes. Broil approximately four inches from source of heat for four to five minutes. Turn fish carefully and continue to broil four to five minutes longer until fish flakes easily when tested with a fork. Combine Parmesan cheese, margarine, mayonnaise, green onion, salt and liquid hot pepper sauce. Spread sauce evenly over fish. Broil two to three minutes longer or until lightly browned. Makes six servings.

Maria Latto

SNAPPER AND SPAGHETTI CASSEROLE

2 c. cooked, flaked snapper	2 T. margarine or butter, melted
1 can (4-oz.) sliced mushrooms, undrained	1 c. Cheddar cheese, grated
	2 T. pimento, chopped
2 T. all-purpose flour	2 c. cooked spaghetti
1 t. salt	1 c. dry bread crumbs
¼ t. pepper	2 T. margarine or butter, melted

Drain mushrooms, reserving liquid. In a two-quart saucepan combine flour, salt and pepper into two tablespoons margarine. Add milk and mushroom liquid gradually. Cook until thick and smooth, stirring constantly. Add fish, mushrooms, cheese and pimento; stir until well-blended. Layer half of the spaghetti, then half the fish mixture into a well-greased one-and-a-half quart casserole. Repeat layers. Combine crumbs and two tablespoons margarine; sprinkle over top of casserole. Bake in moderate oven, 350 degrees for 15 to 20 minutes or until hot and bubbly. Makes six servings.

Maria Latto

POACHED RED SNAPPER IN ASPIC

For a spectacular and ambitious cocktail party centerpiece, try cold, whole, poached red snapper in aspic. A 16-pound snapper should serve from 50 to 100 people. The preparation and service of such a large fish requires some special equipment or an inventive imagination. A submersible candy thermometer is absolutely essential. A large washtub or a roasting pan that can fit over two eyes on top of the stove is also needed.

1 16-lb. snapper	Caviar Dip
water	1 c. Hellman's mayonnaise
1 c. wine or cider vinegar for every qt. water	1 c. sour cream
	2 T. onions, finely chopped
Aspic	2 eggs, hard-boiled, finely chopped
1 c. vermouth or white wine	juice of 1 fresh lime
3 envelopes unflavored gelatin	1 garlic clove, mashed
1 T. red food dye	¼ t. white pepper, finely ground
Garnish	
cherry tomato or radish	
endive	
parsley	

Carefully scale the fish and clean out all the loose connective tissue in the foil to maintain a full shape. Completely wrap the fish in a fold of damp cheesecloth the gills and the eyes. Brush the skin off the fish back from head toward tail. Stuff the head and abdominal cavity with loosely wadded aluminum and lift it into the cooking container.

Add water until the fish is covered by about one inch. For every quart of water, you may also add a cup of wine or cider vinegar. At this point, baste the cook with a little wine; you're in for a long wait.

Turn the stove on full force for the first 45 minutes and bring the water up to around 160 degrees. Pay close attention to the temperature. For the second 45 manipulate the burners to maintain temperature at around 160 degrees. At the end of the second 45-minute sequence, turn the heat completely off and let the pot stand for 45 minutes more.

Carefully lift the fish from the liquid and place it on a large platter or board. Very gently remove the cheesecloth. Don't be alarmed over any breaks in the skin. These will be covered later with the aspic. Chill and firm the fish by placing it in a refrigerator or a large cooler over ice.

The aspic consists of one cup vermouth or white wine into which is poured three envelopes unflavored gelatin and one tablespoon red food coloring. Pour the dry gelatin into the liquid at room temperature and stir it until it is completely dissolved. Heat it very gradually on low heat.

When the fish has thoroughly chilled, stick strips of wax paper underneath its outside edges and fill the eye cavity with a cherry tomato or a radish. Begin painting on the liquid red gelatin with a soft-bristled paint or pastry brush. Do not use a stiff-bristled basting brush. Thoroughly cover again and again in smooth, even strokes until all the aspic is gone. Reheat the pan of glaze mixture if it stiffens before you are through.

With the point of a small paring knife, draw around the bottom edge of the fish to separate the excess gelatin and carefully pull out the wax paper.

Begin tucking leaves of curly endive and parsley around the fish to give the appearance of its lying in a bed of lush greenery. You may also tuck some greenery into the gill opening.

After an appropriate viewing time, cut a window through the skin atop the fish to expose the white meat underneath. Cut the skin completely. Lift up a tab of skin from one corner and peel the skin off. It should be easy to peel.

The fish, as an hors d'oeuvre, is very simple to serve. Your guests do it themselves. Have them each remove a small portion of meat with a cocktail fork and a small knife, put it on a bland cracker like a Bremmer wafer and top it with a dab of caviar dip.

The caviar dip is made of a base of one cup each Hellman's mayonnaise and firm sour cream. When these ingredients are thoroughly mixed, stir in two tablespoons of finely chopped onions, two finely chopped hard-boiled eggs, the juice of one fresh lime, one mashed clove of garlic and one-quarter teaspoon of finely ground white pepper.

Refrigerate to firm mixture and blend the flavors. Just before serving, gently fold in five or six heaping tablespoons of caviar. This rich dip also goes well with crisp raw vegetables or just with crackers.

Ben McC. Moise

CAYMAN FISH

1 lb. firm fleshed fish such as
    wahoo, king mackerel or tuna
    (steaks or fillets) cut ½ to ¾
    inches thick
garlic powder
salt
pepper
¼ c. vegetable oil

½ green bell pepper in julienne
    strips
½ red bell pepper in julienne strips
½ to 1 hot pepper, seeded and
    chopped
1 med. onion, cut in strips
1/3 c. cider vinegar

Cut fish into pieces ½ to ¾ inch thick and pat dry. Season with salt, pepper and garlic powder. Heat about ⅛ inch of vegetable oil in heavy skillet (med. hot). Fry fish about three to four minutes on each side until lightly browned. Remove cooked fish to serving dish and keep warm.

In oil remaining in skillet, fry peppers (sweet and hot) and onion until lightly cooked. Add vinegar to deglaze skillet. Bring to boil and pour vinegar sauce/vegetable mixture over fish. Let set for a few minutes for flavors to blend. Can be served hot or at room temperature as an appetizer or with white rice for a main course.

Glenn Ulrich

TANGY BLUEFISH FILLETS

2 lb. bluefish fillets, fresh or frozen
1 bottle (8 oz.) French dressing
1½ c. crushed cheese crackers

2 T. cooking oil
paprika

Thaw fish if frozen. Skin fillets and cut into serving-size portions. Dip fish in dressing and roll in cracker crumbs. Place on a well-greased baking sheet, 15 by 12 inches. Drizzle oil over fish. Sprinkle with paprika. Bake in an extremely hot oven, 500 degrees for ten to twelve minutes or until fish flakes easily when tested with a fork. Makes six servings.

Maria Latto

BLUEFISH SALAD SUPREME

3 c. cooked, flaked bluefish
½ c. salad oil
¼ c. wine vinegar
2 T. onion, finely chopped
2 T. green pepper, finely chopped
2 t. chopped parsley
½ t. salt

¼ t. oregano leaves
⅛ t. garlic powder
⅛ t. pepper
¼ c. dairy sour cream
salad greens
pimento
tomato wedges

In a large mixing bowl, combine fish, oil, vinegar, onion, green pepper, parsley, salt, oregano, garlic powder and pepper; toss gently. Chill thoroughly. Just before serving, stir in sour cream. Serve on salad greens. Garnish with pimento and tomato wedges. Makes six servings.

Maria Latto

BAKED TILEFISH WITH VEGETABLES

6 tilefish fillets
salt and pepper
juice of 1 lemon
1/3 c. olive oil
1 lg. onion, chopped
1 bunch fresh onions, chopped
1 lb. canned stewed tomatoes
   (pureed in blender)

2 garlic cloves, minced
½ c. water
½ c. dry wine, red or white
¼ c. chopped parsley
2 carrots, sliced into small cubes
4 stalks celery, chopped
2 T. fresh dill
salt and pepper to taste

Cut the fish into serving portions. Pat dry with paper towels. Sprinkle with salt and pepper, lemon juice and arrange in a baking dish which has been oiled with a little olive oil. Set dish with fish in refrigerator while preparing sauce. In medium saucepan heat the olive oil and cook the onions and garlic until tender, but not brown. Add the tomatoes, water, wine, and stir. Cook for three minutes. Add the parsley, carrots, celery, dill, salt and pepper, stirring and simmer for 25 to 30 minutes until sauce is slightly thickened. Adjust seasonings. Pour sauce over the fish. Sprinkle with additional parsley and bake for 40 to 50 minutes, or until fish flakes off with a fork. Makes six servings. Serve over hot cooked rice.

Maria Latto

MARINATED KING MACKEREL STEAKS

king mackerel steaks, ¾ in.-1 in.
   thick
1/3 c. Teriyaki sauce
1/3 c. lemon juice

1/3 c. olive oil
med. onion, cut in rings
bell pepper

Cut fish in three-fourths to one inch steaks and marinate in mixture of Teriyaki sauce, lemon juice and olive oil for two hours. Cut medium onion and bell pepper into rings. Just before you put the fish on the grill, press ring of onion and pepper into the fish on the side you are going to put toward the fire. Grill on a low fire until the meat is white and flaky and baste constantly with the marinade. This is also ideal for wahoo. *Talk about good!*

Senator Jim Waddell

MARINATED SHARK

3 lb. shark
¼ c. Teriyaki sauce
½ c. soy sauce
2 garlic cloves (minced)
2 T. oil

4 T. catsup
juice of ½ lemon
¼ c. vodka
dash of: salt, pepper, oregano
   and parsley, minced

Marinate shark for one hour in all of the remaining ingredients mixed together. Then place in greased, shallow baking pan and bake 20 minutes at 350 degrees or grill on charcoal grill like steak. Serve with lemon slices.

Joan Joyce

SHARK STEAKS ON THE GRILL

shark fillets	seasoning salt
lemon juice	pepper
garlic salt	butter

Marinate shark fillets overnight (or so) in lemon juice, garlic salt, seasoning salt and pepper (other spices can be added). Place on charcoal grill, basting with butter. Slightly char on each side. Serve with anything that you would eat with fish. *This is also delicious using fillets of catfish, striped or largemouth bass and other large fish.*

Billy DuRant

ORIENTAL SWORDFISH STEAKS

2 lb. swordfish steaks, fresh or frozen	2 T. chopped parsley
¼ c. orange juice	1 T. lemon juice
¼ c. soy sauce	1 garlic clove, finely chopped
2 T. catsup	½ t. oregano
2 T. melted fat or oil	½ t. pepper

Thaw fish if frozen. Cut into serving-size portions and place in a single layer in a shallow baking dish. Combine remaining ingredients. Pour sauce over fish and let stand for 30 minutes, turning once. Remove fish, reserving sauce for basting. Place fish in well-greased, hinged wire grill. Cook about four inches from moderately hot coals for eight minutes. Baste with sauce. Turn and cook for seven to ten minutes longer or until fish flakes easily when tested with a fork. Makes six servings.

Maria Latto

BARBECUED SWORDFISH STEAKS

2 lb. swordfish steaks, fresh or frozen	1 can (8-oz.) tomato sauce
¼ c. onion, chopped	2 T. lemon juice
2 T. green pepper, chopped	1 t. Worcestershire sauce
1 garlic clove, finely chopped	1 t. sugar
2 T. melted fat or oil	1 t. salt
	¼ t. pepper

Thaw fish if frozen. Cook onion, green pepper and garlic in fat until tender. Add remaining ingredients and simmer for five minutes, stirring occasionally. Cool. Cut steaks into serving-size portions and place in a single layer in a shallow baking dish. Pour sauce over fish and let stand for 30 minutes, turning once. Remove fish, reserving sauce for basting. Place fish in well-greased, hinged wire grill. Cook about four inches from moderately hot coals for eight minutes. Baste with sauce. Turn and cook for seven to ten minutes longer or until fish flakes easily when tested with a fork. Makes six servings.

Maria Latto

Shellfish

Coastal residents are lucky as far as shellfish go. With cast net in hand, we go wading in creeks and come back with brown shrimp to boil. We dangle chicken necks off piers and then slowly pull up a fat little blue crab. We roll up our britches and go clamming at low tide or brave tidal creeks with hammers for clusters of oysters. Every year we reap a tasty harvest from the sea.

Shrimp

Shrimp headed the list of shellfish recipe submissions to this cookbook, a fact which reflects its "most popular seafood" status. Shrimp support a valuable seafood industry.

When buying fresh shrimp, look for firm, translucent flesh free of black spots. If heads are not already removed, they should be firmly attached. Make sure the shrimp have a fresh odor. Sizes indicate number to a pound: there are 15 "jumbos" to a pound and 60 "smalls" to a pound.

Once caught or bought, dehead and freeze or cook within two days. Shrimp can be frozen cooked or raw, shell on or off, but maximum life (six months) is obtained by freezing them raw, headless and unshelled.

To clean: Remove head. Hold tail in one hand, slip thumb of other hand between swimmerettes (little legs) and lift off all shell except tail. If desired, pull off tail. To remove the black "sand vein," cut one-eighth-inch deep along outer curve and rinse out with cold water.

To freeze: Wash thoroughly, put in heavy plastic bag. Freeze. When frozen (about six hours), take bag out, fill with cold water, and refreeze. The ice coating will prevent freezer burn.

To boil one-and-a-half pounds unpeeled shrimp: Thaw if frozen. For added flavor, leave heads on fresh shrimp while boiling. Bring one quart water and one-fourth cup salt to boil in a four-quart saucepan. Add shrimp. Reduce to simmer for three or four minutes or until shrimp are opaque in center when cut in half. Drain. Rinse under cold water. Remove shells and veins. Rinse and chill. Yields three-fourths pound cooked shrimp.

(If you shell, devein, and rinse before boiling, they may take a minute less to cook.)

Canned shrimp can be substituted in shrimp recipes. Allow three cans (four-and-a-half ounces each) for three-fourths pound cooked shrimp. Soak in ice water for five minutes to remove some salt. Always add last in cooking process.

SHRIMP SALAD

6-29-99 Wonderful

Serve cold as hors d'oeuvre or cool semi-supper on lettuce and tomato wedges.

1 lb. boiled, cleaned shrimp (best if cooked in spices)

celery (enough to color and "crunch")

capers (enough so each spoonful "gets some." The small capers are better than the large.)

mayonnaise (enough to hold mixture together)

eggs (hard-boiled and chopped fine; two or three for two people)

Worcestershire to taste

Mix, chill and serve. If you are going to do this for hors d'oeuvres, chop the shrimp very fine or run through a food mill.

Mrs. C.B. Prevost *Served with Saltines - English peas*

FLAVORFUL SHRIMP SALAD

3 lb. jumbo shrimp

box of McCormick's crab and shrimp boil with cloth bag

1 t. McCormick's seafood seasoning

½ c. salt

½ c. vinegar

3 qt. water

4 crisp lettuce leaves

orange sections

2 t. lemon juice

4 eggs

¼ c. French dressing

Wash unshelled shrimp and place in sauce pan. Combine crab and shrimp boil, seafood seasoning, salt, vinegar and water. Pour over shrimp. Cover. Bring to a boil; reduce heat and allow about ten minutes. Stir once, coating shrimp well with spiced liquid. Remove from heat and drain. Remove shells and devein.

Use crisp lettuce leaves around green bowl. Place cleaned shrimp and sections of orange alternately around bowl on lettuce leaves. Sprinkle lemon juice over all. Slice four boiled eggs lengthwise and place over salad in sections. Pour French dressing over all. De-licious!

Lula S. Coleman

ALLIGATOR PEAR AND SHRIMP SALAD

First concocted as a toothsome salad, another shrimp dish is being used more frequently as a light but showy summer luncheon entree. Two avocados (also called alligator pears) stuffed with shrimp will make a delectable meal for four.

2 ripe but firm avocados
lemon juice
1 lb. raw, headless, peeled, deveined
   shrimp (buy 2 lb. if fresh,
   unpeeled)
1 sm. can pineapple rings, drained
   and minced

½ c. bell pepper, thinly sliced
½ c. celery, stringed and sliced
2/3 c. firm sour cream
1 t. onion salt
lettuce
1 c. Swiss cheese, shredded

Cut avocados in half and remove the pits. Carefully separate the skin by running a large tablespoon just under the skin surface. Hollow out the centers slightly to allow room for the shrimp stuffing and rub well with lemon juice to preserve color. Put shrimp in lots of boiling water for about three minutes and pour into a colander to drain.

Mix together pineapple, bell pepper, celery, sour cream and onion salt. Stir in shrimp and refrigerate 30 to 45 minutes to set flavors.

Place the avocados in a nest of lettuce leaves. Mound the shrimp mixture over the hollow of the avocados and cover with cheese.

Ben McC. Moise

MARINATED SHRIMP I

1½ lb. cooked shrimp in shells
½ c. olive oil
¼ c. red wine vinegar
2 T. spaghetti sauce
2 T. horseradish mustard
¾ c. celery, minced

½ c. green onions, minced
½ c. drained capers
2 cloves garlic, minced
1½ t. paprika
½ t. salt
dash cayenne pepper

Peel shrimp, leaving tails on. Mix remaining ingredients in medium bowl; stir in shrimp. Refrigerate covered overnight, stirring three to four times. Spoon onto lettuce-lined plate and garnish with lemon wedges. Makes six servings.

Maria Latto

MARINATED SHRIMP II

2 lb. shrimp, peeled, deveined and
   cooked
3 sm. onions, in rings

2 green peppers, quartered
2 bottles of your favorite Italian
   dressing

Mix all ingredients and marinate in dressing overnight. Excellent party hors d'oeuvre.

Doris Akers

FRIED SHRIMP

1 c. sauterne wine
3 c. milk
1 t. hot sauce
¼ t. butter
1 t. garlic powder

1 t. onion powder
4 eggs
3 t. salt
shrimp, optional amount
2-3 c. pancake mix

Combine the above ingredients, except pancake mix. Let shrimp soak three to four hours. In bag, place pancake flour mix. Place shrimp in bag and shake well. Cook in deep-fat fryer at 365 degrees until golden brown. About three to five minutes.

Mrs. Stanley Vick

BEER BATTER FOR FRIED SHRIMP

1 egg, beaten
½ c. sifted flour
½ t. salt

beer (enough to make batter thick or thin as you prefer)

Enough for one pound shrimp.

Ginny Prevost

SHANGHAI STIR-FRY VEGETABLES WITH QUICK-FRY SHRIMP

1 T. safflower or peanut oil
2 carrots, sliced diagonally or in
vertical strips
2 zucchinis, sliced in thin strips
1 lg. onion, sliced in half-moons
1 sm. bell pepper, chopped
1 t. powdered ginger
1 c. fresh shrimp, peeled
½ T. salt
1½ T. cornflour or wholewheat
flour

1 egg white
2 slices of ginger root or 2 t.
powdered ginger
vegetable oil for deep frying or
½ pt. for shallow frying
1 T. oil or lard
1½ T. dry sherry or white wine
2 t. sesame oil

First prepare the shrimp and vegetables for cooking. Set the peeled shrimp aside. As you are almost finished slicing the vegetables, heat on medium one tablespoon of the oil in a frying pan, iron skillet or wok. If using a wok, be sure to coat the sides with oil. When the oil is hot, begin to stir-fry the vegetables, starting with the carrots and bell peppers, which take the longest to cook. After about one or two minutes, add the zucchini and onions. To this add one teaspoon of ginger as you stir-fry. If necessary add a *small* amount of oil.To stir-fry, toss the vegetables until they are coated in oil, then continue tossing for a few minutes. The point is to produce cooked, but somewhat crunchy, and therefore more flavorful and nutritious, vegetables. Do not overcook. Once your vegetables are prepared, remove from pan and set aside.

Now rub the shrimp in the salt, one tablespoon of flour, and beaten egg white. Mix the remainder of the flour with two tablespoons water until well blended. Chop the ginger finely if using ginger root. Heat the oil in a separate frying pan or deep-fryer. Add the shrimp a few at a time and fry for no more than one minute. Remove and drain.

Heat the oil or lard in the same frying pan you used for the vegetables. Add the ginger and stir in the oil. Add the sherry, the flour mixture, and shrimp dipping stock. Stir until the sauce thickens. Put the shrimp and the vegetables in the pan, add the sesame oil, stir, and toss quickly for 30 seconds. Serve immediately over rice on a well-heated dish. Serves two to four.

The subtle taste of ginger and sesame oil combined with the freshness of the shrimp and vegetables are characteristic of this dish. A delicate flavor, but a filling meal. Provides a delightful change from more traditional shrimp recipes.

Julie Lumpkin

SHRIMP WITH SNOW PEAS

1 lb. shrimp
¼ c. soy sauce
3 T. dry sherry or white wine
½ c. chicken broth
2 t. minced fresh ginger
2 T. cornstarch
¼ c. oil

1 (6-oz.) package frozen snow peas, thawed and patted dry, or ½ lb. fresh snow peas
3 green onions, cut in 1 in. pieces
1 c. water
½ can (8-oz.) water chestnuts, sliced

Peel shrimp and if large, split in half lengthways. Combine soy sauce, sherry or wine, chicken broth, ginger and cornstarch and set aside. Heat oil hot. Cook the shrimp, snow peas, onions and water chestnuts by adding each separately to the pan or wok over high heat and stirring rapidly for 3 to 4 minutes. When one is finished, remove from the pan or wok, set it aside and put in another ingredient. Cook the shrimp only until they are pink and the vegetables until they are hot and become soft. Put all ingredients back into the pan or wok, stir and add the soy sauce mixture and cook until the sauce thickens slightly, about 2 to 3 minutes. Serve over hot rice. Makes 4 servings.

Donna Florio

LOWCOUNTRY BREAKFAST

1 lb. shrimp
2-3 T. butter
salt
pepper
garlic powder

pot of grits
1-2 green tomatoes
bacon
biscuits

Cook grits. Fry green tomatoes and enough bacon for number of people eating breakfast. Sauté shrimp in butter, season with salt, pepper and garlic powder. Serve shrimp over grits with rest of food.

Mrs. Stanley Vick

CHARLESTON SHRIMP BREAKFAST

Venturing out on the ebb tide with cast net or seine and catching the small sweet creek shrimp is a favorite pastime. Properly prepared, they are an incomparable treat. A memorable breakfast menu features shrimp gravy over hominy alongside buttered toast with fig preserves, crisp bacon, slices of brilliant vine-ripened tomatoes, and a pot full of steaming coffee.

1½-2 lb. fresh small white or brown
   creek shrimp
3-4 T. bacon fat
2 T. onions, finely chopped

¼ t. ground black pepper
2-3 T. flour, maybe more
hominy

Pick and devein shrimp while still raw. If freshly caught, head them and refrigerate for about one hour to make shelling a bit easier. Bring three cups of water to a rapid boil and add the shrimp. Gently stir for about five minutes. Pour them into a colander, saving the liquid.

Heat fat in a large frying pan. Add onions and pepper. After about two or three minutes, add flour and stir around in the pan until all fat is absorbed and the mixture begins to turn brown. Pour on the liquid in which the shrimp was boiled and stir vigorously around the bottom of the pan. After two or three minutes, stir in the shrimp, lower the heat, cover, and let simmer for four or five minutes before serving over hominy.

It is said that, upon first sampling this dish, one spontaneously lowers the head in a moment of silent prayer.

Ben McC. Moise

SHRIMP CREOLE I

¼ c. butter or margarine
2 med. onions, diced
1 c. diced celery
1 clove garlic, finely minced
½ lb. fresh mushrooms, sliced
2 T. flour
1 t. salt
⅛ t. pepper

¼ t. paprika
½ t. chili powder
1 t. Tabasco sauce
1 No. 2 can tomatoes (2½ cups)
1 green pepper, finely shredded
1 lb. cooked, cleaned shrimp
rice

Preheat frypan to 300 degrees. Add butter, melt; add onion, celery, garlic and mushrooms. Sauté until tender, stirring. Blend in flour and seasonings. Add tomatoes. Cover, close vent. Simmer about ten minutes, stirring twice. Add green pepper and shrimp. Heat. Serve over hot cooked rice. Serves four to six. Recipe may be doubled if desired.

Rice for Shrimp Creole

½ lb. grated cheese
1 T. grated onion

1 T. butter
6 c. cooked rice

Adding cheese, onion and butter to rice, stir in lightly with a fork. Rice can also be packed into a well-buttered ring mold, then unmolded.

Lonie Laffitte

SHRIMP CREOLE II

3 lb. cooked shrimp, peeled
1½ c. raw rice, cooked
¾ c. whipping cream
1 stick butter

1 sm. bell pepper, chopped
1 sm. onion, chopped
1½ can tomato soup

Sauté onion and pepper in butter. Mix all ingredients. Cook for about one hour at 300 degrees. Makes eight to ten servings.

Sarah P. Lumpkin

SHRIMP CREOLE III

1 lb. boiled shrimp
4 slices bacon
2 c. tomatoes (I used canned stewed
tomatoes)
½ c. bell pepper, chopped
1 c. onion, chopped

½ c. celery, chopped
1 t. Worcestershire sauce
1 t. salt
4 shakes Tabasco
chili powder to taste
rice

Fry bacon, remove from pan. Brown onions, celery, peppers. Add tomatoes, chili powder, Worcestershire sauce, Tabasco and salt. Cook slowly till thick. Add shrimp and bacon 30 minutes before serving. Serve over rice.

Mrs. J.J. Ward

SHRIMP CREOLE IV

1-26-10

2 strips bacon, chopped
½ c. butter
¾ c. chopped celery
6 T. minced onion
¼ c. chopped green peppers
¾ c. chopped mushrooms
3 c. chopped tomatoes
¾ c. sliced olives

1 t. salt
1 T. Worcestershire sauce
1 T. paprika
⅛ t. pepper
2 lb. shrimp
½ c. sherry
cooked rice

Fry bacon in butter until crisp; add celery, onion, green pepper and mushrooms. Cook gently until tender. Add tomatoes and olives; simmer for at least one hour. Add seasonings and shrimp; simmer for ten minutes longer. Stir in sherry; simmer two minutes longer. Serve over hot fluffy rice. Yield: eight servings.

Doris Akers

SHRIMP AND RICE

1 lb. shelled shrimp	½ c. fresh mushrooms, sliced
1 med. onion, chopped	(optional)
1 med. bell pepper, chopped	soy sauce to taste
2-3 strips bacon, cut in small pieces	salt to taste
1 c. cooked rice	pepper to taste

In pan or large pot, fry bacon until crisp. Remove bacon. Drain all grease but two tablespoons. Sauté shrimp, onion, bell pepper and mushrooms until done. Add rice and bacon. Shake soy sauce over mixture until rice is coated. Let warm. Season to taste. Serve with rolls and salad.

Mrs. Stanley Vick

SHRIMP 'N RICE

Quantities are up to you

long grain rice	salt
shrimp	Tabasco sauce
bacon	

Cook shrimp and peel. Cook rice. Fry bacon and crumble into small pieces. Put shrimp in bacon grease and toss to coat. Add shrimp and bacon to cook rice. Heat ten to fifteen minutes. Can add salt and dash of Tabasco for flavor.

Mrs. C.B. Prevost

SHRIMP FRIED RICE

2 c. raw rice	1 can water chestnuts, sliced
1 c. onions, chopped	mushrooms
1 c. bell pepper, chopped	3 or 4 c. boiled shrimp
bacon drippings	soy sauce
1 c. celery, chopped	

Cook rice. Sauté onions, bell pepper and celery in bacon drippings. Add water chestnuts, mushrooms, shrimp and rice. Season with plenty of soy sauce. Serves eight to ten.

Mrs. Rembert C. Dennis

SHRIMP FRIED RICE WITH BACON

4 to 5 strips bacon	2 celery sticks, chopped
1 lb. shrimp	soy sauce
2 green onions, chopped	1 c. uncooked rice
1 sm. can mushrooms, cut in small pieces	salt and pepper to taste

Fry bacon until crisp. Remove from pan. Sauté onions, celery, mushrooms and shrimp in bacon grease until shrimp turn pink and other ingredients are soft. Cook rice according to package directions. Add cooked rice, soy sauce, salt and pepper to shrimp mixture. Stir with fork and add crumbled bacon. Cover and simmer on low heat about 20 to 25 minutes.

Irene Richards Bennett

SHRIMP RICE

3 c. rice
soy sauce (replaces salt)
raw, peeled shrimp (amount
  optional)
butter
1 can bean sprouts

1 can water chestnuts, sliced
1 c. mushrooms (fresh or canned),
  sliced
1 c. celery, sliced
1 lg. onion, diced
1 med. bell pepper, diced

Cook rice (using soy sauce to season water instead of salt). This will turn the rice a light brown.

Sauté shrimp until done. Sauté each vegetable in butter until half done (still crisp). It is important to sauté each ingredient separately in order to retain their distinct tastes. Season to taste with soy sauce. (You may wish to increase, decrease, or substitute the amount of vegetable ingredients, according to your preference). Stir each ingredient into cooked rice as it finishes sauteing.

Serve with additional soy sauce. Serves 12.

Kathie Dennis

CHARLESTON SHRIMP BAKE

1 lb. peeled, deveined and cooked
  shrimp
1 c. onion, chopped
1 c. celery, sliced
1/3 c. margarine

1 can tomato wedges, undrained
3 c. cooked rice
1 t. dill weed or oregano
4 oz. crumbled feta cheese
½ c. sliced black olives

Cook onion and celery in margarine until tender. Add tomato wedges and heat. Stir in rice, dill weed, shrimp, cheese and olives. Bake at 350 degrees for 25 minutes or until shrimp is cooked. Makes six servings.

Doris Akers

SHRIMP IN WINE SAUCE

1 lb. shelled shrimp
2 T. butter
1 T. corn starch
½ t. seafood seasoning

¼ c. dry sherry
2 T. water
rice

Sauté shrimp in butter; mix corn starch, seafood seasoning, sherry and water in a separate bowl. Put mixture into pan with shrimp. Let cook for about five more minutes. Serve over hot rice with French bread and white wine. Serves two or three.

Mrs. Stanley Vick

SHRIMP CURRY

½ c. onion, finely chopped
2 cloves of garlic, minced
4 T. butter or 4 lg. dabs
4 T. flour or 4 lg. dabs
2 T. curry powder
½ t. powdered ginger or 4 lg. pinches

½ t. salt or 4 lg. pinches
2 c. chicken broth
1 lb. shrimp, peeled
2 T. lemon juice or 4 squirts or squeezes
1 c. milk
1 liter dark rum, chilled

Sauté onion and one clove garlic in butter over low heat until onion is wilted. Stir in flour, one tablespoon curry powder, ginger and salt. Add chicken broth and milk, blend by stirring occasionally and cook until it thickens to a light paste. Add the shrimp and lemon juice. Cook over low heat for 20 minutes. Do not boil.

Correct the seasoning by taking a sample on a spoon, let it cool and taste it. Add more curry powder if you like it hotter, and more garlic if you don't have a date. If you burn your tongue, apply an ice cube immediately and yell and scream. Serve over hot rice and garnish with goodies. Makes four servings.

If it does not taste as good as you expected, and your tongue is still burning, open the rum, cool your tongue with it, and try to figure out where you went wrong.

James C. Holt

SHRIMP STEW

5 pieces lean bacon
3 med. onions, chopped
3 T. brown flour
2½ c. water
½ t. Worcestershire sauce

dash of Tabasco sauce
2 T. white wine
2 c. small creek shrimp
salt and pepper to taste
1 t. garlic powder

Fry bacon; add onion; add flour and brown to make gravy, then add water and other seasonings. Simmer until gravy thickens; add shrimp and more water if necessary. Serve on grits. Serves eight.

Doris Akers

SHRIMP AND WILD RICE

1 box of Uncle Ben's long grain rice
1 can celery soup
1 t. green peppers, chopped
1 sm. onion, chopped
2 t. melted oleo

1 t. lemon juice
½ t. dry mustard
¼ t. pepper
½-1 c. mild cheese, cubed
½ lb. cooked shrimp

Mix all ingredients and pour into a greased casserole dish. Bake at 375 degrees for 35 minutes.

Mrs. Alfred M. Avant

SHRIMP QUICHE

½ c. mayonnaise
½ c. milk
2 eggs
1 t. corn starch
1½ c. Swiss cheese
1/3 c. onion, chopped

dash of salt
1 lb. cooked, cut shrimp
1/3 c. green pepper, chopped
1 4-oz. can mushroom stems and
  pieces

Mix first seven ingredients. Then add shrimp, green pepper and mushrooms.
Place in a nine-inch pie crust and bake at 350 degrees for 45 to 60 minutes. This can be made into a seafood quiche by adding one cup of crabmeat.

Betty M. Sanders

SHRIMP-STUFFED POTATOES

1 lb. shrimp, peeled and cooked
4 med. baking potatoes
½ c. butter or margarine
¼ c. half and half
4 t. finely chopped green onions

1 c. sharp cheddar cheese, shredded
1 t. salt
paprika
parsley

Scrub potatoes thoroughly; bake at 425 degrees for 40 to 60 minutes or until done. When cool, cut potatoes in half lengthwise. Scoop out pulp, and leave a firm shell ¼ inch thick. Combine potato pulp, butter, half & half, onion, cheese and salt. Whip until smooth. Stir in shrimp and stuff shells with potato mixture and sprinkle with paprika. Bake at 425 degrees for 15 minutes. Garnish with parsley. Makes four servings.

Doris Akers

GOLDEN SHRIMP CASSEROLE

2 c. boiled shrimp
6 slices day-old bread
butter
½ lb. sharp cheese, grated
1 4-oz. can sliced mushrooms
1½ c. milk

3 eggs
½ t. salt
½ t. dry mustard
dash of pepper
dash of paprika

For bread crumbs, toast bread, butter and cut into cubes.
Grease two-quart casserole. Mix in casserole shrimp, mushrooms, half of bread crumbs, half of cheese. Beat eggs, milk and seasonings in small bowl. Pour over items in casserole. Top with cheese and remaining bread crumbs. Bake at 325 degrees for 40 to 50 minutes. Serve hot. Serves eight to ten.

Mrs. Nancy D. Cromer

SHRIMP SCAMPI

lg. shrimp
butter
onion, chopped
garlic powder

paprika
lemon juice
parsley flakes

Wash and peel shrimp. Butterfly by cutting one-half to three-fourths way through (starting on the upper curve). Put shrimp in cake pan (or whatever). Dot each shrimp with butter. Sprinkle with chopped onion and spices. Broil about four inches from broiler for ten to fifteen minutes. Serve with rice and juices from shrimp.

Ginny Prevost

SHRIMP DEVILS

8 lg. eggs
4 T. mayonnaise
1 c. cooked, chopped shrimp or *1
   (4½-oz.) can shrimp, chopped
2 T. minced celery

2 T. minced onion
1 T. finely chopped pickle relish
salt
pepper
paprika

Hard boil, peel and halve eggs. Remove yolks carefully (a teaspoon works well) and mash. Add mayonnaise, shrimp, celery, onion and pickle relish. Stir. Add salt and pepper to taste. Replace yolk mixture in whites, using a pastry tube if desired. Garnish with paprika or small shrimp. Makes 16 appetizers. *When using canned shrimp, drain well. Cover with ice water and two tablespoons lemon juice or vinegar. Chill for 20 minutes and drain thoroughly.

Donna Florio

STUFFED SHRIMP EGGS

6 eggs
½ c. shrimp
celery

mayonnaise
med. onion

Boil eggs, cut in half, remove yolks. Add shredded celery, onion, shrimp. Add enough mayonnaise to make a paste of the yolks. Now stick well and put back into whites of eggs.

Mrs. Alfred M. Avant

SHRIMP MOLD SPREAD

1 can tomato soup, undiluted
2 envelopes Knox gelatin
1 8-oz. pkg. cream cheese
1 lb. shrimp, chopped fine
½ c. onions, chopped

½ c. bell peppers, chopped
½ c. celery, chopped
½ c. mayonnaise
dash of salt
dash of Worcestershire sauce

Heat soup till very hot. Put cream cheese in blender and add soup and blend. Dissolve gelatin in one-half cup cold water and add to soup mixture and blend. Mix together shrimp, onions, celery, mayonnaise, bell peppers, salt and Worcestershire sauce in bowl. Then combine both mixtures, pour into oiled mold, and chill for at least six to eight hours. Makes six cups. Serve on crackers.
NOTE: Chicken-in-a-Biscuit cracker is very good with this spread.

Kathy T. Johnston

SHRIMP DIP

1 lb. cooked, peeled, and deveined
   shrimp
2 8-oz. blocks cream cheese
1 T. horseradish

1 med. onion, chopped
¼ c. mayonnaise
dash of Tabasco
dash of Worcestershire

Clean and cook shrimp until pink. Soften cream cheese at room temperature. Chop shrimp and onion. Mix with all other ingredients and serve with crackers. May serve up to 20 people as an hors d'oeuvre.

Doris Akers

Rock Shrimp

A deepwater cousin to the brown and white shrimp, the rock shrimp is caught only at night, far offshore at 20 to 30 fathoms deep.

When buying rock shrimp, look for firm white flesh with only a little odor. Remember that two pounds yields one-and-a-half or two cups meat.

To store: Rock shrimp freeze very well. Keep frozen till ready to use. Thaw under water as you clean them and use immediately.

To shell: Lay shrimp, legs down, on a flat surface. Crack lengthwise through spine with knife or cut through shell with kitchen shears along outer curve. Make an eighth-inch groove through the shrimp. Pull sides of shell apart and remove the meat. Wash in cold water to remove vein.

To cook: Rock shrimp are said to have the flavor of shrimp and lobster and can be substituted for either in recipes. Rock do cook faster, however, so they must be watched.

Broiling is said to be the best way to prepare rock shrimp. If you wish to broil them, place on a flat surface with legs up. Cut with knife between legs (actually called swimmerettes) through meat to the shell. Spread the shell open until flat and wash in cold water to remove the vein. Butter and season. Broil two to three minutes four inches from the heat source.

To boil, first thaw if frozen. For one-and-a-half pounds raw, peeled rock shrimp, boil a quart of water with two tablespoons salt (also bay leaves and peppercorns, if desired). Put shrimp in and simmer 30 to 45 seconds or until opaque. If unshelled, simmer two minutes. Drain. Rinse with cold water to stop cooking quickly.

To fry, place in hot (375-degree) oil and cook 35 to 45 seconds till light brown. Serve immediately.

ROCK SHRIMP HORS D'OEUVRES

rock shrimp
soy sauce
lemon juice

liquid margarine
garlic salt
paprika

Split rock shrimp and wash thoroughly in cold water to remove sand vein. Lay flat on a baking pan with meat exposed. Sprinkle with other ingredients. Bake 350-375 degrees for five to seven minutes. Rock shrimp are done when tails turn up.

Dottie Lewis

Blue Crab

There are other crab species in Southeastern waters, but the blue crab is the only one of any commercial or recreational importance.

After shedding their old exoskeleton, a process known as ecdysis and necessary for normal growth, the crab is totally defenseless for four to six hours and is known as a softshell. With time, the new shell begins to harden and commercial crabbers have designated the successive stages as leather, papershell and buckram. Less than two days are required after ecdysis for the crab's new shell to harden; those with recently hardened shells exhibit clean white sternums and are unaffectionately known as white bellies.

Crabs require about 18 to 20 molts to mature. Upon achieving maturity, male crabs continue to molt and grow, but females cease molting. All their energy is channelled into egg production. Females carrying a visible orange or brown sac are called sponge crabs and by law must be returned to the water if caught. Crabbers also must return all hard crabs less than five inches across the back between spine tips.

Mature female crabs are most abundant in high salinity waters such as the front beach areas immediately accessible to the ocean. Mature male crabs are most abundant in low to moderate salinity waters, so fishing location generally determines sex composition of your catch.

To pick up a crab, hold its claws down with something and grab it at the base of either last leg (paddle fin). If it grabs a finger, place it in the water or on the ground and it will usually let go.

Crabs are sold alive or steamed whole, and crabmeat is sold fresh picked, frozen, pasteurized or sterilized.

When buying live crabs, make sure they are moving. If they die, throw them out; never cook a dead crab. Allow three hard-shell live crabs per person.

Fresh crabmeat can be either pasteurized or non-pasteurized, which is high quality, but very perishable. Both may be used in any recipe calling for cooked crabmeat. Crabmeat should have a clean, moist appearance and a mild odor.

Picked crabmeat is available in four forms: (1) lump meat — white meat from the backfin (highest quality, good for "appearance"); (2) special or flaked meat — small pieces of white meat from the body; (3) claw meat — brownish meat from the claws (cheaper and popular for recipes where looks don't matter); (4) crab claws or fingers — brownish meat left on claw (ready for serving cold, fried or breaded).

For casseroles, soups and stews, fresh or frozen crabmeat is best. One pound of crabmeat serves six.

Commercially sterilized canned crabmeat can be bought in a grocery store and kept on a shelf indefinitely.

To store: Fresh crabs should be kept alive in a moist, cool place until ready for cleaning or boiling. Don't freeze cooked or uncooked whole crabs. Cooked crabmeat will stay fresh five to seven days if packed in ice in refrigerator. Picked crabmeat doesn't feeze well but is acceptable in dips or casseroles if frozen for under six months. The crab core, that part left after debacking and cleaning, can be rapidly frozen and stored for six to nine months without a significant loss of quality. After thawing, pick skeletal parts out before eating.

Once a container of fresh, frozen or pasteurized crabmeat is opened, use within one to two days of purchase. Pack in ice in refrigerator. Pasteurized will last three months unopened.

To boil: Put live crab in a large pot of boiling water, seasoned with seafood seasoning mixture. Let water return to a boil and cook for 20 minutes. Don't cook a dead crab and don't return crabs to original container without washing it thoroughly with soap or detergent.

To steam: Alternate layers of live crabs with salt and seafood seasoning in top of a double boiler with water boiling in bottom pot. Leave about 20 minutes. Test a top crab; its meat should be white, firm and opaque.

To clean: (1) Remove and save the two large claws. Crack the claws with your knife and remove the meat in them. Pull up lower apron and remove back.

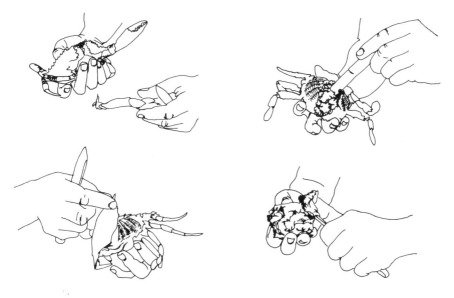

Remove all legs except the back two (broader than the others), and save any meat clinging to them. (2) Scrape away the gray spongy gills ("deadman"), the yellow liver and/or eggs, and the mouth parts. Clean off with napkin or rinse. (3) Break the body into two halves lengthwise. Then break each of these halves again, leaving a large piece of lump backfin meat attached to the base of each leg. Pick meat out of the chambers.

SHE-CRAB SOUP

When all of the methodology is thoroughly explored, it's difficult to make a bad she-crab soup. There are people, however, who have been known to burn a tossed salad.

Roe is found in female or "sook" crabs in the late spring and summer. The orange roe is found on the inside of the female's shell. It should not be confused with the orange sponge of eggs on the outside of female undershells which are ready to deposit their larvae.

Some people substitute hen eggs for the crab roe, but their flavor really isn't the same.

1 lb. white crab meat (10 or 12 crabs)	1 pt. light cream
4 oz. hard orange crab roe	4 or 5 T. dry sherry
1 sm. onion	½ t. mace
1 stalk of celery, stringed	pinch of salt
½ stick sweet butter	pinch of ground white pepper
1 T. flour	several healthy dollops of
7 c. milk	Worcestershire sauce
	chopped parsley or paprika

Mince onion and celery, and sauté in a pan with butter. Sauté until the onions and celery are translucent. Then sprinkle flour over them and stir. This light coating helps the vegetables float in the soup instead of sitting on the bottom of the bowl.

Begin warming milk and cream in a double boiler. Pour the crab meat (not the roe) in the pan with the sautéed vegetables and warm while stirring in sherry, mace, salt, pepper and "wooster" sauce. When this mixture is warm, add it to the milk and cream in the double boiler and cook over an extremely low heat for just under an hour.

If you like, more sherry may be added to the individual servings at this point as the hard roe is crumbled in the bottom of each soup bowl. Top-garnish each serving with chopped parsley or a light dusting of paprika. This recipe serves from four to twelve depending on their appetites and the generosity of the cook.

Ben McC. Moise

CREAMY CRAB SOUP

1 lb. crab meat	4 c. milk
1 stick butter	1 c. heavy cream
1/3 c. flour	1 t. salt
1 c. chicken broth or stock	1 c. dry sherry
1 t. pepper	

Pick crab meat to remove all remaining cartilage. In a large saucepan, melt butter. Blend in flour, stirring until smooth. Slowly stir in chicken broth, and continue stirring until mixture is smooth. Simmer for two minutes. Add milk and cream. Cook over low heat, stirring constantly until thickened. Do not boil. Add crab, sherry, salt and pepper. Remove from heat and serve. Makes six servings.

Doris Akers

FRIED HARD CRABS

1 doz. crabs
about 6 c. pancake mix
about 4 t. seafood seasoning

3 to 4 c. milk
hot cooking oil

Catch crabs and clean off all but the legs and claws (leave attached to body).

Mix up pancake mix, seafood seasoning and milk. Dip each crab in the mixture and thoroughly coat all over. Then deep-fry in hot cooking oil (med-high) or 350 degrees for about three to four minutes or until brown all over).

J. Oscar Sullivan

BOILED CAROLINA BLUE CRABS

crabs
2-3 T. vinegar
2-3 T. salt

Have one inch of water in the pot in which crabs are to be cooked. Add two or three tablespoons of vinegar and salt to this. Put crabs in water when water comes to a boil. Steam crabs for 25 to 30 minutes. The vinegar and steam make the crabs easy to pick. Keep clean crab shells in the refrigerator before using.

Barbara Jones

HOT CRAB DIP

1 c. Miracle Whip or mayonnaise
1 c. crab meat

1 c. Parmesan cheese
2 cans artichoke hearts, mashed fine

Mix and bake about 15 minutes. Serve with crackers. This serves a crowd. I often prepare only half the recipe and it's truly good.

Margaret Meynardie

CRABMEAT DIP

2 blocks cream cheese, room
   temperature
½ c. mayonnaise
1 T. horseradish
1 T. Worcestershire sauce

1 t. lemon juice
½ c. sharp Cheddar cheese,
   shredded
½ to 1 lb. crab meat
1 sm. onion, chopped

Mix all ingredients well and serve with crackers.

Doris Akers

DORIS'S CHEESEY CRAB DIP

1 can Harris Atlantic she crab soup
1 6-oz. can crab meat (fresh is
  better)
4 T. butter

½ to 1 c. sharp Cheddar cheese,
  grated
1 T. Worcestershire sauce
dash of Tabasco
sherry or brandy to taste

Mix together and heat in microwave.

Doris Akers

CRAB IMPERIAL

1 egg
1 T. mustard
pinch of salt
pinch of white pepper
heavy dash of Worcestershire sauce
parsley flakes to taste

dash of sugar
2/3 c. mayonnaise
1 lb. crab meat (preferably back
  fin)
paprika

Mix above ingredients lightly and avoid breaking up the larger pieces of crab meat. Place in four ramekins or crab shells. Sprinkle heavily with paprika. Bake at 425 degrees for 15 minutes.

Note: If crab meat is frozen, squeeze out excess water before using.

David Allen

DEVILED CRABS

1 pkg. saltines
3 eggs
1 c. diced onions
½ c. thinly sliced celery
1 stick oleo
½ c. sweet relish

1 T. prepared mustard
1 T. Worcestershire sauce
2/3 c. mayonnaise
2 lb. crab meat
14 shells
paprika

Crumble saltines. Boil and chop up eggs. Cook onions and celery in oleo.

Mix saltines, relish, onions, celery and eggs. Add mustard, Worcestershire and enough mayonnaise to hold the final mixture together. Add crab meat last and gently.

Put in shells. Sprinkle with paprika. Bake 25 minutes at 350 degrees. Serves 14.

Mrs. Stiles M. Harper

SEAFOOD TRIANGLES

1 c. Bechamel Sauce (see below)
6 oz. frozen crab meat
2 T. butter
2 T. onion, chopped
2 scallions, chopped
½ c. fresh mushrooms, chopped
2 T. parsley, finely minced
⅛ t. dill weed
¼ t. red pepper

⅛ t. ground nutmeg
½ t. salt
2 T. dry sherry
8 T. crumbled feta cheese
1 T. grated Parmesan cheese
1 egg yolk
½ c. cornflake crumbs
½ lb. filo pastry
½ lb. sweet butter, melted

Prepare bechamel sauce.

Thaw and drain crab meat. (Reserve one tablespoon of liquid.) In large saucepan, melt butter and sauté onion, scallions and mushrooms until tender, about three minutes. Remove from heat.

Slowly add bechamel sauce, stirring. Add all remaining ingredients (except filo and half-pound sweet butter). Return to very low heat and cook about five minutes until cheeses have melted. Stir in one tablespoon crab liquid. Set aside in refrigerator overnight or several hours (this will enhance the flavor and mixture will be easier to use).

Prepare triangles: Filo is usually packaged in one-pound cartons. There are approximately 20 to 24 sheets of filo per pound. Each sheet measures approximately 13 by 17 inches.

Filo should be placed in refrigerator from freezer two to four hours before using or left at room temperature for an hour to thaw for handling. When ready to use, unroll filo and cover with foil or wax paper and top with a damp towel to prevent filo from drying. Pin towel to foil at one end so they can be lifted together when getting sheets of filo.

Melt the half-pound sweet butter. Place one sheet of filo lengthwise on a cutting board. Brush with butter. Top with second sheet of filo and brush with butter. With pastry cutter, divide filo equally into six strips (each strip will be approximately 2 by 13 inches). Place full teaspoon of crab mixture in bottom corner of one strip. Fold pastry over in triangular shape, folding over and over to end of strip. Brush triangle with butter. Prick with a toothpick. Place on baking sheet, seam side down. Bake 15 to 20 minutes or until golden. Makes approximately 30 triangles. Delicious as an hors d'oeuvre!

Bechamel Sauce

2 T. butter
2 T. flour
1 c. warm milk

salt to taste
dash of white pepper
dash of nutmeg

Melt butter over moderate heat and add flour, stirring until well blended. Cook a few seconds until mixture is bubbly. Remove from heat. Stir in warm milk, two tablespoons at a time until you have used one-half cup. Blend well. Return to low heat and add remaining milk slowly, stirring constantly until thickened. Season with salt, pepper and nutmeg to taste. Makes one cup.

Maria Latto

DEVILED CRAB

½ stick margarine	1 t. prepared mustard
½ sm. onion, chopped	1 T. Worcestershire sauce
½ bell pepper, chopped	1 dash of Tabasco sauce
1 stem celery, chopped	½ t. salt
3 eggs, beaten	black pepper
12 Ritz crackers, crumbled slightly	½ c. milk
1 heaping T. mayonnaise	1 lb. claw crab meat

Melt margarine in heavy saucepan. Sauté onion, celery and pepper until tender, but not browned. Beat eggs, add all other ingredients, and toss together lightly until well mixed. Turn into one-quart casserole, sprinkle with additional cracker crumbs and paprika. Bake at 325 degrees about 25 to 30 minutes or until firm. Serves six.

I like to serve my deviled crab with spoonbread and cole slaw for a cold winter night supper.

Betty L. Waskiewicz

CRAB DABS

4 6-oz. cans crab meat or use fresh crab meat	4 t. chives
1-1/3 c. bread crumbs	4 t. dry mustard
8 T. sherry	¾ t. salt
	1 lb. bacon

Drain crab and combine all ingredients except bacon. Mix well and chill 30 minutes. Roll in balls about 1 tablespoon each. Wrap in 1/3 slice bacon and skewer with toothpick. Place on broiler pan and broil 8 to 10 minutes on one side, turn and broil 4 minutes on other side. Excellent hors d'oeuvre.

Doris Akers

CRAB IN SHELLS

1 shell per person	1 c. light cream
vegetable spray	dash of salt
1½ c. Swiss cheese	½ t. lemon peel
crab meat	¼ t. dry mustard
2 green onions	dash of mace
3 eggs, beaten	

Spray each shell with vegetable spray. Sprinkle cheese, crab meat and onions in shells. Combine eggs, cream, salt, lemon peel, dry mustard and mace. Mix and spoon over crab. Bake 20 minutes at 325 degrees on cookie sheet.

Sarah P. Lumpkin

CRAB MEAT CASSEROLE

6 strips bacon	1 bay leaf
1 med. onion	1 t. Worcestershire sauce
½ lb. Cheddar cheese	3 T. cooking sherry
1 lb. crab meat	1 c. cream sauce
2 T. butter	salt and pepper to taste
1 can she-crab soup with ¼ c. water	bread crumbs

Fry bacon till crisp. Drain and crumble. Finely chop onion and sauté in bacon grease. Chop cheese and mix with crab meat, butter, soup, bay leaf, sauces and sherry. Salt and pepper to taste. Add bacon and onion. Sprinkle bread crumbs on top and bake at 250 degrees for approximately one hour. Serves six.

Doris Akers

CRAB CASSEROLE "TO TASTE"

½ c. chopped onions	hot sauce to taste
1½-2 c. crab meat	Worcestershire sauce
cracker crumbs	pepper
butter	

Preheat oven to 350 degrees. Grease sides and bottom of baking dish. Line the bottom of the dish with cracker crumbs. Combine onions and other ingredients to taste in a bowl. Mix well. Place in a baking dish. Dot the mixture with butter. Bake at 350 degrees for about 20 to 30 minutes. Serves four to six.

Mrs. Stanley Vick

SISTER'S CRAB MEAT CASSEROLE

6 oz. fresh dark or Harris' canned crab meat	1 sm. can evaporated milk
	1 c. mayonnaise
2-3 slices of white bread, trimmed and broken up	salt
	pepper
1 sm. onion, chopped	Worcestershire sauce
2 hard-boiled eggs	Tabasco sauce, optional

Mix first six ingredients in a bowl. Add seasonings, including a dash of Tabasco if you have it. Bake in a casserole dish at 350 degrees for 45 to 60 minutes.

Camilla Murphy

SIX-EGG CRAB CASSEROLE

1 lb. crab meat	1 c. milk
6 hard-boiled eggs, mashed up	1/3 c. onions, grated
20 crumbled saltines	salt, pepper and Tabasco sauce to taste
1 stick margarine, melted	
½ c. mayonnaise	

Grease casserole. Mix all together and cover with cracker crumbs. Bake at 350 degrees for 30 minutes or until done.

Gail B. Smith

MAMA RUTH'S CRAB CASSEROLE

1½ c. white crab meat
3 c. thick white sauce
2 c. American cheese, grated
1 c. bell peppers, chopped
1 c. onions, chopped

1 c. celery, chopped
1½ c. pieces and stems mushrooms
salt and pepper to taste
1½ c. buttered bread crumbs

Boil together celery, onions and bell pepper until tender. Drain. Make three cups of thick white sauce. Add cheese, celery, onions, peppers, mushrooms, seasoning and crab meat. Mix lightly.

Pour into buttered casserole dish; sprinkle generously with buttered bread crumbs. Place in pre-heated oven and bake for 30 minutes at 350 degrees.

Shrimp and/or oysters may be added to the above for a real delicious seafood casserole.

Ruth M. Reynolds

CRAB AND GUINEA SQUASH CASSEROLE

1 lg. ripe eggplant, known also as a
  guinea squash
1 lb. crab meat (8 or 10 picked
  crabs)
5 or 6 vine-ripened tomatoes,
  skinned and diced

3 lg. fresh eggs, well-beaten
½ c. toasted bread crumbs
butter
pinch each of salt and pepper
1 t. sugar

Steam or boil the diced eggplant until tender. Drain and pour into a large buttered baking dish. Then pour in the crab meat. Mix the eggs, salt, pepper and sugar with the tomatoes and pour evenly over the crab meat.

Cover the surface with the toasted bread crumbs and generously dot with butter. Set oven at 350 degrees and bake for around one-half hour.

Ben McC. Moise

DINNIE CAMPBELL'S CRAB CASSEROLE

1 c. milk
2 eggs, well-beaten
½ t. salt
1 t. black pepper
½ t. paprika
1 T. mayonnaise

2 T. Worcestershire sauce
dash of mace *or* juice of ½ lemon
½ lb. Ritz crackers, crushed
1 lb. crab meat, picked
2/3 stick butter, melted

Mix first eight ingredients together. Add to mixture crackers and crab meat. Mix lightly, then add butter and mix very lightly. Put in 350-degree oven and cook about 30 to 40 minutes. (I use a shallow Pyrex casserole dish for baking.)

Dinnie Campbell

CRAB PIZZA

12 oz. cream cheese (softened)
2 T. Worcestershire sauce
1 T. lemon juice
2 T. mayonnaise
1 sm. onion, grated

dash of garlic salt
½ bottle chili sauce
1 c. crab meat
parsley flakes

Mix first six ingredients until blended and soft. Spread evenly on a nine-inch round pan. Spread chili sauce on top. Sprinkle with the crab meat. Sprinkle to taste with parsley flakes.

This makes a quick and easy hors d'oeuvre to be served spread on your favorite cracker. Can be made ahead and refrigerated.

David Allen

SPOLETO SPIRAL SALAD

½ lb. rotini (spiral) pasta
1 bunch fresh broccoli
12 oz. white crab meat

1 c. sweet red pepper, diced
Dressing (see below)

Cook pasta according to package directions; drain and place in a large bowl. Remove florets from broccoli, blanch and drain. Add broccoli, crab and red peppers to pasta. Pour dressing over all and toss. Makes four to six servings.

Dressing

1 T. capers
¼ c. red wine vinegar
1 clove garlic
1 t. salt

½ t. oregano
½ t. lemon pepper
½ t. seasoning salt
¾ c. virgin olive oil

Combine all ingredients except oil in small bowl or work bowl of food processor. Slowly add the oil, whisking or processing until smooth. Makes approximately one cup.

Donna Florio

SOFTSHELLS
by Jim Bishop

Crabs are seldom captured in the field as softshells. The best time to do so, however, is at low tide (preferably at night) about the time of the full moon in April. It is during this period that large numbers of immature females molt to their mature stage. Oyster reefs, submerged objects and shallow mud flats in areas of moderate salinities (10 to 20 degrees/OO S; full strength sea water equals 35 degrees/OO S) are probably the best areas to search.

Commercial softshell crab producers obtain crabs just prior to molt and hold them in tanks until they shed their shell.

Softshells are considered by many to be one of the most delicious seafoods. In addition to better taste, the biggest advantage that softshells have over hardshell crabs is that the entire crab can be consumed. Contrary to popular opinion, the "deadman" or gills are not toxic, but in hard crabs, the gills are objectionable in flavor and texture and eaten only accidentally. In soft crabs, however, the gills are totally innocuous and commonly removed for cosmetic purposes only.

I cook the entire crab and have served literally hundreds to guests without a single complaint. In fact, few were even cognizant of eating the gills. This is not to suggest that softshells should always be served whole.

Softshell preparation for cooking may simply involve rinsing with fresh tap water or excising the gills, face, flap (abdomen), dirt sac (intestines), and in extreme cases, the carapace. To remove the gills, lift one of the lateral spines of the carapace and cut exposed gills with scissors. The face can be removed by cutting along the anterior edge of the carapace just behind the eye stalks.

Stone Crab

by Charles Moore

The meat held within the claw of the stone crab (*Menippe mercenaria*) is a delicacy and when boiled and dipped in lemon-butter is one of our finest seafoods. The flesh has the consistency of large pieces of blue crab but a more lobster-like flavor.

They are near-shore inhabitants, but are rarely seen by the casual observer, as they live in burrows and seldom venture far from the safety of their homes. Burrows are found from just below the low tide line out to depths in excess of 40 feet.

In many states, only the larger of the two claws of any stone crab may be removed and the live crab must be returned immediately to the water. In fact, it is illegal to possess a stone crab, live or dead, except while removing the claw.

As with blue crabs, female crabs with a visible egg mass on the underside of their body are completely protected by law and neither claw may be removed.

Most individuals seeking stone crabs use a three-foot stick with a wire hook on the end to pull these powerful clawed crabs from their burrows. Stone crabs have the reputation of being slow, but their powerful claws should always be respected.

The claws of stone crabs are excellent eating, either steamed and served with a sauce, or used in recipes that call for lobster or blue crab.

As the claw meat tends to stick to the shell if the claws are frozen raw or iced, the claws are frequently cooked as soon as they are landed, and sold cooked and frozen.

Stone crab claws are often found fresh in seafood markets, and are a good buy with rich, delicious flesh and moderate prices. When purchasing, remember that approximately two and one-half pounds of whole claws will yield about one pound of cooked meat.

STEAMED STONE CRAB CLAWS

6 stone crab claws
3 qt. boiling water
½ c. salt

clarified butter, cocktail sauce or
Mustard Sauce (see below)

In a six-quart saucepan, bring water and salt to a boil. Place stone crab claws in pot and cover. Bring water back to the boiling point. Reduce heat and simmer for about eight to ten minutes. Drain. Rinse in cold water for one minute. Crack claws and serve with butter or sauce.

Mustard Sauce

1½ T. prepared mustard
2 t. butter or margarine, melted
½ t. parsley flakes

⅛ t. salt
½ c. sour cream

Combine all ingredients. Heat at a very low temperature until just warm, stirring occasionally. Do not boil. Makes approximately two-thirds cup sauce.

Northern Clam

The most common clam species in the Southeast is the hardshell (or quahog) northern clam. Clams are sold in three sizes: littlenecks, cherrystones, and chowders. Considered the most choice, littlenecks are the smallest and most expensive. They are best eaten raw or steamed. Cherrystones are good for minced clam recipes. Chowders are the largest and are used in soups, such as Manhattan (tomato-based) or New England (milk-based) clam chowder.

Clams are sold in the shell, shucked, or canned. Don't ever buy or cook dead clams. Like oysters, the shell should be unbroken and closed or should close when tapped. Shucked clams are rarely available. Two dozen chowders, three dozen cherrystones or littlenecks, or one quart of shucked clams serves six.

To store: Live clams can be covered with wet cloth and kept in the refrigerator for up to seven days. Though rarely available at markets, fresh shucked clams will keep in a sealed container in the refrigerator for seven to ten days.

Clams can be frozen in their own shell for up to six months. Shucked clams should be frozen in their own juice. Thaw under running water or in ice in the refrigerator. Don't refreeze clams.

To shuck: Wash well. Clams will open if steamed for eight to ten minutes. OR you can put them in the freezer for two hours. Then insert a sharp knife between the valves and cut around the shell, twisting to open and cutting the muscle that holds it shut. Cut the meat out.

CAMPFIRE CLAMS

clams   catsup
melted butter   horseradish

Place washed clams on coals, cover with a dampened sack, and bake until done. (We prefer ours "rare.") Oysters may be prepared in the same manner, and served with a sauce of melted butter, catsup and horseradish. Good with simple saltines. And beer.

Barbara Bara

STEAMED CLAMS WITH BROTH

3 qt. soft clams (steamers)
½ c. boiling water
butter

Wash clams thoroughly. Place in a steamer, add the water and cover. Steam for five to ten minutes or until clams open. Discard any that don't open. Drain clams, reserving broth. Add butter to broth and serve steaming hot in individual bowls. Serve in soup plates.

Maria Latto

BENNETT'S CLAM CHOWDER

½ lb. fatback   pepper
1 lg. onion   ½ t. thyme
½ bunch celery hearts, including 1 qt. tomato juice
   leaves   1 lg. can tomatoes
4 med. carrots   1½ doz. cleaned fresh clams or 3
4 med. potatoes, diced   6½-oz. cans minced clams
1 sm. bunch parsley

Fry fatback till crisp in large pot. Chop and sauté onion, celery, carrots, potatoes, parsley, pepper and thyme. Add tomato juice and enough water to cover. Simmer vegetables for a half hour. Add tomatoes and clams.

My parents come from New Jersey once a year and make this treat!

Joan Joyce

MURRELLS INLET CLAM CHOWDER

1 peck clams   salt
1 lb. onions   pepper
5 lb. potatoes   Texas Pete
16-oz. can crushed tomatoes   Worcestershire sauce, optional
4-oz. can tomato paste   all seasoning salt, optional
4 slices bacon

Coarse-grind first five ingredients, saving clam juice. Fry bacon, saving grease. Put it all in a pot, adding clam juice and one to two quarts water. Season to taste with salt, pepper, Texas Pete. May add Worcestershire sauce and all seasoning salt. Cook at slow boil for two to three hours and stir frequently. Should make about eight quarts.

Holmes B. Springs

140

"KRICK" CLAM DELITE

clams
Tabasco sauce
1½-inch cut of bacon/clam

½-inch sq. sharp Cheddar
cheese/clam

Obtain a number of silver-dollar-sized clams, big enough to just fit in the hole of a muffin pan where it will stay upright and not lose any of the juice. Freeze the clams hard and run a little tap water over them. When they open up, separate the shells, and put a half shell with the clam with the meat in it in each hole in the muffin pan. Put several dashes of Tabasco on each clam and place a square of cheese and bacon over each clam. Place in oven and bake at 350 degrees for ten minutes. Then switch to broil for five minutes. Retreive from oven and "scoop 'em up."

Seabrook Platt, Martin North

FRIED CLAMS

1 qt. shucked soft clams (steamers)
1 egg, beaten
1 T. milk
1 t. salt

dash pepper
1 c. dry bread crumbs
fat for frying

Drain clams. Wipe dry. Combine egg, milk and seasonings. Dip clams in egg mixture, and roll in crumbs. Fry in a basket in deep fat, 375 degrees, for two to three minutes or until golden brown. Drain on absorbent paper. Serve plain, sprinkled with salt, or with your favorite sauce.

Maria Latto

BEACH CLAM 'DURVES'

12 med. to lg. clams
1 c. Pepperidge Farm herbed bread
  crumbs, finely crumbled
½ stick sweet butter, melted

1 t. dried parsley
juice of half a lemon
a healthy "dollop" of Tabasco
paprika or chopped fresh parsley

This recipe is for basically a dozen medium to large clams, but for additional clams, just add to the amounts of each ingredient.

First scrub the shells until they are clean. Then open them up and cut out the meat. Save the juice and one half of the shells. Chop up the clam meat or run it through a blender or food processor, and pour out into a colander. Wash off and drain.

Mix together in a bowl the clams, bread crumbs, butter, parsley, lemon juice and Tabasco sauce. If mixture is too dry to stir, add some of the clam juice. Divide mixture evenly between 12 of the clam shells, and bake in the middle of a hot 425-degree oven for ten minutes or so.

This makes a pretty good little 'durve' to serve company at the beach.

P.S. You can sprinkle the top with a little paprika or chopped fresh parsley.

Ben McC. Moise

CLAM DIP

6 T. butter
2 sm. onions, diced
1 bell pepper, diced
½ lb. Velveeta cheese
½ c. catsup

2 T. Worcestershire sauce
2 T. cooking sherry
1½ t. red pepper
1 lb. clams, minced

Sauté onions and bell peppers in butter until clear. Melt cheese, catsup, Worcestershire sauce, sherry and red pepper. When mixed together, add clams, onions/pepper mixture. Serve warm in chafing dish. This mixture can be frozen.

Mrs. Stanley Vick

CLAMDIGGER DIP

1 7½ to 8 oz. can minced clams
1 8-oz. pkg. cream cheese, softened
1 t. Worcestershire sauce
1 T. lemon juice
1 T. onion, grated

1 t. parsley, chopped
¼ t. salt
⅛ t. liquid hot pepper sauce
assorted chips, crackers or raw
   vegetables

Drain clams and reserve liquor. Cream the cheese. Add seasonings and clams. Mix thoroughly. Chill at least one hour to blend flavors. If necessary to thin dip, add clam liquor gradually. Serve with chips, crackers or vegetables. Makes approximately one and one-third cups dip.

Maria Latto

Eastern Oyster

Unlike shrimp and crab, which were considered rather ordinary food in colonial days, the oyster has always been extremely popular in America. Oysters were the favorite shellfish of the Indians on both the East and West coasts. John Smith raved over the oysters served by the Indians at the first Christmas meal in America. In the 19th century, they were used like we use salt today; they were eaten raw, baked, fried, fricasseed, in soup, in pies, in stuffings and on steaks. An 1853 gumbo recipe calls for 100 oysters.

The only commercial oyster on the East Coast is the eastern oyster, which is usually found on marsh creeks and river banks.

To buy: Oysters can be bought in the shell, fresh shucked, frozen shucked, frozen breaded and canned. Oysters in the shell should be closed, or should close when tapped. Singles are larger, choice, and easier to shuck, clusters yield smaller oysters and are cheaper.

Fresh shucked oysters are plump, naturally creamy with a clear liquid, and have a mild odor. They are sold by size: "Counts" are very large and rare; "selects" are usually the largest available and are good for frying or on-the-half-shell; "standards" are average and good for chowders, casseroles or hors d'oeuvres.

When buying in the shell, figure six oysters per person. One quart of fresh shucked oysters will provide six servings.

To store: If kept cool and moist, oysters can live out of water for a few days. In the shell, covered with a moist towel, they'll live seven to ten days in the refrigerator. If packed in ice in a sealed container, shucked oysters will stay fresh for a week in the refrigerator.

Oysters frozen in the shell become brittle, so it's best to freeze only a few hours to retain the juices and then shuck into a plastic container and return to the freezer.

To shuck: Rinse thoroughly. Wear glove on hand that will hold oyster. Insert knife into small crevice near the hinge. Twist knife while pushing in. Slide it along inside of top shell and cut connecting muscle loose. Remove top shell and slip knife under oyster to remove from bottom. Don't mutilate it.

OR oysters can be steamed for five to ten minutes in one inch of water in a roaster pan in a hot oven. Shells will open slightly.

The outdoor oyster roast is a popular coastal tradition in the fall and winter. A heavy metal sheet is heated over an open fire. Oysters are placed on the sheet and covered with wet burlap. In a few minutes, they're ready for eating.

GOLDEN OYSTER STEW

1 can (15-oz.) oysters, undrained
1 c. chopped onion
1 c. sliced celery
1 c. butter
2 c. sliced fresh mushrooms
1 c. all-purpose flour
1 t. salt
1 t. pepper
2 c. milk
1 c. grated sharp Cheddar cheese
1 can (10-oz.) cream of potato soup
1 jar (2-oz.) diced pimento
1 t. liquid hot pepper sauce

Remove any remaining shell particles from oysters. Cook onions and celery in butter until tender. Add mushrooms and cook one minute. Over low heat, stir flour, salt and pepper into vegetable mixture. Add milk gradually and stir until thickened. Add cheese, stir until melted. Add oysters, soup, pimento and liquid hot pepper sauce. Heat 5 to 10 minutes or until oysters begin to curl. Makes six servings.

Doris Akers

PICKLED OYSTERS

Smug purists will quickly proclaim that the best way to eat oysters is raw on the half shell, freshly plucked from their briny beds. They are probably right. But Southerners also delight in oysters as a pickled hors d'oeuvre.

The one disadvantage of this recipe is the virtual impossibility to fix enough of it.

3 doz. fresh med. oysters	1 whole bay leaf
3 or 4 c. rapidly boiling water	½ c. cider vinegar
1 med. red onion	½ t. salt
2 red cayenne peppers	Tabasco sauce
whole peppercorns	

Shuck oysters and plunge them into boiling water. Remove the saucepan from the heat and let them sit for about five minutes before draining oysters in a colander. Thinly slice onion and separate the slices into rings. Cut peppers in half lengthwise. Flatten and scrape out all the seeds and pulp. Cut the peppers into long thin slivers. Begin layering in a pint jar the oysters, the onion and the hot peppers, along with about one-half tablespoon of whole peppercorns. Place a whole bay leaf about halfway up the jar. When the jar is full or as full as it's going to get, pour in a mixture of the vinegar, salt and a dash or two of Tabasco.

Hide the jar in the very back of your refrigerator for at least three days and get ready to pick some more oysters for another batch. The first jar is not going to last long.

Ben McC. Moise

OYSTER RAMEKINS

12 slices of bread	½ c. cream
1 stick butter	salt, pepper and nutmeg (salt
1 qt. oysters	depends on saltiness of oysters)
½ c. oyster juice	

Toast bread and roll into crumbs. Melt butter and add to crumbs. Place a layer of crumbs in bottom of each ramekin. Add a layer of oysters. Sprinkle with salt, pepper and a dash of nutmeg. Repeat and end with crumbs. Pour about two tablespoons of oyster juice and cream over each. Bake at 350 degrees for 30 minutes. Makes six servings.

Sarah P. Lumpkin

OYSTER PIE ✓

2 pts. lg. oysters	2 eggs
1 can cream of mushroom soup	salt
2 packs Townhouse Crackers from	pepper
box of four packs	butter

Drain oysters, save liquid. Mix oyster liquid, cream of mushroom soup and eggs together.

On bottom of casserole dish, layer crushed Townhouse Crackers, oysters and then liquid mixture. Sprinkle with salt, pepper and bits of butter. Makes two layers. Finish with cracker crumbs and butter. Bake at 350 degrees for approximately one hour.

Debbie Faithful

SCALLOPED OYSTERS WITH MACARONI

1 c. elbow macaroni
12 saltine crackers, crumbled
1 pt. oysters, drained
½ t. salt

¼ t. pepper
1 c. milk
¼ c. margarine
¼ c. saltine cracker crumbs

Cook macaroni according to package instructions. Sprinkle half of cracker crumbs in a greased one-and-a-half quart casserole; top with half of macaroni. Spoon half of oysters over macaroni; sprinkle with one-fourth teaspoon salt and one-fourth teaspoon pepper. Repeat layers. Pour milk over oyster mixture. Dot with butter; sprinkle cracker crumbs over top. Bake at 350 degrees for 45 minutes or until brown. Makes four servings.

Gail B. Smith

ALDERMAN'S CARPET BAG

Many Southeasterners pride themselves on their English heritage. One recipe which comes from this background involves oysters, a thick prime sirloin, and sturgeon caviar.

1 thick prime sirloin
butter
ground black pepper

about 2 doz. med.-sm. raw oysters
Ben's Variation on Bearnaise Sauce
3 heaping t. caviar, optional

Cut a deep pocket into the side of the steak. Rub the inside of the pocket with butter and a pinch of ground black pepper. Stuff the pocket with raw oysters. The number of oysters depends on their size. A good-size steak should be able to hold anywhere from 18 to 24 medium to small oysters. Before you stuff them, though, pat the oysters dry on some paper towels. When the pocket is full, secure it with round wooden toothpicks.

Cook the steak over a charcoal fire or under an oven broiler for five minutes or so per side, depending on the thickness of the steak and the heat of the fire.

When the steak is cooked, pour the sauce over it. If this is not already rich enough for your taste, add caviar as a garnish on top of the sauce.

Ben's Variation on Bearnaise Sauce

1 T. spring onion, finely chopped
½ T. each tarragon and chervil
half a bay leaf
½ c. each cider vinegar and white
   wine
pinch of salt and pepper

3 egg yolks
1 to 1½ stick butter, warm or
   melted
squeeze of lemon wedge
pinch of cayenne

Combine spring onion, tarragon, chervil, half a bay leaf, salt and pepper in cider vinegar and white wine. Boil all ingredients until they cook down to about two tablespoons of liquid. Strain and set aside to cool for about five minutes.

In another small pot, put egg yolks into one tablespoon warm water. Constantly and vigorously beat this mixture while very gradually warming on a low heat.

As soon as the yolks show the first signs of thickening, slowly drip in two tablespoons of the reduced liquid while still vigorously beating. Whip in butter thoroughly, then add lemon juice and cayenne to accent the flavor.

This recipe should yield slightly more than one cup. Keep the sauce warm in double-boiler arrangement until just before the steak with oysters is to be served.

Ben McC. Moise

Calico Scallop

The scallop is a mollusk with two shells, like clams and oysters. The calico scallop inhabits Southeastern waters, but is seldom caught by recreational fishermen. Fish markets carry scallops, however, and therefore we included here our three scallop submissions.

To buy: Make sure fresh scallops are creamy white or pink with a mild sweet odor. Whether fresh or frozen, scallops should have a little liquid in them. They are best if used the day of purchase, but they can be kept on ice for two days.

Raw frozen scallops will keep for three or four months.

To shuck: Open like an oyster or clam, but be sure to remove all the viscera until all that's left is white muscle. Wash and put on ice immediately.

SCALLOP-VEGETABLE SALAD

1½ lb. scallops, fresh or frozen
1 qt. boiling water
2 T. salt
1 1-lb. can cut green beans, drained
1 c. celery, sliced

¼ c. onion, chopped
¼ c. green pepper, chopped
1 T. pimento, chopped
Marinade (see below)
6 lettuce cups

Thaw scallops, if frozen. Rinse with cold water to remove any shell particles. Place in boiling salted water. Cover and return to the boiling point. Reduce heat and simmer three to four minutes, depending on size. Drain and cool. Slice scallops. Combine all ingredients except lettuce. Cover and chill for at least one hour. Drain. Serve in lettuce cups. Makes six servings.

Marinade

½ c. cider vinegar
1 T. sugar
½ t. salt

dash pepper
¼ c. salad oil

Combine vinegar, sugar, salt and pepper. Add oil gradually, blending thoroughly. Makes approximately two-thirds cup marinade.

Maria Latto

CHARCOAL BROILED SCALLOPS

2 lb. scallops, fresh or frozen
½ c. melted fat or oil
¼ c. lemon juice
2 t. salt

¼ t. white pepper
½ lb. sliced bacon
paprika

Thaw scallops, if frozen. Rinse with cold water to remove any shell particles. Place scallops in a bowl. Combine fat, lemon juice, salt and pepper. Pour sauce over scallops and let stand for 30 to 40 minutes, stirring occasionally. Cut each slice of bacon in half lengthwise and then crosswise. Remove scallops, reserving sauce for basting. Wrap each scallop with a piece of bacon and fasten with a toothpick. Place scallops in well-greased, hinged wire grills. Sprinkle with paprika. Cook about four inches from moderately hot coals for five minutes. Baste with sauce and sprinkle with paprika. Turn and cook for five to seven minutes longer or until bacon is crisp. Serves six.

Maria Latto

SCALLOP KABOBS

1 lb. scallops, fresh or frozen
1 13½-oz. can pineapple chunks,
    drained
1 4-oz. can button mushrooms,
    drained
1 green pepper, cut into 1-inch
    squares

¼ c. melted fat or oil
¼ c. lemon juice
¼ c. parsley, chopped
¼ c. soy sauce
salt
dash pepper
12 slices bacon

Thaw scallops, if frozen. Rinse with cold water to remove any shell particles. Place pineapple, mushrooms, green pepper and scallops in a bowl. Combine fat, lemon juice, parsley, soy sauce, salt and pepper. Pour sauce over scallop mixture and let stand 35 to 40 minutes, stirring occasionally. Fry bacon until cooked, but not crisp. Cut each slice in half. Using long skewers, alternate scallops, pineapple, mushrooms, green pepper and bacon until skewers are filled. Cook about four inches from moderately hot coals for five minutes. Baste with sauce. Turn and cook for five to eight minutes longer or until bacon is crisp. Serves four to six.

Maria Latto

Seafood Combinations

SEAFOOD GUMBO I

1 c. salad oil
1 c. all-purpose flour
2 lg. onions, chopped
3 stalks celery, chopped
6 cloves garlic, minced
1 gal. warm water
2 c. okra, sliced
1 No. 2 can tomatoes, chopped
2 t. salt
black pepper to taste
2 t. Old Bay seafood seasoning
1 pt. oysters, undrained
1 lb. fresh crab meat
1 doz. fresh crab claws
2 lb. fresh peeled shrimp
1 doz. sm. fresh clams, chopped
hot cooked rice
gumbo filet

Combine oil and flour in a large heavy pot over medium heat. Cook, stirring constantly until roux is the color of a copper penny (about 15 minutes). Add onion, celery and garlic until vegetables are tender. DO NOT LET ROUX BURN, or it will ruin the gumbo. Reduce heat if necessary.

Gradually add one gallon warm water, blending well. Add okra and tomatoes. Bring mixture to a boil. Reduce heat; simmer, stirring occasionally for one and one-half hours. Stir in salt, pepper, seafood seasoning and the seafood.

Bring the gumbo to a boil and simmer for around 15 minutes. Gumbo can be thickened by adding gumbo filet. Serve over hot rice. Serves 12 to 14.

Susan McIntyre

SEAFOOD GUMBO II

¾-1 c. flour
½ c. shortening
2 qts. water
1 can tomatoes
1 can tomato sauce
3 ribs celery, chopped
1 bell pepper, chopped
1 lb. okra
2 lg. onions, chopped
3 pods garlic, minced
¼ c. parsley
½ c. green onions
3 lbs. shrimp, peeled
1 lb. crab meat

In heavy skillet, brown flour in shortening until richly brown. Transfer to deep heavy pot. Add water, tomatoes and tomato sauce. Cook five minutes. Add celery, pepper, okra, onions and garlic, cooking ten minutes. Add parsley, onion tops, shrimp and crab meat. Season. Cook 30 minutes longer. Add more water if gravy becomes too thick.

Serve in soup bowls over steaming rice with tossed salad and garlic bread. Serves ten hungry people.

LaMae Strange

GUMBO WITH SHRIMP AND CRAB

One day I was talking to Jim Bishop about a gumbo recipe and he said, with great alacrity, "I hope you start with a roux!" — and I was damned glad I did. Just like when you're fixin' catfish stews, if you don't have your ingredients together, you can lose credibility in a big hurry.

People seem to be very serious about their gumbos. A study of the literature will reveal that there are two essential ingredients to differentiate a bonafide gumbo from just any old raggy stew, and those are okra and filet (a powder made from the leaves of the sassafras tree).

½ c. olive oil
4 cloves garlic, mashed flat and finely chopped
1½ c. flour, well rounded
1 sm. can tomato sauce
1 sm. can tomato paste
3 healthy "dollops" of Tabasco sauce
3 big onions, chopped
1 head of celery, leaves and all, strung and finely chopped
5 c. water

3 c. dry white wine, plus some for the cook
2 pts. fresh okra, cut in ½-in. pieces
2 bell peppers, chopped
½ to ¾ lb. lean ham, cubed
a good handful of fresh parsley, finely chopped
2 T. Worcestershire sauce
2 lbs. raw peeled shrimp
1 lb. crab claw meat
hot rice
gumbo filet

To begin, pour oil in the bottom of a two-gallon pot. Bring up to medium heat, sauté garlic. After about four or five minutes, stir in flour. Stir constantly with a fork until the flour "cooks" and turns a good dark brown. You might have to add a little more oil of it is too pasty. Then stir in tomato paste and stir around until it begins to darken. Pour in tomato and Tabasco sauce, still stirring, so it doesn't scorch. Then stir into the roux onions and celery. Keep stirring and begin pouring in little by little a mixture of the water and wine. This should produce a bubbly mixture a little thicker than an average soup.

Bring up to heat and stir in okra, bell peppers, ham, parsley and "wooster" sauce.

Simmer all of this for about one and one-half to two hours, adding water if you need it. At the end of two hours, add shrimp and crab claw meat, and cook at a simmer for about 20 to 30 minutes more. This will be longer than you need to cook the shrimp, but you need to let the flavor "sink in."

Now, from this point on, you are faced with the "art" of using the filet in the correct way. "Everybody" says you don't put the filet in the pot and cook it. "They" say sprinkle it over the gumbo, either over each individual serving, which I don't like 'cause it doesn't mix in well that way, or stir it into the pot just before serving, which leaves you the problem of the leftovers getting stringy when you reheat it (when it's even better).

I think it works best if you ladle out some gumbo into another pot or into a serving bowl, say a good quart to quart-and-a-half of gumbo, and stir in about two to two-and-a-half teaspoons of the filet.

How you dish it up depends on the "politeness" of the occasion, but most of the time it is best served in an individual bowl over hot rice.

You can also use oysters (about one or two pints) or cooked, chopped-up duck in the gumbo.

Ben McC. Moise

LOWCOUNTRY FETTUCINI

4 oz. fettucini
¼ lb. sm. shrimp, peeled
¼ lb. crab meat
¼ lb. sm. bay scallops
1 T. pimentos, diced
½ c. frozen baby green peas
1/3 stick butter

½ t. salt
½ t. pepper
Garlic-Dill Cream Sauce (see below)
sherry or white wine to taste
   (optional)
fresh parsley to garnish (optional)

Cook the fettucini according to the directions on the box about the same time as starting the sauce. Start the seafood about five minutes before the sauce and fettucini are done. The peas are best when lightly cooked. They may be placed in a wire mesh strainer or colander in the boiling fettucini water the last minute or two.

Sauté the pimentos, scallops, shrimp and crab meat with the salt, pepper and butter in skillet until almost done (only two-three minutes). Stir in sherry or wine and cook until just done (about a minute more). Stir in the cream sauce and the peas and ladle over individual plates of fettucini. Serve immediately. Serves two-three.

Garlic-Dill Cream Sauce

1/3 stick butter
1 T. self-rising flour
1 c. half and half

½ t. sugar
½ t. dill weed, dried
½ t. garlic powder

Melt butter in top section of double boiler. Add flour and stir well. Cook two minutes, stirring often. Slowly stir in the half and half and add the sugar, dill and garlic powder. Stir almost constantly as the sauce gradually thickens.

Eddie Collins

BEAUFORT STEW

10 lbs. smoked beef sausage in long
   links
2 doz. ears shucked, cleaned corn
½ bushel crabs

15 lbs. shrimp, headed
2 boxes Rex seafood seasoning (a
   commercial brand that comes in
   small bags)

Use a big 20-gallon pot filled to about half full. The best thing to do is clean the crabs before you put them in the pot. You can use the whole crab too, but it takes up more room in the pot and is messier to eat.

Cut sausage in one-inch sections. Bring water to a boil. Put sausage and seasoning bags in water and let boil for about ten minutes or so.

Put corn in and bring back to a boil. Then put the crabs in and bring back to a boil. Finally add the shrimp, and when the water comes back to a boil, pour off water. Serves thirty people.

Ed McTeer

CRAB STEW

a couple lbs. smoked pork meat or
    fat
3 lbs. onions, diced
3 lbs. potatoes, diced
approximately 3 doz. cleaned crab
    bodies

1 lb. crab claw meat
2 lbs. med. to lg. raw shrimp, peeled
    and diced
1 stick butter
salt and pepper to taste
rice

First fry out smoked pork meat or fat in a pot. Then add onions and brown (just like you're preparing for a fish stew). Then add water and pour in potatoes (dice 'em up real fine) and boil until it's like a thin soup. Then add cleaned crab bodies (take off back, fingers, deadman, etc.) and crab claw meat and shrimp. Put in butter and salt and pepper. Serve over rice.

Ivan Holden

Note: Ivan said this gets better after you "warm it up." He also said this recipe is "dangerous." "It's so good, your tongue will beat you half to death."

CREOLE BOUILLABAISSE

2 T. margarine or butter
2 T. olive oil
¼ c. flour
1 c. onions, chopped
½ c. celery, chopped
1 clove garlic, minced
4 c. fish stock or water
1 lg. can (1 lb., 12 oz.) tomatoes,
    undrained, cut up
½ c. dry white wine
2 T. parsley, chopped

1 T. lemon juice
1 bay leaf
½ t. salt
¼ t. cayenne pepper
¼ t. saffron (optional)
1 lb. fresh fish filets, cut in 1½-inch
    chunks
½ pt. fresh oysters
½ lb. fresh shrimp, peeled and
    deveined

In large boiler pot over medium heat, melt margarine and add olive oil. Prepare roux by slowly blending in flour, stirring constantly until mixture is light brown. Add onion, celery and garlic, and continue stirring until vegetables are tender. Gradually stir in fish stock or water. Add remaining ingredients except seafood. Bring to a boil, then simmer for ten minutes. Add fish and simmer ten minutes more. Add shrimp and oysters and cook for five minutes more, or until all seafood is done. Makes eight servings.

Maria Latto

COLD DAY'S SEA ISLAND CHOWDER

The following recipe makes a very rich chowder to be used as an appetizer or a cup of something hot to take away the chill of being on a frozen marsh.

4-5 sm. crabs (boil, pick and chop meat)
1 c. liquid from boiling crabs
1 lb. shrimp (shelled, deveined and chopped)
3 strips bacon
1 lg. onion, chopped fine
3 med. potatoes (cubed, playing dice size)
2 stalks celery, ribbed and chopped fine
½ t. thyme
salt
pepper
½ t. Worcestershire sauce
2 T. butter
3 c. milk
cream sherry to taste

Set boiled, pickled and chopped crab meat aside, along with chopped shrimp. Fry bacon strips in large skillet. Remove and crumble when crisp. Add minced onions, diced potatoes and celery to bacon grease, along with bacon crumbs. Brown. Add crab liquid, crab, shrimp, thyme, salt, pepper and Worcestershire sauce.

Bring to a slow boil until shrimp are done. Remove from heat. Add butter and milk. Slowly reheat until hot but not boiling. Add cream sherry to taste and top with pat of butter. Serve.

Greg R. Alexander

JAMBALAYA

½ c. green onion, chopped
½ c. white onion, chopped
1 lg. green pepper, cut in strips
½ c. chopped celery with a few leaves
1 t. minced garlic
1/3 c. butter
1 lb. raw shrimp, peeled and cleaned
2 doz. (about 1 c.) raw oysters (1 c. cubed, cooked ham may be used instead of oysters)
1 lb. can tomatoes
1 c. chicken broth
½ t. salt
1 t. cayenne
1 c. raw rice

In a large pan, sauté onion, green pepper, celery and garlic in the butter until tender, but not browned. Add shrimp and oysters and cook five minutes. (If ham is used instead of oysters, add the ham when rice is added.) Add the tomatoes, chicken broth, salt, cayenne and rice; stir and cover. Cook 25 to 30 minutes over low heat or until rice is done. If mixture becomes too dry, add tomato juice. Taste for seasoning. Serves four to six.

C. Laffitte

SHRIMP PUFF CASSEROLE

butter
12 slices bread
½ lb. cooked shrimp or one can
    shrimp
1 can minced clams and juice
dehydrated onion

6 slices American cheese
6 whole eggs
1½ pt. milk (3 c.)
salt
pepper

Grease casserole generously. Trim bread slices. Butter bread generously. Put six slices of bread in bottom of casserole. Sprinkle shrimp, clams and clam juice over bread. Sprinkle onion over mixture. Put a slice of cheese over each slice of bread. Cover with remaining six slices of bread. Beat eggs. Add milk, salt and pepper and beat again. Pour over bread and shrimp mixture. Let stand in refrigerator 12 hours. Cook at 350 degrees for 45 minutes. DO NOT OPEN OVEN DOOR WHILE COOKING! Use immediately. Will fall if left for any length of time.

Gail B. Smith

KIAWAH CASSEROLE

1 6-oz. pkg. each wild and white
    rice
1 lb. fresh crab or 2 7-oz. cans crab
2 lbs. cooked and peeled shrimp
    (may substitute frozen or canned)
3 10-oz. cans condensed cream of
    mushroom soup
1/3 c. grated onion

1 c. green pepper, chopped
1 c. celery, chopped
1 4-oz. jar pimento, drained and
    chopped
2 T. lemon juice
black olives, optional
lemon wedges, optional

Cook wild and white rice mixes as package labels direct. Preheat oven to 325 degrees. Lightly grease a four-quart casserole. Combine all ingredients right in casserole and stir to mix well. If desired, reserve a little crab meat and shrimp to garnish top of casserole. Sometimes you can find canned clams in the shell and this is good to garnish the top of casserole along with black olives and wedges of lemon. Bake uncovered at 325 degrees for approximately one hour.

Mrs. Benjamin Gause

BAKED SEAFOOD SALAD

¾ c. mayonnaise
1 t. Worcestershire sauce
1 t. lemon juice
½ lg. green pepper, diced
1 slice onion
½ t. salt

pepper
2 lbs. cooked shrimp
1 lb. crab
6 saltine cracker crumbs
½ c. grated cheese

Blend first eight ingredients in blender. Add crab. Mix with sauce. Put in casserole. Mix crumbs and cheese and cover casserole with mixture. Bake 350 degrees for 30 minutes. Makes eight servings.

Sarah P. Lumpkin

CRAB AND SHRIMP PIE

1 lb. cooked crab meat, or 2 lbs.
    cooked shrimp, or combination of
    the two (Fantastic with both.)
4 eggs
1 c. celery, diced

1 c. sharp cheese, grated
3 T. sherry
1½ c. mayonnaise
1¼ t. Worcestershire sauce

Beat eggs till frothy. Add all ingredients. Pour into casserole dish. Bake for one hour at 325 degrees or till knife inserted in middle comes out clean. This can be made ahead and refrigerated. If so, allow additional time to cook. I haven't microwaved this, but it will probably do A-OK. Can probably cook as any egg-based casserole.

Mrs. A.H. Lachicotte, Jr.

SEAFOOD QUICHE

1 cooked 9-inch pie crust
1 med. Vidalia onion, chopped
1 c. raw, peeled shrimp
¾ c. crab meat
3 lg. fresh eggs

1½ c. light cream (or milk)
a dash each of salt and pepper
¼ t. mace
butter

Sauté in butter the onion and shrimp until the shrimp are curled and pink and the onions translucent. Then pour in the crab meat and stir. Pour the mixture in the bottom of the pie crust. Beat together eggs, cream, salt, pepper and mace. Pour the frothy mixture over the seafood. Liberally dot the surface with butter. Bake in a 375-degree oven approximately 30 minutes until nicely browned and very puffed.

Good hot or cold. A quiche will settle as it cools. Serves four.

Ben McC. Moise

Unusual, But Still Good

Many of us are picky about what we eat. It may be because we know what tastes good, or it may be simply that we're not open to different foods. In this chapter we've collected those recipes from animals which suffer from a poor public image or perhaps have no image at all. After all, how many people have seriously considered eating periwinkles?

The main reason people screw their noses up at the idea of eating something like squid is simply prejudice. We assume that if an animal looks ugly, then it is unpalatable too. Compared with countries like Italy and Japan that relish squid and octopus, Americans are peculiarly prejudiced against the unusual food.

But where folks have a heritage of "living off the land," the prejudices appear less ingrained. Frog's legs, for example, are a regular feature of restaurant menus in many small towns. At a time when high prices really hurt at the supermarket, it would be wise to take advantage of the unusual but nutritious and reasonably priced foods that are available. Eel, squid, octopus and frog's legs are often overlooked at the seafood counter because they are unfamiliar. Yet they may be the best buy of the day and taste just as good as the normal fare - if not better.

Call them what you will - survival foods, economy-cuts, or taste treats - they should add a new dimension to your dining adventures.

Snapping Turtle

TURTLE STEW

Prefer to use snapping turtle, the meat of which resembles in taste, texture and color all types of meat, like chicken, beef or pork, in different parts of the turtle's body. Cut around the upper shell with a sharp knife and pry off both upper and lower shell.

snapping turtle meat	**corn, cut off cob**
salt	**potatoes, cubed**
pepper	**onions, chopped**

Cut off head, but use meaty neck, as this is very large and extends far under the shell. Boil down the meat in seasoned water and pull off bones, into very small pieces. Return meat to juices and add corn (cut off cob if in season), cubed potatoes, chopped onion and simmer until done.

Also, the small cap-sized turtle can be cut into chunks and batter-fried in hot oil.

Mr. and Mrs. Joe B. Norris

MOISE'S SNAPPING TURTLE STEW

This recipe calls for about five pounds of cleaned snapping turtle meat, which is a process all by itself, for a "snapper" can put up quite a fight. Kill and plunge the whole bloomin' turtle into boiling hot water for about five minutes. Remove it, rinse it and scrape the dark outer skin with a steel pot scrubber or a stiff wire brush. Cut the skin at upper shell level around the front from shoulder to shoulder and also along the back side. Then with pure brute strength, separate the top shell from the bottom. Remove the guts and then begin removing the meat with a boning knife. Rinse and drain the meat in a colander.

snapping turtle meat
salt and pepper
½ c. fat
2 or 3 garlic cloves, finely chopped
1 c. flour
1 sm. can tomato paste
2 8-oz. cans tomato sauce
6-8 onions, chopped

1½ c. celery, de-stringed and
    chopped
2 bell peppers, chopped
juice from 2 or 3 fresh squeezed
    lemons or limes
3 T. Worcestershire sauce
couple dollops Tabasco

Salt and pepper the meat and sauté in fat in a large pot until just browned and pour back in the colander. Wipe pot out and cover bottom with half-a-cup melted fat and two or three finely chopped garlic cloves and bring up to heat. Then stir in about one cup of flour and keep stirring until the flour is nice and brown. Then add one small can of tomato paste, stirring constantly all the while. When this has made a good thick brown mixture, add two regular cans of tomato sauce.

Stir well until thoroughly mixed and add the onions, celery, bell peppers, the lemon or lime juice, "wooster" sauce, and a couple of healthy dollops or so of Tabasco. Keep turning at medium-low heat for a half-an-hour or so, and then add the turtle meat with a little water (and then more, along and along as necessary). Cover and simmer for another couple of hours, stirring every now and then. You may add salt, pepper or other seasonings to suite your taste. Serve over hot rice. *There really isn't anything exactly like it!*

Ben McC. Moise

Bullfrog Legs

Bullfrog legs are delicacies, and they are easy to prepare. To dress frog legs, cut skin across the top of the back at the small part of the body. Slip off the skin like removing a glove inside out. Cut off the feet at the ankles. Cut off hind quarters at small part of body. There you have a pair of legs, which when washed in cold water, is ready for cooking.

FROG'S LEGS

doz. pr. of frog's legs	onion, several slices
2 c. milk	bell pepper, several strips
2 eggs	flour

Clean and split pairs of legs. Make a mixture of the milk, eggs, onions, bell pepper and pour over legs. Let soak in refrigerator for several hours. Dredge legs in flour, salt and pepper and fry in cooking oil.

Ben McC. Moise

FROG LEGS WESTFIELD

6 pr. frog's legs	2 T. lemon juice
olive oil	2 T. parsley
1 c. white wine	1 sm. can mushrooms
salt and pepper to taste	paprika
garlic powder to taste	cornstarch

Coat skillet bottom with oil and add wine. Sprinkle legs with salt, pepper and garlic powder to taste and place in skillet. Sprinkle with lemon juice and parsley and cook at low heat (250 degrees), covered, for about 20 minutes or until tender. Remove to warm platter. Add mushrooms to remaining liquid and thicken with cornstarch. Pour sauce over legs and sprinkle with paprika.

David Allen

FROG'S LEGS A LA CREOLE

This recipe is wonderful if you are lucky to have the frog legs. My husband does all kinds of hunting and fishing, so I have wild everything all of the time. I myself read everything on wildlife. I have learned a lot of things I didn't really know. I fix most of the wild meat in my microwave. I had a recipe on how to make earthworm cookies, but I can't find it. I made some chickweed salad too.

16 frog's legs	2 eggs, well beaten
boiling water	fine dry bread crumbs
juice of ½ lemon	fat for deep frying
salt and pepper	Onion Cream Sauce (see below)

Put frog's legs in boiling water with lemon juice and salt and pepper. Scald for four minutes. Drain legs and pat dry. Dip legs into eggs and roll in bread crumbs. Fry in deep fat for four or five minutes, until legs are tender. Serve with onion cream sauce.

Onion Cream Sauce

2 T. margarine or butter	½ t. salt
2 T. all-purpose flour	2 T. onion, minced
1½ c. light cream or evaporated	1 T. parsley, minced
milk	1 egg, well-beaten

Melt margarine or butter and stir in flour. Gradually stir in cream. Add salt, onion and parsley. Cook over low heat, stirring constantly until smooth and thickened. Beat some of sauce in egg. Add to remainder of sauce and cook for two minutes. *This recipe I've had for forty years - a favorite of ours.*

Helen Carter

Crawfish

I remember growing up in Lee County where just about every old ditch, branch and swamp would abound in crawfish, or "crawdads" as we called them. We used to put empty tin cans in shallow water and go back days later and quickly lift each can up to see if a crawdad was hiding inside. It seemed like the rustier the can, the better they liked 'em. We used to pop off the tails and boil 'em in a tin can over a campfire. The head, body and feet of the crawdads are removed, the tails being all that are eaten. Boiled in water, then peeled and seasoned with a little salt, they are just as delicious as shrimp. As a matter of fact, you can substitute crawdads for shrimp in just about any shrimp recipe.

CRAWFISH IN THE BUSH

½ lb. salted butt meat, diced
1 box frozen spinach, thawed
1 c. water

1 c. boiled and peeled crawfish tails
1 c. shredded cooked fish
pepper and cinnamon

Bring the fry pan up to medium hot heat and get the butt meat to frying. When it begins to brown a little, pour in the spinach and stir around for a couple of minutes until the water off the spinach is sizzling. Then add about a cup of hot water and let simmer for about five minutes or so and add the crawfish, fish and pepper and a wee bit of ground cinnamon. Cook until the water boils away. This dish, in which spinach is aptly characterized as "the bush," is usually eaten with rice.

Ben McC. Moise

CRAWFISH LINGUINE

1 lb. peeled crawfish tails
½ c. butter
¼ c. olive oil
1 clove garlic, minced
1 c. mushrooms, sliced

½ c. green onions with tops, chopped
¼ c. parsley, chopped
1 pkg. (8 oz.) linguine, cooked
Parmesan cheese (optional)

Melt butter with olive oil in large skillet. Sauté garlic and mushrooms until mushrooms are just tender. Add crawfish tails and green onions.

Cook five minutes over low heat. Stir in chopped parsley. Serve over hot cooked linguine and sprinkle with Parmesan cheese. Four servings.

Note: The crawfish mixture also makes an excellent filling for omelets. If using in omelets, omit the olive oil.

Donna Florio

FLO'S ETOUFFEE

1 lb. peeled crawfish meat
1 can (6 oz.) tomato paste
1 c. cooking oil
3 cloves garlic, minced
5 c. diced onions
1½ c. minced celery
1½ c. chopped green onions

crawfish fat reserved from cleaning
   crawfish
½ t. sugar
½ t. salt
¼ t. pepper
1½ c. water

Cook tomato paste in oil over medium heat, stirring constantly, until oil turns light brown and paste loses its bright red color, about ten minutes. Add garlic, cook until golden. Add onions, celery and green onions. Cook, stirring occasionally, until onions are translucent. Stir in crawfish fat, sugar, salt, pepper and water. Simmer for five minutes. Add crawfish meat. Simmer five minutes longer. Serve over hot cooked rice. Four servings.

Flo Triska

BELL PEPPERS STUFFED WITH CRAWFISH

1 lb. peeled crawfish tails and fat
5 med. bell peppers
3 med. onions, minced
2 c. green onions with tops,
   chopped
1 med. bell pepper, minced
5 cloves garlic, minced

½ t. black pepper
½ t. red pepper
½ t. salt
½ c. Crisco oil
1 c. parsley, chopped
2 c. stale French bread crumbs or
   seasoned bread crumbs

Wash, halve and core peppers. Boil for five minutes in lightly salted water and drain well. Grind or chop tails. Place in a large mixing bowl. Add onions, green onions, bell pepper, garlic, black and red pepper and salt. Mix well by hand. Heat oil in a large skillet. Add crawfish mixture and cook five to seven minutes, or until vegetables are tender-crisp. Remove from heat and add parsley. When cool, stuff into peppers and place in well-greased baking dish. Sprinkle with bread crumbs. Bake at 350 degrees, for 20 to 30 minutes, or until lightly browned. Five servings.

Donna Florio

CRAWFISH JAMBALAYA

1 lb. peeled crawfish tails
½ c. margarine or butter
1 c. chopped onions
½ c. chopped celery
½ c. chopped bell pepper
4 cloves garlic, finely chopped
2 T. crawfish fat
½ t. salt

¼ t. black pepper
¼ t. cayenne
½ t. cornstarch
4 c. cooked rice
½ c. green onion tops, chopped
½ c. parsley, chopped
2 pieces pimento, chopped

Melt margarine and add onions, celery, bell pepper and garlic in heavy pot. Cook, uncovered, over medium heat until onions are wilted. Add crawfish fat and 1½ cups of water. Season with salt, pepper and cayenne. Cook, uncovered, for about 20 minutes, stirring occasionally. Add crawfish. Continue cooking and stir another five minutes. Dissolve cornstarch in ½ cup of water and add to mixture; cook another five minutes. Mix ingredients with cooked rice. Add green onions, parsley and pimento. Mix again. Six servings.

Donna Florio

Eel

I learned about eels at a Parker's Ferry landing on the Edisto River from an old black gentleman. I had observed a large number of dead eels lying around the bank and commented on it to the old man. He said that "when most people catch 'em, they just take 'em off the hook and throw 'em on the bank," but, he said, he keeps his and "skins 'em and either fries 'em or stews 'em." To skin 'em, he said, he ties a piece of strong string around their neck just below their gills and makes a loop. He hooks his loop over a nail in a tree in his yard and cuts a circle all the way around the eel, just below the string, and then loosens the skin down just a bit to make a "hold" for a pair of plyers. "You just pull the skin right off, just about like a catfish," he said.

"Gut it and cut off the fins with some scissors," he said, and then cut 'em loose just below the string. He said he parboils them some (just at the simmer) for 20 minutes in some water and a little bit of vinegar. Then he rolls them in flour or corn meal and fries 'em 'til good and brown. He says he pours a little "wooster" on 'em, and they taste pretty good. For the stew he says "you do it just like you would any stew, but you use eel."

Ben McC. Moise

REGGIE'S FRIED EEL

eel cut in 2-in. slices
buttermilk
flour

salt
pepper
lemon slices or vinegar

Cut, clean and skin eel into two-inch slices. Coat with buttermilk, then dip into flour, salt and pepper. Deep fry or panfry till golden. Serve with lemon slices or sprinkle with vinegar.

Small eel are delicious when cut into three-inch slices and then split in the middle and fried in butter, salt and pepper.

Joan Joyce

Garfish

The longnose garfish *(Lepisosteus osseus)* is a common denizen of coastal waters and an unused resource. Commonly considered trash fish, there is no commercial market for this species. When properly prepared, however, the flesh is mild, boneless, and can be obtained in large quantities for social gatherings. Gar are the bane of shad fishermen, who are more than happy to pass these net tanglers on to anyone willing to accept them.

Cleaning garfish involves some effort, but this lessens with experience. Beginning at the head, split the shell (armored scales) open down the back with a hatchet or suitable instrument. Remove head and tail, separate shell from meat along sides with a knife. Scrape exposed meat from carcass with a large spoon, fork or serrated fish scaler. Gar meat is permeated with tendons and fascia, and this procedure leaves most gristle behind. Grind meat if necessary.

GAR BALLS TOOGOODOO

2 lb. garfish meat
1 lb. boiled potatoes, mashed (use
   ratio 3 units meat, 1 unit
   potatoes)

2 lg. onions, chopped fine
1 c. (or more) parsley, green onions,
   celery tops; chopped

Mix above ingredients, salt and pepper to taste. Shape into one and one-and-a-half inch balls. Roll in mustard sauce (see page 88), flour, deep fat fry.

James M. Bishop

Octopus

Octopus is a cephalapod mollusk with nearly globular body and eight arms covered by suction cups for grasping prey. Generally, the arm span reaches two to three feet. A parrot-like beak at the junctions of the eight arms is well-adapted to crunching lobster, crabs, shrimp and scallops on which the octopus feeds. This diet yields the octopus meat a very flavorsome taste, often compared to chicken.

To clean an octopus, use a very sharp knife, split it open and remove all the internal organs, etc. To do this, place the knife blade at the junction of the legs where the mouth is and force the blade up through the top of the head. Next scrape the octopus clean with a blade and be sure to cut out the beak. Wash the body thoroughly, including the tentacles, the tastiest part. Cut into pieces no larger than one by one inch. Octopus meat needs to be tenderized. This can be done by beating the pieces with a wooden mallet for several minutes or simply boil in water for ten minutes.

Do not cook the meat too long, since it is very delicate and will toughen quickly. Or you may want to marinate the octopus overnight. This will also tenderize the meat.

CHARCOAL-BROILED OCTOPUS

2 lb. octopus
1 c. dry sherry wine
2 T. olive oil

Clean octopus as described above. Cut small hunks of the mantle meat into whatever pattern you desire, keeping each piece no bigger than one inch around or long and one-half inch thick. Marinate overnight in the wine and olive oil. When ready to cook, place on charcoal grill and cook for about 10 to 15 minutes until lightly browned. Makes four servings.

OCTOPUS IN TOMATO WINE SAUCE

3 lb. octopus
3 lb. sm. whole onions, peeled
1 c. olive oil
2 c. dry sherry wine
2 garlic cloves, minced
salt and pepper to taste

2 sm. bay leaves
1 stick cinnamon
2 whole cloves
1 can (8-oz.) tomato sauce
1 can tomato paste, diluted with
   ¼ c. water

Clean octopus and pound meat with a wooden mallet to soften. Cut mantle into one inch pieces. In a deep Dutch oven place the octopus, whole onions, olive oil, sherry wine, garlic, bay leaves, salt and pepper, cinnamon, cloves, tomato sauce and tomato paste. Bring to a boil and simmer for 45 minutes or until octopus is tender. Check seasonings. If needed, add a little salt and pepper. Remove cloves and cinnamon before serving. Makes six servings. Serve over hot rice.

Maria Latto

Squid

STUFFED SQUID A LA MARIA

5 lb. whole squid, fresh or frozen
  (16 lg. squid)
juice of 1 lemon
½ t. pepper
Rice Stuffing (see below)
1 can (15-oz.) tomato sauce
1 c. dry sherry wine

1/3 c. olive oil
2 T. flour
½ t. salt
½ t. oregano
¼ t. pepper
3 garlic cloves, crushed

Thaw frozen squid. Cut through arms near the eyes. With thumb and forefinger, squeeze out the inedible beak, which will be located near the cut. Reserve tentacles. Feel inside mantle for chitinous pen. Firmly grasp pen and attached viscera; remove from mantle. Turn mantle inside out and remove membrane from interior of mantle. Wash thoroughly in cold running water and turn back right side out. Wash mantle thoroughly and drain. It is now ready for stuffing. Make rings by cutting across mantle. Arms can be chopped, minced or left whole. Drain squid, making sure all excess water is removed. Place squid in a shallow pan and sprinkle with lemon juice and salt and pepper. Set pan in refrigerator until ready to stuff squid.

Rice Stuffing

½ c. olive oil
2 lg. onions, chopped
chopped tentacles
1 box (6¾ oz.) long grain and wild
  rice (Do not use seasoning packet
  that comes with rice.)
1/3 c. fresh parsley, chopped

5 T. fresh dill, chopped or 1 t. dried
½ t. salt
¼ t. pepper
1/3 c. toasted almonds, coarsely
  chopped
1½ c. fresh mushrooms, sliced

Cook onion in hot oil or until tender. Add tentacles and cook for two to three minutes. Add rice and cook for ten minutes, stirring occasionally. Add parsley, dill, salt and pepper. Cook for another two minutes and add fresh sliced mushrooms. Stir and check seasonings and cook for three minutes. Add almonds and stir. Cool stuffing. While stuffing is cooling, PREPARE SAUCE:

In a large sauce pan or bowl, combine the tomato sauce, dry sherry, olive oil, flour and seasonings. Stir thoroughly. Set aside. Stuff squid loosely (do not overstuff, or squid will split open while cooking). Close opening with a toothpick. Place squid in a single layer in a well-greased 17 by 11 inch pan. Pour sauce over stuffed squid, making sure squid is well coated. Cover pan with aluminum foil and place in 350-degree pre-heated oven and bake for 40 to 45 minutes or until squid is tender. Uncover last ten minutes of baking and baste. Continue baking until done. Serves eight.

Maria Latto

SQUID VINAIGRETTE

1½ lbs. squid, cleaned and
   cut into rings
6 T. olive oil
2 T. wine vinegar
1 T. lemon juice

1 8-oz. can artichoke hearts
1 T. parsley, chopped
1 t. garlic powder
1 c. small mushrooms, sliced
romaine lettuce

Combine oil, vinegar, lemon, salt, pepper and garlic powder. Add artichoke hearts and marinate for at least two hours.

Immerse squid rings in boiling water for 30 seconds. Drain and cool. Add squid, mushrooms and parsley to vinaigrette. Marinate for 30 minutes. Serve over bed of romaine lettuce.

Doris Akers

Whelk

Whelks or conchs may often be found in shallow water during periods of low tide along the coast. To remove the animal from the shell, break off the whirled portion with a hammer. When the muscle attachment is severed, the animal will slide out easily. If the shell is to be saved intact, several minutes in a steamer or boiling water will loosen the animal enough that it may be pried out with an ice pick or fork. Cut away the soft entrails, the hard operculum and the tough gray skin. The remaining white meat may be prepared in a variety of ways, but the flavor and texture are best when eaten raw.

CONCH STEW

3 c. conch meat, finely chopped
¾ c. fatback
1 lg. onion
2 T. flour
3 c. stewing tomatoes
½ c. tomato sauce

1 c. water
pinch of oregano
salt to taste
2 c. potatoes, cubed
1 chili pepper, diced
1/3 stick butter

Sauté fatback and remove cracklings. Lower temperature and add conch and onion to fat. Blend in the flour, tomatoes, tomato sauce, water, oregano and salt. Cover and simmer for three to four hours or place in crock pot all day. Add potatoes, bell pepper and chili pepper. Simmer another half hour or until potatoes are done. Add cracklings and one third stick of butter.

SEVICHE (Marinated Raw Fish)

Prepare a marinade by combining:

2 c. lime juice	several tomatoes, chopped
1 lg. onion	2 t. salt
several chili peppers, chopped	pinch of oregano

Pour over thinly sliced conch meat, shrimp, diced fish, picked crab claws and hard portion of clams, then marinate in refrigerator for 4 to 24 hours. Serve cold with chips or crackers as an hors d'oeuvre or light summer meal.

GROUND CONCH SEAFOOD CAKE

¾ c. cracker or toast crumbs	½ t. salt
2 eggs, beaten	paprika

Pat mixture into cakes and sauté or fry.

Steve Hopkins

MORE WHELK

There are two kinds of whelks commonly found in the creeks and beaches of the coast - the knobbed whelk and the channel whelk. The knobbed whelk has a grayish pear-shaped shell, and the opening is usually a rich orange-red. It is distinguished from the channeled whelks by the "knobs" or prominent horns around the whirls of the shell. The channel whelk is more yellowish-gray on the outside shell, and the opening is yellow instead of red and the whirls are somewhat smoother and without the "horns." They are locally referred to as conchs, but they aren't.

The best way to get the whelk out of its shell is to plunge it in boiling water for four or five minutes, and when it is cool enough to handle, pry the meat out with a stout knife or screw driver. Then peel off the hard, plate-like operculum from the foot. Cut the muscular foot off from the other parts and skin or scrape it. (This foot is the only part of the whelk you use.) Then parboil it (you will probably need about five or six whelks to make enough for your people) until tender or cook in a pressure cooker under 15 pounds for half an hour. Another way you can tenderize the whelk meat is to put it on a heavy board or chopping block and pound it with a mallet or hammer, but not so hard as to squash it to a pulp, but just where it is rather flattish. Anyway, when it is tenderized, cut it into thin slices and set aside.

WHELK STEW

whelk meat
olive oil
2 garlic cloves
1 med. onion, chopped
1 celery stalk, de-stringed and
  chopped

1 bell pepper, chopped
2 can sm. Italian tomatoes
2 T. tomato sauce
½ t. ea. oregano, basil, salt
2 bay leaves
¼ t. Tabasco sauce

Bring a large pot up to medium heat with enough olive oil to cover the bottom. Mash two cloves of garlic flat and finely chopped and add to the olive oil along with one medium-sized, finely chopped onion and one de-stringed stalk of celery (not a whole head of celery), one chopped bell pepper and the prepared whelk meat. Stir around with a spoon until the onions are just browning and add the Italian tomatoes and tomato sauce and simmer for about five minutes or so. Then stir in the remaining seasonings, cover and cook for five more minutes. This makes a good thick stew-like dish.

If you want to make a chowder out of it, add one more can of Italian tomatoes and one medium can of tomato juice and two cups of peeled, diced Irish potatoes, and simmer until the potatoes are tender. You can also sauté the parboiled or tenderized, thinly sliced meat in a mixture of sweet butter, lemon juice, and mashed, finely chopped garlic, or stir 'em in scrambled eggs for breakfast.

Ben McC. Moise

More Oddities 'n Ends

PERIWINKLES

Periwinkles are the black and brown snail-looking mollusks seen clinging to stalks of marsh grass or found leaving arabasque trails in marsh mud.

periwinkles
lightly salted water

melted butter
dill or garlic

Gather a goodly number of periwinkles and thoroughly scrub the mud off the shells. Boil them in lightly salted water for 20 minutes or until "lid" opens. Pick them out of their shells with a nut-pick or toothpick and dip them in either plain melted butter or dill or garlic butter.

Ben McC. Moise

COQUINA SOUP

Coquinas are the tiny rainbow-hued clams found along the beach. Their open butterfly shells are seen more frequently than the whole closed bivalve which lives just beneath the surface of the sand where washed by the waves.

2 gal. thoroughly washed coquinas	2½ c. heavy cream
1 onion, finely chopped	a pinch ea. salt and pepper
2 c. white wine	paprika

Put one chopped onion in the bottom of a large kettle and add the coquinas. Pour in one cup of water and the wine and bring to a boil about 15 to 20 minutes until the tiny shells open and their juice blends with the wine. This should produce about one to one-and-a-half quarts of broth. Carefully strain through several thicknesses of cheesecloth in a colander and then stir in the cream. Heat; but do not bring to a boil, and serve with a light top garnish of paprika. *Serves four blissfully.*

Ben McC. Moise

FRESHWATER MUSSELS

These are found in rivers, creeks and branches, usually under water in varying size from tiny to big. I bring them home after duck hunting, choosing those that are about the size of saltwater clams. I wash them in cold water, let them sit in the refrigerator overnight.

steamed freshwater mussels	Worcestershire sauce
melted butter	lemon juice
salt and pepper	

Using a biscuit pan and a little water, steam the mussels open in the oven. Foil over the pan helps. Remove temporarily and break off the now-open top shell and discard it. Mix the remaining ingredients and pour over the meat on the half-shell. Leave off the foil and return to the oven, but this time to the broiling lower section. In just a few minutes, they are ready to eat.

Dana Crosland

SEA TROUT AIR BLADDERS

Save air bladders from about a dozen trout. Rinse in tap water, cut into strips, dredge in seasoned flour, fry until crisp. *Provides a great mystery dish.*

James M. Bishop

SAUTÉED MULLET GIZZARDS

The common striped mullet (Mugil cephalus) consumes large amounts of plant matter. To facilitate the digestive process of this food substrate, mullet posses a pyloric stomach not unlike the gizzard of a chicken. When obtained in quantities, mullet "gizzards" offer a spendid change for the adventurous appetite.

mullet gizzards	chopped parsley
butter	lemon twist

To prepare, simply clean the gizzards and sauté in butter. Seasonings may include chopped parsley and a twist of lemon slice.

James M. Bishop

ALBERT'S BARBECUED PIGEONS

This recipe comes from the late Albert Williams, Mrs. F.M. Moise Sr.'s Edisto Island-born cook, whose straightforward approach to almost any recipe began with "First, you take an onion." This recipe transformed tough old pigeons into a pretty fine meal.

6 old birds
water to cover
2 stalks celery in ½-in. slices

¼ c. catsup
2 med. onions, sliced

Sauce

1 bottle catsup
½ bottle chili sauce

2 T. Worcestershire sauce
2 med. onions, chopped

Boil birds in water, celery, catsup and onions for a long time until tender. You may have to add more water while boiling. Then place birds in a baking pan. Mix sauce ingredients and pour over birds. Bake at 350 degrees for 30 to 45 minutes, basting often. *Reprinted from "Cookbook of the Family Favorites" by Ethel McCutcheon Moise.*

Ben McC. Moise

PRAIRIE OYSTER

yolk of 1 fresh egg (whole)
½ c. V-8 juice
1 t. "Wooster" sauce
vinegar, several drops

squeeze of fresh lemon
pinch of salt and pepper
Tabasco, 1 dash

Mix and serve in small glass. Bottoms up! *Cures bilious remitting and unremitting fevers, agues, some symptoms of gout and will rid one's self of fleas.*

Ben McC. Moise

Wild Plants

Woodland Harvest

Before you can munching through the woods on just anything organic, learn all you can about the plants you plan to eat. An experienced wild plant eater, a field guide, or both are must companions. Keep an eye on the plants through the seasons, noting where you can find them and which time is right.

Be sure you have the landowner's permission. Many of the following plants are very nutritious, but be sure your fern or berry hasn't been sprayed or polluted. Don't gather from the shoulder of roads. Give your stomach time to adjust to wild foods by adding only one plant to your diet at a time. Don't use plants and berries for medicine.

The only time to eat a plant before it's been identified is when starvation is the alternative. If you haven't learned the poisonous plants, at least obey these rules of thumb: (1) Avoid all mushrooms; (2) Don't eat anything that looks like, but doesn't smell like, an onion; and (3) Don't eat any lacy-leafed plants that resemble carrots, parsley or Queen Anne's lace.

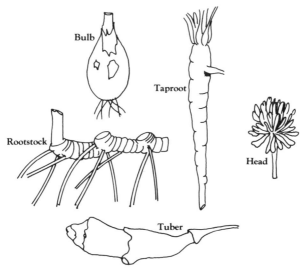

Wild Vegetables

POKEWEED *(Phytolacca americana)*

Also known as poke, poke salad, pigeonberry, garget, skoke, ink berry, cancer root, wild spinach.

Indians and early settlers once treated countless ailments, from ulcers to hemorrhoids, with pokeweed or its parts, and even mixed it with gunpowder as a cancer remedy. In the Lowcountry, pokeweed root is still boiled and applied to the head for relief of high blood pressure.

These uses may be unusual and impractical, but pokeweed, prepared like a potherb or asparagus, is one of the most commonly eaten wild plants. Although most people boil it one or two times and throw off the water to get rid of the bitter taste, some say poke still surpasses most vegetables in iron, vitamin C and other nutrients. Like many country folk in the springtime, Roxie Oglesby gathers the young shoots when six to twelve inches high and fixes the now-famous "poke sallet."

"I parboil the tender parts one time to get the bitter out," she says. "Then I fry some meat grease and put the poke in with fresh green onions. And I usually put turnip greens with it. My whole family loves it."

Dr. Wade Batson, professor of botany, says he has eaten poke every spring of his life. "I don't cultivate it. Like most people who eat it, I just know where it grows. You can dig up the roots in the fall and bed them down in the basement or some other dark spot. Put rich soil over them. When the shoots come up about six inches, just pull them off. Others grow back and you can keep eating all winter."

The tender shoots can also be cooked like asparagus by immersing in or steaming over boiling water and adding salt, pepper, and butter or sauce. The whole leafy plant can be used to make pickles or sliced and fried like okra.

The scientific name of this extremely useful plant nonetheless warns us of the phytolaccin contained in its poisonous root. The stems, when purple, and the berries are also said to be poisonous.

Poke can be found in waste places and cultivated fields.

CATTAILS

Cattails can be recognized by their long, linear, sheathed leaves, and by their erectly stalked, sausage-shaped brown flowerheads. All cattails grow these "sausages" which in actuality are tightly packed, minute flowers. These plants form dense stands in ponds, wet ditches, freshwater swamps, sluggish or standing waters, brackish marshes and pools, and river banks. All stages of the cattail have been used for food as the plant provided starch, flour, gruel (from the seeds) and vegetables for man's plate. Leaves were used in rush seating, thatching, sleeping mats, sandals, baskets and small toys such as ducks and dolls. Stalks were used extensively for caulking barrels. The familier brown spikes were used in dried flower arrangements, candle molds, "sweeps" for chimneys and other hard-to-reach places, and torches were made by dipping the flowerheads in coal oil or kerosene.

During springtime, the new shoot rises from the cattail's tall, swordlike leaves. When about three feet tall, the stalk can be pulled from the leaf cluster and peeled. The exposed 6 to 12 inch core of crisp vegetation can be sliced and tossed in salads (the taste and texture is similar to hearts of palm) or boiled for three to five minutes and then buttered with a taste similar to freshly cooked asparagus.

If the shoot is left to grow, the spike will elongate and fatten as it develops the familiar flowers — the brown "tail." At this stage, the center part of the plant will look similar to unripened ears of corn wrapped in their husks. When filled out with newly formed green flowers but before the spike bursts through its sheathed leaves and develops pollen, stalks can be collected, boiled for five to ten minutes, drained, buttered and eaten like corn on the cob. In addition, the buds can be scraped and used in cold salads or added to egg omelettes. There is a core in the middle of the flower spike, and like corn on the cob, is inedible.

Later in the spring, the bloom spikes which have not been harvested will develop a coat of yellow pollen. While this pollen is an integral part of the plant's sexual reproduction, the Indians found it to be quite nutritious. The bright, golden grains can be collected by placing the flowerheads in an enclosed bag to avoid scattering the fine grains in the wind. After sieving, the pollen can be substituted for flour and adds a nut-like taste to pancakes, breads, and muffins, and as a bonus, contains protein, sulphur, phosphorus, carbohydrates, sugar and oil.

CATTAIL PANCAKES

1 c. cattail pollen
1 egg
1 c. white or whole wheat flour
2 T. vegetable oil
¾ t. salt
1 t. baking soda

2 c. milk (more milk can be added as the pollen quickly absorbs the milk. Use much more milk for thinner pancakes.) Buttermilk can be substituted for regular milk.

Mix together cattail pollen, flour, soda and salt. Stir together the milk, egg and oil. Mix liquid ingredients with the dry mixture and set batter aside until it thickens — about 5-10 minutes.

Grease and bake pancakes on a hot griddle (about 375 degrees), turning cakes once. Remove as soon as the second side is browned. Serve hot with butter, maple or corn syrup, or honey.

Just before spring arrives and warms the earth again, the cattail produces a bulb-like root on the leading ends of the rhizome and roots. These root sprouts can be peeled, boiled, buttered, and eaten like a vegetable or made into an excellent pickle. In addition, at the base of the plant where the stalk joins the rootstock, the starchy, white sprout found there can also be boiled and seasoned with butter, or added to a stew or roasted in the same way one would use potatoes.

Lin Dunbar

EDIBLE FERN TIPS

bracken tips (fiddleheads)
water
salt
butter

flour
milk or cream
light toast

Our usual fern found in woods is known as the bracken fern (Pteridium aquilinum). In the spring, the new shoots come through the ground and begin growing in a curly shape like a pig's tail. When these are still finger size, cut them even with the ground, carry them home, remove the husk down to the tender stems, wash and put into a small pot. Cover with water and bring to a boil. Throw away this water. Do the same thing again and throw away the second water. Cover stems a third time. This time, add salt and cook until tender. These will look and taste somewhat like asparagus. Make a cream sauce using butter, flour, and milk or cream. When ready, serve on light toast.

Dana Crosland

COMMON DANDELION (Taraxacum officinale)

The solitary yellow flower and downy white seed clusters of the dandelion are familiar to all who keep a well-groomed lawn. Few realize that the dandelion can serve as a nutritious salad, cooked green, fritter, or coffee substitute. But once its value is recognized, the little weed usually becomes the first plant tried by those experimenting with edible plants. Novices must be sure, therefore, to gather the young leaves *before the flowers appear* or the bitter taste may turn them against wild foods permanently. The blanched part below the soil level is best.

174

Dr. Wade Batson, professor of botany, parches and grinds roots to make dandelion coffee. To do this, scrub the roots and place them on aluminum foil in a 100-to 500-degree oven for four to five hours or until dark. When the roots have cooled, grind it in a coffee grinder or blender. Boil one heaping teaspoon of this dried root with one cup of water for three minutes, strain, and serve with sugar or honey.

When still tucked down in the rosette of leaves, the flowerbuds can either be boiled or pickled. "When they blossom, dandelion flower heads can be pulled, dipped in a light batter, and fried in a small amount of grease. They are quite good," Dr. Batson says.

Like poke, dandelions may be brought into the cellar, covered with leaf litter, and raised in winter for good salad greens without bitterness.

DANDY DANDELIONS

12 to 18 long dandelion stems with
   buds
boiling salted water
3 hard-cooked eggs
3 T. olive oil

3 T. lemon juice
½ clove garlic, finely chopped
salt and freshly ground black
   pepper to taste

Remove the dandelion buds and discard. Tie the stems in a bundle and cook in boiling salted water to cover in an uncovered skillet until tender, about ten minutes. Drain.

For each serving, wind two or three dandelion stems in a basket shape and place in small ramekin. Top with hard-cooked egg half.

Combine the remaining ingredients and drizzle over the eggs and stems. Serve cold or warm. To warm, heat in a 300-degree oven five minutes. Makes six servings.

Mrs. Helen B. Lee

DANDELION GREENS

2-3 lbs. dandelions
2 T. salt

juice from approximately 2 lemons
¼ to 1/3 c. olive oil, or as needed

Gather dandelions from a field or your yard. Cut off root end and wash throughly several times in cold water. Drain.

Fill a large kettle or pot with cold water and salt, bring to a boil, and add dandelions a little at a time until all are immersed in the boiling water. Bring to a boil, turn down heat, and simmer for approximately one hour, or until dandelions are tender.

When cooked, drain in colander (or you may want to save hot liquid to drink). Place dandelions in a large bowl and sprinkle with lemon juice, olive oil, and salt (if needed).

Serve with homemade fresh bread, feta cheese, and Greek olives. Delicious! Makes six servings.

NOTE: *Save dandelion liquid and serve in a cup with a little lemon juice and salt. Stir and drink. Delicious!*

Maria Latto

SASSAFRAS *(Sassafras albidum)*

Also known as white sassafras, root beer tree, ague tree, saloop.

Sassafras is likely to be sold in supermarkets, but it's seldom recognized because it's sold as filet gumbo used to thicken soups. Carrying on a practice of the Choctaw Indians, Southerners cut and dry the young tender stems and leaves and grind them to a fine powder to make filet gumbo, which is especially popular in the Bayou country.

SASSAFRAS TEA

Though recent studies have shown that too much sassafras tea can be harmful to one's health, a moderate intake of the tea is harmless.

The sassafras tree, *Sassafras albidum*, is a medium-sized to large tree with spicy-aromatic twigs and different shaped leaves: egg-shaped, mitten-shaped (two-lobed) and three lobed. Leaves are smooth and bright green above and smooth to slightly downy beneath. Sassafras trees can be found growing along fence rows, woodland borders and old fields. Typically, a number of small, young trees surround the mature ones, and these are easier to harvest when collecting roots for tea.

Gather the roots by pulling or digging the small trees from the ground. (Since many of the young trees are produced by underground runners from the parent plant, collecting the young trees will not harm the others, and additional trees will grow from these same runners.) Roots can be used fresh or dried for later use. Peel off the outer bark of the root and scrub clean. Place the roots in a large kettle filled with water and boil until the water turns reddish-brown. Strain. The tea can be served hot or is delicious cooled and sweetened.

Lin Dunbar

SWEET GOLDENROD TEA

Goldenrod flowers are a pleasant, roadside addition to much of the state's golden autumn color. Only *Solidago odora* has leaves that give a distinctive anise or "licorice" smell when crushed. Sweet goldenrod is found in woodlands, along roadsides, savannahs and pine barrens.

The fresh or dried leaves make an excellent tea. Steep a teaspoonful of crushed leaves in a cup of boiling water for 5 minutes. Sweeten with sugar or honey and serve.

Lin Dunbar

CURLED DOCK *(Rumex crispus)*

Also known as yellow dock, narrow-leaved dock, or common dock.

Dock should be gathered in the early spring when the nights are still nippy and the leaves still young and tender. They can be boiled ten to 15 minutes or used fresh in salads. Later in the spring or summer it must be boiled two to three times to remove bitterness. Dock can be fried in hot grease or mixed hot with onions, horseradish, sour cream and bacon and spread on toast.

As a folk remedy, dock was credited with purifying the blood, tightening loose teeth, and sharpening vision. Dock contains more vitamin C than orange juice and four times as much vitamin A as the famous A source, the carrot. In the pre-refrigerator days, winter diets consisted almost entirely of dried and salted foods, causing a deficiency of vitamin C (ascorbic acid), which eliminates impurities (thus "purifying the blood") and combats scurvy. A symptom of scurvy is soft gums and loose teeth. Likewise, the body uses vitamin A to form an essential pigment in the retina of the eye.

In late summer and fall, the flowering stalks of dock make lovely dried arrangements, but the seeds, as close relatives of buckwheat, can be used to make flour. Boiling water poured over the halved roots makes a medicinal tea, which acts as a gentle laxative.

Docks are found most commonly in fields and waste areas.

GREENBRIER *(Smilax, various species)*

Also known as catbrier, bullbrier, chainy-brier, ground nut, saw brier, prickly bamboo, China brier, biscuit leaves.

The young shoots, leaves, and tendrils of greenbrier can be cooked like spinach as a potherb or served fresh in salads. Greenbrier grows in thickets or open woods.

Dr. Wade Batson says the roots are built up with fiber cells and people crush them in cold water to separate the starch from the fiber and make a powder to use as a gelatin substitute. Naturalist William Bartram, in his 1791 *Travels through North and South Carolina*, watched the Indians in this process. After straining out the fibers and pouring off the water a couple of times, the Indians had a fine red powder, used to thicken soup or make bread and jellies.

Making the powder is a lot of trouble when you can buy gumbo or gelatin, but the young shoots are highly recommended, and their price in an open field compares well with the grocery store charge for asparagus.

CHAINY-BRIER

The tender shoots of smilax begin to appear in early spring and when properly prepared are a splendid addition to any meal.

smilax shoots	**lemon juice and salt**
boiling water	**OR**
1½ t. salt/qt. water	**butter**

The shoots may be fat or thin.

Prepare by removing any long tendrils and tying in bundles as you would asparagus and plunging into a large pan of boiling water. Add about one-and-a-half teaspoons of salt per quart of water and boil for about eight to ten minutes until tender but not limp. Keep testing with a fork so they don't overcook.

The water will turn purple. Serve with either lemon juice and salt or melted butter or lemon butter.

Ben McC. Moise

VIOLETS (*Viola*, various species)

Dr. Wade Batson, botany professor, says, "I tell my classes to put the tender young violet leaves and flowers in a salad. The leaves are good boiled for ten or 15 minutes like greens. Since they are mucilaginous (slick like okra), they can also be used as a soup thickener." Like most dark greens, violet greens are said to be slightly laxative. The plant is very rich in vitamin A and C.

A wild violet might be too pretty to pick, particularly if it's not caught in a large crowd of violets. If you just pick the blossoms, however, the plant will produce more flowers, and you haven't harmed it.

The marsh blue violet and the common blue violet are found in sunny damp hardwood areas, the birdfoot violet in sandy fields and slopes.

VIOLET JELLY

1 pt. violet blossoms   1 pkg. powdered fruit pectin
2 to 3 c. boiling water   3 c. sugar
juice of 1 lemon

Put violet blossoms in a large jar, cover with boiling water, allow to stand 24 hours, strain, and discard blossoms. To two cups of this infusion, add lemon juice and fruit pectin. Bring this just to a boil, then add sugar. Bring back to a boil and boil for two minutes. Pour into jars and seal.

Mike Farmer

WOOD-SORRELS (*Oxalis*, various species)

Also known as sour-grass, shamrock. Mistakenly called clover.

The sweet stems and sour leaves of wood-sorrel have long been popular with hikers and mountain climbers as a refresher on a warm day.

Dennis Gunter says wood-sorrel has a delicious sour taste and loses a lot of flavor if you cook it. "Just wash it and eat it raw. A lot of people use it in a salad. Sour-grass is common in hardwood forests around here and most common in the Piedmont."

When added to a salad, it should be used in small quantities because of its oxalic acid content. Gunter says excessive consumption may inhibit the body's absorption of calcium. Biologist Doug Rayner says collecting it in the city is dangerous because of the accumulation of lead, pesticides and animal wastes. It is found in dry, open, sunny places.

"Besides enhancing salads, wood-sorrels serve as a poor man's lemonade," Dr. Wade Batson says. The leaves can be boiled for ten to 15 minutes and the resulting beverage is cooled, strained, and flavored with honey or lemons.

ROSE (*Rosa*, various species)

Also known as sweetbrier (*Rosa eglanteria*) and pasture or Carolina rose (*Rosa carolina*).

John Reid Clonts, park naturalist, highly recommends adding rose petals to salads, if only for looks and vitamin C.

Many vitamin C tablets contain rose hips as their natural source of the vitamin. "The hip is the fruit of the rose," says Clonts, "which develops in late summer and fall as a swelling that encloses the seeds. They are usually gathered in the fall and can be dried and saved. Simply crush the fruit, fresh or dry, and steep several minutes to make tea. A cup of rose hip tea has considerably more vitamin C than orange juice. Mixing rose hips with hibiscus flowers enhances the flower, making an excellent purple tea. Sweeten with honey or sugar."

Jelly, jam or syrup can also be made from rose hips or petals. You can find them around old homes, in pastures and clearings, or in most gourmet shops.

ROSE HIP SYRUP

Place rose hips in a shallow pan and heat in an oven on low for half an hour or until dried. Store in an airtight jar out of direct sunlight. To make syrup, place berries in a pan and cover with water. Boil until the water turns a dark pink. Add a cup of sugar for every 1½ cups of juice. Boil on full heat for five minutes. Cool and serve on pancakes or biscuits.

Ann Casada

PETALS

The petals of the rose, yucca, violet and spiderwort can be candied as a sweet treat.

Wild roses (*Rosa* species) grow along roadsides, low woods, streams and ponds, though cultivated rose petals can be substituted. Spiderworts (*Tradescantia* species) prefer dry woods and sandy soil and are especially plentiful around the barrier islands. They can be recognized in early spring by their long, grasslike leaves, three purple petals and bright yellow stamens.

Three species of yucca or Spanish bayonet (*Yucca* species) grow in the Southeast, and all provide edible flowers and fruit. Yuccas can be found in dry, sandy soils and along edges of brackish marshes. They are easily recognized by their long, linear, sharply pointed leaves, with a single, large cluster of white, bell-looking flowers arising from the center of the plant. (The flowers can be added to salads, but if left on the plant, will turn into thick, green pods which are edible and can be prepared like okra.) Since the flowering times can differ from plant to plant and habitat to habitat, yucca flowers are generally plentiful.

Violets are one of spring's earliest flowering plants and are most often found in moist, alluvial woods. Colors of petals vary from white to violet with great variations in leaf shape. The young violet leaves can be cooked as greens, and the flowers also make a colorful, mild-tasting jelly.

CANDIED PETALS

flower petals   **finely granulated sugar**
egg whites

Wash and pat-dry flower petals. Violets, spiderworts and yucca can be kept entire and dried in their original flower shape. (These make a wonderful cake decoration.) Remove the white part of the rose; it's bitter.

Dip the flowers or petals in beaten, frothy egg whites; then dip into the finely granulated sugar. Gently pour additional sugar over the flowers to make certain that all surfaces are coated. Place on waxed paper-covered cookie sheets. Dry in a 200-degree oven until sugar crystalizes. Time will vary according to the petal's thickness. Rose petals, violets and spiderworts take about 30 to 60 minutes, while yucca petals may take up to 1½ hours. Store in a tightly covered container.

Lin Dunbar

POOR MAN'S PEPPER

Growing in the early spring along roadsides, in fields, gardens and disturbed soils is the rosette of poor man's pepper, *Lepidium virginicum*. Leaves are serrated to deeply dissected, and the racemes of tiny, four-petaled white flowers appear from April to June (although the plants may occasionally flower throughout the year). The fruits of this plant are small, flat, heart-shaped seeds, which hang from a short stalk and have a tongue-biting, peppery taste. Collect the seeds while still green by running entire stalk through the hand. Young leaves and green seeds make an excellent addition to salads.

POOR MAN'S PEPPER DIP

1 large container (8 oz.) softened cream cheese
1 cup poor man's pepper seeds (green)

Combine above ingredients and serve with crackers or fill celery stalks for a "zippy" treat.

Lin Dunbar

GLASSWORT

In brackish marshes grows the common, succulent glasswort, *Salicornia* species. This plant has thick fleshy stems (green in summer and red in the fall) with small, scalelike leaves. The taste is very salty, but glasswort, used in small quantities, makes an interesting addition to salads. Simply collect the fleshy stems, rinse well, and chop into a green salad.

Lin Dunbar

180

Wild Fruits

BERRY COBBLER

7.30.13

Works with any kind of berry.

1 c. sugar	2 t. baking powder
1 c. all-purpose flour	½ stick butter
1 c. milk	2-4 c. berries

Make a batter from first four ingredients, using a wire whisk to stir until smooth. Next melt butter and pour into the batter. Pour butter and batter mixture into a pan (9 inches by 13 inches is ideal size). Use 2 to 4 cups of berries (according to taste preference) and pour directly into the batter/butter mixture. Bake at 350 degrees for thirty to forty minutes or until crust is golden brown (the batter will rise to the top to make a crust). Serve with ice cream, milk or by itself.

Ann Casada

DEEP DISH BERRY PIE

Use any type of berry.

1 qt. berries	2 T. lemon juice
1 T. all purpose flour	pastry
¼ c. sugar	

Preheat oven to 400 degrees. Wash and drain berries. Mix flour and sugar together, then lightly toss the mixture with the berries until they are coated. Pour into a deep casserole dish. Sprinkle the lemon juice over the berries. Place a layer of pastry over the berries and flute the edges. Cut slits into the pastry to let steam escape during the baking process. Bake for thirty to thirty-five minutes or until the crust is nicely browned.

Ann Casada

PAWLEY'S ISLAND BLACKBERRY COBBLER

1 stick butter or margarine	1 c. flour
1 c. milk	2 c. blackberries
1 c. sugar	Cool Whip or vanilla ice cream

Melt butter or margarine in casserole. Mix milk, sugar, and flour and pour into butter. Do not stir.

Pour in blackberries. Do not stir, but attempt to pour berries evenly into mixture. Bake at 375 degrees for 30 minutes. Delicious served warm, topped with Cool Whip dollop or vanilla ice cream.

D. Pierce

CAMP COBBLER (using Coleman folding oven)

1 pt. blackberries, freshly picked
   and washed
¼ c. water

1/3 c. sugar
1 box white or yellow cake mix
liquid or melted margarine

Place berries and water in nine-inch square cake pan. Mash approximately one dozen berries and sprinkle entire surface with sugar. Cover with cake mix, spread evenly one-fourth to one-half inch deep (approximately one-third to one-half box). Squeeze spiral pattern of margarine over surface, leaving one-half to one-inch spaces between spirals. Bake 40 minutes in folding Coleman oven at 400 degrees.

NOTE: Most fruits and berries can be substituted for blackberries. If canned, use approximately 20-ounce can; omit water and sugar if canned in heavy syrup. If peaches are used, mash with fingers and stir one teaspoon flour into juice. Mincemeat may be subsituted for fruit for a seasonal variation.

Eugene W. Braschler

CAMP COBBLER (without Coleman oven)

1 pt. blackberries, freshly picked
   and washed

½ c. sugar
pie crust or pie crust mix

Slowly cook berries over low heat with sugar to taste. Roll pie dough and cook on top of Coleman pancake grill, slowly cooking both sides. Break cooked crust into cooked berries and serve.

Eugene W. Braschler

FRESH HUCKLEBERRY PIE

Tame blueberries can be substituted

1 nine-inch baked pie shell, cooled
4 c. fresh huckleberries, divided
1 envelope gelatin
¼ c. water

¼ t. salt
¼ t. cinnamon
1 T. butter (can be omitted)

Line the shell with two cups of berries, uncooked. Cook remaining berries with sugar, salt and water over medium heat. Boil for one minute, then add butter and cool slightly. Add gelatin and stir. Cool the mixture and pour over uncooked berries in the shell. Chill until set.

Anna Lou Casada

PERSIMMON PUDDING

1 qt. persimmons	2 T. vanilla
3 c. buttermilk	1 t. soda
1¾ c. sugar	3½ cups flour
2 eggs (beaten)	1 t. cinnamon
½ t. salt	1 t. allspice
½ c. butter (melted)	2 c. grated, raw sweet potatoes

Pour milk over cleaned persimmons and mash through a strainer. To this mixture add other ingredients, melted butter last. Use two well-greased 2-quart casseroles. Bake at 325 degrees forty-five minutes or until done. Serve in squares topped with whipped cream. Rum or sherry flavoring may be added to the whipped cream.

Mrs. Wendell H. Tiller

STRAWBERRY FREEZER JAM

2 c. cleaned, sliced strawberries	1 box commercial fruit pectin
4 c. sugar	

With fruit at room temperature, stir sugar into fruit thoroughly and let stand for ten minutes. Then mix ¾ cup of water and fruit pectin in a pan. Bring this to a full boil for one minute, stirring steadily. Stir in fruit at once, continuing to stir for three minutes. place in previously prepared glass or plastic containers with tight-fitting lids. Cover immediately. Allow the containers to stand for twenty-four hours at room temperature and then place in the freezer.

Ann Casada

KEISLER'S ICE CREAM DELIGHT

1 pack vanilla instant pudding	2 c. milk
4 c. ripe fruit (wild fruit or peaches, strawberries, blueberries, etc.)	2 T. lemon juice
2 c. sugar	1 pt. whipped cream or Dream Whip

Mix first five ingredients together and pour into an electric or hand-cranked ice cream maker. Then pour half of the whipped cream on one side of the dasher and half on the other. Churn till desired consistency.

Herbert Keisler

ELDERBERRIES

Along the meandering roadways, flattish white flower clusters play a peek-a-boo from dense, emerald green shrubs. These flowers belong to the elderberry shrub, *Sambucus canadensis*, which grows three to ten feet tall with opposite, oddly compound leaves edged with minute teeth. Clusters of flowers are actually hundreds of five-petaled, fragrant white blossoms no larger than ¼ inch wide. In late summer when heavy with juice, the glossy, purple-black berries hang temptingly from the plants. Elderberries grow in moist, rich soil and are especially apparent along our sunny wood edges and roadsides.

Elderflowers have been used in many ways — to make tea and wine, as an addition to egg dishes, pancakes, muffins and fritters. To collect the flowers, snip the clusters at the base of the stem, rinse gently under water and pat dry with paper toweling.

ELDERFLOWER FRITTERS

1 c. flour	1 T. sugar
1 egg	¾ c. milk
1 t. baking powder	½" deep oil for frying
20-30 flower clusters	

Remove as many stems as possible without the flower cluster falling apart. Blend above ingredients. Add more milk if batter is too thick. Heat oil to 360 to 375 degrees. Dip flower clusters into mixture and fry until lightly browned. Drain. Top with confectioner's sugar.

Lin Dunbar

ELDERFLOWER MUFFINS

1¼ c. flour	½ c. elder flowers
2½ t. baking powder	1 beaten egg
2 T. sugar	¾ c. milk
¾ t. salt	1/3 c. melted shortening

Sift together the flour, baking powder, sugar and salt. Add elderflowers. Make a well in the center and add egg, milk and shortening all at once and stir until ingredients are just blended — do not overbeat. Mixture should be lumpy. Fill muffin tins 2/3's full and bake in a 400 degree oven for 25 minutes. The results are sweet, moist, delicious muffins!

Remember to leave enough flower clusters to mature into those delicious berries for pies and jams later in the summer!

Lin Dunbar

ELDERBERRY JAM

Collect about five to six pounds of ripened fruit. Pick berries from stems and wash. Place fruit in a stainless steel pan and add water to about ¼ or ½ the depth of the fruit (the less water, the stronger the flavor). Bring to a boil and simmer about 15 minutes, crushing fruit during this time to release the juice. Cool for 30 minutes and place in a jelly bag or several thicknesses of cheesecloth. Let juice drip through without squeezing the bag (squeezing will result in cloudy jelly).

3¾ c. prepared juice (above)	1 box powdered pectin
¼ c. lemon juice	5 c. sugar

Place elderberry, lemon juice and pectin in a deep stainless steel pot. Stir and bring to a boli over high heat. Add sugar, continue to stir, and bring to a full, rolling boil (one that cannot be stirred down). Boil hard, stirring constantly, for two minutes (any less and the jelly will be too soft). Remove from heat and skim off any foam. Pour into jelly jars and seal with a boiling bath (covered canner) for 10 minutes.

Lin Dunbar

ELDERBERRY JUICE

1 qt. elderberries
1 c. water

Add water to berries. Simmer for 10 to 15 minutes, mash, simmer another 10 minutes. Strain through several layers of cheesecloth. Add sugar to taste and serve chilled. The taste is similar to grapejuice, though somewhat heavier. Add equal amounts of lemon-lime soft drink or lemonade to the elderberry juice for a different, lighter-flavored beverage.

Lin Dunbar

WILD MUSCADINE JUICE

Easy method: Place two cups of wild grapes and one cup of sugar in quart Mason jar, then fill with boiling water. Seal immediately. Cool and store for at least ten weeks before serving. Strain and serve.

Old time method: Mash grapes without crushing seeds, add enough water to cove, then heat for twenty minutes. Strain and add sugar to taste (normally two cups of fruit to one cup of sugar).

Ann Casada

JELLIES

Fruits used for jellies should be picked before they are completely ripe. The juices are more likely to gel if the fruit is slightly green, whereas ripe and over-ripe berries are often contaminated with molds.

Crab apples, quinces, gooseberries and wild plums should give no worry about gelling. These fruits contain high amounts of natural pectin within their skins.

Wild blueberries, raspberries, blackberries and grapes are low in natural pectin. Their gelling properties can easily be improved by adding apples or a commercial pectin product when cooking.

General Instructions For Making Jelly From Wild Fruit: After picking over the fruit, wash and drain it. Then boil, in as little water as possible without scorching, until the fruit is soft and the skin or pomes pop open.

The cooked berries are then mashed to free the juices. For jellies, the juice is strained through several layers of fine cheesecloth. For marmalades and jams, the pulp and juices are both used after being forced through a sieve.

The resulting juice, or juice and pulp, should then be measured into a large enamel or steel pot. Any additional apple juice or commercial pectin, if needed, should be added at this time. Add an equal amount of warm granulated sugar, unless your taste or recipe specify a different amount.

Boil this mixture vigorously. In five to ten minutes, it should begin to gel. To test, pour a small amount from the side of a spoon. When two large drops come together and fall as a single drop, the syrup will form a firm jelly. If the jelly does not gel after 15 minutes of cooking, additional sugar is required.

The jelly is now ready to be poured into hot, sterile jars and sealed. Leave one-half inch of space at top of jar. Dome lids or paraffin can be used to seal the jars. If paraffin is used, remember to melt it in a double boiler to prevent flare-ups of the liquid. Usually two layers of paraffin are poured into each container since the first layer will draw away from the sides as it cools. Allow the jelly to stiffen for three days before using.

Other native wild fruits which make good jellies include red mulberries, mayapples, chokeberries, rose hips, elderberries (see above), persimmons, and the root stock of cattails.

The crabapple and mayapple also make delicious marmalades. Only the fruit of the mayapple should be used since the foilage and root are poisonous. Crabapple is good to add to blueberries or wild grapes as a source of needed pectin and as a touch of tartness. The combination makes for superb jelly. Both crabapples and grapes add flavor to elderberry jelly.

Chokeberries, although very puckery when raw, make a very heavy, sweet, dark red jelly. They are abundant in natural pectin.

PYRACANTHA JELLY

Pyracantha jelly is a delightful and colorful confection, good with both bread and meat. The berries have been unfairly maligned as poisonous.

berries	**juice of 2 lemons**
1 c. water/lb. of berries	**pectin**
7 c. sugar	**5 T. vinegar**

For each pound of berries, add one cup of water to a large pot. Boil 20 to 25 minutes, until berries pop open.

Drain through cheesecloth. Boil three cups of juice, sugar, and lemon juice. Add pectin and vinegar. Boil two minutes, then pour into sterile jars and seal.

Anne Moise

CRABAPPLE HONEY

crabapples	**sugar**
water	

Wash and core crabapples but do not peel. Cut into small pieces and put in an enamel pot with enough water to cover. Boil ten minutes. Measure the pulp and add three-fourths as much sugar as pulp. Cook until clear, with jelly-like consistency. Seal in clean hot jars.

Anne Moise

SPICED GOOSEBERRIES

2 qts. ripe gooseberries	**½ t. cinnamon**
1½ lbs. brown sugar	**½ t. ground cloves**
1 c. cider vinegar	**½ t. ground nutmeg**

Wash and stem gooseberries. Bring brown sugar and vinegar to a boil; slowly add the berries. Cook about 40 minutes or until the fruit is tender.

Season with cinnamon, cloves, and nutmeg. Pour into hot sterile jars and seal. Good served over yogurt or as a sweet.

Anne Moise

WILD GRAPE JELLY

grapes
½ c. water/4 c. grapes
1 apple, quartered
*3 c. vinegar

*4 2-inch sticks cinnamon
*2 T. whole cloves, without heads
sugar

Wash the grapes. Place in pot with half cup of water for each four cups of grapes. Add apple. If spices are desired, add vinegar, cinnamon, and cloves.

Boil until the grapes are soft and beginning to lose their color. Strain through cheesecloth. To each cup of juice, add three-fourths to one cup of sugar. Cook until mixture begins to gel, then pour into hot sterile jars and seal.

* optional

Anne Moise

CRABAPPLE JELLY

crabapples
water

sugar

Wash, quarter, and core crabapples. Put in saucepan and add water until you can see it through the top layer of fruit. Cook until soft. Pour through cheesecloth. Add three-fourths to one cup of sugar for each cup of juice. Cook until it begins to gel, then seal in hot sterile jars.

QUINCE PRESERVES

8 c. quince, cleaned
4 c. sugar

4 ambrosia leaves
2 c. water

Peel quince and cut into long thin strips. Add sugar, ambrosia leaves, and water. Cook over slow fire until fruit is soft and syrup has thickened. Makes eight servings.

Great on ice cream or served with whipped cream or by itself!

Maria Latto

FRESH FIG PRESERVES

2 lbs. fresh figs
4 c. sugar

3 c. water
juice of ½ lemon

Wash figs and trim stems. If fig skin is tough, peel before cooking. If figs are tender, leave skin on.

Make syrup by boiling sugar and water together with lemon juice until it begins to thicken. Place figs in syrup and let stand overnight.

The next day, bring figs and syrup to a boil and simmer until figs are tender. Remove figs from pot and place in clean dry glass jars. If syrup is still a little thin, simmer until it coats a spoon.

Pour syrup over figs to fill jars. Let cool before sealing.

This is delicious on top of vanilla ice cream, or just eaten by itself. Makes eight to ten servings.

Maria Latto

PRICKLY PEARS (*Opuntia* species)

Opuntia are found in dry, sandy soil. Cacti are native only to the Americas — but different varieties and species have been exported and cultivated around the world. The green, flat part we usually consider the "leaves" are actually modified stems which carry on the job of photosynthesis for the plant. The actual leaves of *Opuntia* are awl-shaped and appear on the new growth of the stem, but since they drop early, they are not usually seen on mature plants. The cacti's characteristic spines are also found on *Opuntia*, and the size and arrangement of these spines help distinguish the different species.

Opuntia drummundii has spines which are thin, approximately 1-3 cm long, and cover the entire plant. The pads are easily detached from one another, and the species is so inconspicuous that one may often notice the plant only after walking around its habitat and finding small pad segments attached to one's shoes.

The spines of *Opuntia compressa* grow in roundish circles containing a multitude of short, sharp spines which are almost flat against the green pads. These circular protuberances are found over the entire plant, including the fruit. The pad segments are held tightly together, and individual plants may reach a height of 4 dm.

Opuntia vulgaris is similar to *Opuntia compressa* in spine formation, but can reach a height of 1 m., with a fruit size of 4-6 cm. tall and 3-4 cm. in diameter. This species is an escape from cultivation, and all three species hybridize easily.

The waxy, bright showy yellow flowers (5-7 cm. broad) appear from May to June. The part which holds the flower to the stem will later develop into the edible fruit. These inverted, pear-shaped green fruits are usually found on stems from August to October, though many pears will remain throughout the winter. As the weather grows colder, the fruit ripens, until it is at its peak when it becomes dark maroon (usually after the first frost). Take care removing the pears from the stems (a pair of gloves is helpful). Peel the spines and the skin from the fruit, using a sharp knife. Slice the pear in half and spoon out the seeds. The fruit can be added to salads, eaten raw, added to ambrosia and made into a delightful drink.

Lin Dunbar

PRICKLY PEAR JAM

4 c. prickly pears, peeled, chopped and seeded (about 25-30 fresh pears, depending on species)	1 pkg. powdered pectin 7 c. sugar 1 c. lemon juice

Combine prickly pears and lemon juice; mash until pulpy. Measure pulp — you should have five cups. You can add a small amount of water to make up the quantity.

Place pulp in a stainless steel pot and add pectin. Stir over high heat until boiling. Add sugar, bring to boil again and boil hard for two minutes, stirring constantly. Remove from heat, and stir for 10 additional minutes while skimming off any foam. Ladle into sterile jelly jars and seal. Give a 10-minute boiling bath in a covered canner to ensure seal.

Lin Dunbar

COCOA PALM

Many people in the Southeast have planted an ornamental palm tree called the cocoa or jelly palm *(Butia capitata)*. Though it looks very similar to the cabbage palm, *Sabal palmetto*, it can be easily distinguished by the way the leaflets are arranged along both sides of the leaf stalk. The palmetto has leaflets only on the tip of the leaf stalk. The cocoa palm bears clusters of round, orange fruit — very sweet tasting — which can be eaten raw or made into a fine jelly.

PALM JELLY

cocoa palm fruit and water for　　　　**1 pkg. powered pectin**
　3¾ c. juice　　　　　　　　　　　　**4 c. sugar**

Wash fruit throughly. Cover with water and boil for one hour, piercing the fruit during the cooking time to release the juices. Pour the juice into a jelly bag or several thicknesses of cheesecloth. Drain overnight. Do not squeeze the bag or the jelly will be clouded.

Measure 3¾ cups juice and one package pectin into a deep, stainless steel pot. Stir and bring to a full boil. Add sugar and while stirring constantly, bring to a full rolling boil (one that can't be stirred down). Boil hard (still stirring) for 2 to 2½ minutes. Pour into sterile jelly jars and seal with a boiling bath (covered canner) for 10 minutes.

Lin Dunbar

Nuts

America has given world civilization no more important horticultural product than the pecan. The history of the pecan is said to relate closely to the history of the American Indian in the South. It traveled roughly down the Missippippi and its tributaries and spread that way through the South. Pecan plantings were found wherever the Indians made a settlement.

Its growth has declined in the Southeast since 1950, but of course it is still popular.

Easy to collect, the pecan will keep several months in the refrigerator or a year in the freezer. The fruitcake and the pie are the most popular recipes for pecans.

PECAN FUDGE PIE

2 2-oz. sq. unsweetened chocolate	¾ c. dark Karo syrup
2 T. butter or margarine	¾ c. pecans
3 eggs	pastry for 1 9-inch pie
1 c. sugar	

Melt butter and chocolate over hot water. Beat together eggs, sugar, syrup and chocolate mixture. Mix in pecans. Pour into pastry-lined pie pan. Bake 40 to 50 minutes at 375 degrees until silver knife inserted into center of filling comes out clean. (I do not bake my pies at 375 degrees for over 15 to 20 minutes. After the filling is set, I turn the temperature down a few degrees, but all stoves are different.)

Mrs. Brock Conrad

FRUIT CAKE

½ lb. butter	1 lb. glazed cherries
1 c. sugar	1¾ c. plain flour
5 lg. eggs, well beaten	½ t. baking powder
4 c. shelled pecans	½ oz. vanilla extract
1 lb. glazed pineapple	½ oz. lemon extract

Cream butter. Add sugar slowly; cream till fluffy. Add eggs. Chop pecans, pineapple, cherries; mix with three-fourths cup flour. Sift rest of flour (one cup) with baking powder and fold into egg-butter mixture. Add extracts. Mix well and fold in fruit-nut mixture. Pout into greased tube pan, put in cool oven, bake at 250 degrees for three hours. Cool in pan, wrap and store in canister for at least two months.

Nancy Coleman Wooten

Cookin'
For That
Outdoor
Taste

We're not sure if it's necessity or boredom that's the mother of invention when it comes to the many ways you can prepare wildlife foods. But today's cook has plenty of techniques to draw from, many of which are part of our heritage and are only improved by the availability of modern utensils and our society's growing interest in nutrition.

In addition to canning, drying, salting and curing - the cook can pot, brew, ferment, smoke, pickle, freeze and age. These methods preserve or enhance food flavor, capturing the natural bouquet of seasons created by moisture, soil, air and light. Unprocessed and unpackaged, wild foods are uncompromisingly of the wild - more delicious and nourishing to the body and soul.

Even though we all may not can our garden tomatoes or put up fruit preserves, we can use several cooking methods to help wild food meals taste like all outdoors, whether home-bound or in the field.

Outdoor Grilling

Outdoor grilling is one of the simplest ways to infuse a rich flavor in about any kind of meat, adding an aroma and zip that no kitchen broiler or even Jenn-air grill can duplicate. Maybe we can remember the days when we barbecued steaks over charcoal because we didn't know beans about cooking. But besides easing the beginner's plight, outdoor grilling provides a fine way to produce delicious dinner fare and so has emerged as a great American pastime.

In his *Southern Wildfowl and Wild Game Cookbook,* Jan Wongrey offers the following pointers for successful grill cookery:

1. Allow food to reach outside temperature before placing it on the grill.

2. Make sure that all charcoal briquets have burned to the point where they are coated with ash before placing food on the grill. (This means starting the coals well in advance of the projected mealtime.)

3. Coat or rub lean meat, such as venison, with a piece of fat or cooking oil to prevent meat from sticking to the grill.

4. Cook game meats over a slow fire and baste constantly to keep them moist and juicy.

5. Apply a basting sauce, the most important addition to grilled game foods, to the meat even before a barbecue sauce is applied. A basting sauce, like a barbecue mixture, is made to suit the cook's taste.

No comments on outdoor grilling would be complete without adding a few companion recipes for barbecue pork. So next time you turn that pig on the spit at an outdoor social, be sure to give these a try:

192

LADDIE BOONE'S BARBECUE SAUCE OR "MOP"

1 pt. Duke's mayonnaise
½ pt. French's mustard
Mix the mayo and mustard together
   thoroughly
1 gal. catsup
dash of sugar

dash of Texas Pete ("A damn good
   shake!")
¼ c. vinegar
salt
pepper

Mix all well together. Put on table to spoon over meat.

Laddie Boone

MUSTARD BASE BARBECUE SAUCE FOR CHICKEN OR PORK

1 gal. French's mustard
1 gal. red White House vinegar
10 lb. margarine
½ box salt

2 oz. box black pepper
½ sm. bottle Texas Pete
½ sm. bottle Worcestershire sauce
2 oz. sugar

Mix and warm all ingredients. Baste meat and place on grill, basting constantly as it cooks.

Bill Peaks

LADDIE BOONE'S HASH FOR A LARGE CROWD

5 lbs. onions, quartered
5 lbs. potatoes, quartered
5 lbs. stew beef, cut in chunks

1 hog head, cleaned, boned and cut
   in chunks
liver, spleen, heart, and scrap meat
   from one hog

Boil all meat and half the onions in water, seasoned with salt and pepper. Use enough water to cover meat. Boil until well-done. This generally takes about two hours. Remove meat from the water, and then add to the water the rest of the onions and all of the potatoes, and cook until half done, about half-an-hour or so. Remove from the water and put with the meat. Grind all ingredients together. Skim the grease off the top of the pot water. Add just enough water back to the brown ground hash where it is not too soupy. Then add one gallon catsup and a couple of good shakes of Texas Pete. Bring back to a good boil and keep stirring. Add more salt and pepper as needed. Serve over rice.

Laddie Boone

HOG ROAST SLAW

2 heads cabbage
2 bell peppers
1 lg. Bermuda onion
1 c. cider vinegar

¾ c. olive oil
1 T. salt
1 t. Coleman's dry mustard
1 t. celery seed

Slice or chop cabbage, peppers and onion, and place in a large container with a cover. Mix all the other ingredients and bring to a boil. Pour over the chopped cabbage, pepper and onion and toss well. Cover and refrigerate for at least 24 hours prior to serving. This gets better the longer it lasts. This will also keep in a large jar.

Ben McC. Moise

RED HORSE BREAD

5 lb. yellow, self-rising corn meal
2 lb. self-rising flour
2 bell peppers, finely chopped
2 lb. onions, finely chopped
2 rounded T. salt

1 rounded T. sugar
1 T. black pepper
1 qt. buttermilk
4 hen eggs
1 heaping T. baking powder

Mix all together. Mix in some plain water if mixture is too dry. Mixture needs to be just thick enough to hold together on the end of a teaspoon, not too dry, not too soupy. Dip mixture, one teaspoon at a time and drop into deep hot grease. When they float and turn brown, they should be done. Keep a cup of water nearby to clean spoon off every so often.

This recipe serves 50 people with a little left over.

Ernestine Boone

HUSHPUPPIES FOR A CROWD

4 c. self-rising flour (about 2 lb.)
4 c. self-rising corn meal
onions, as much as you desire

3-4 eggs
8-oz. can tomato sauce, or paste
buttermilk

Mix flour and corn meal together. Chop onion into mixture. Add tomato sauce and eggs. Use as much buttermilk as needed to make thick mixture suitable to be spooned into hot oil. Using one spoon to dip the mixture and another spoon to push it into the oil is a good way to make pretty, round hushpuppies. Use small teaspoon to make small hushpuppies or large spoon to make large hushpuppies.

Bill Cobb

Iron Cookware

Because the old cast-iron pot was most often used suspended over a log fire or set on top of a wood-burning stove, cast-iron utensils nearly disappeared when the jet-age hit the electric range industry. Recognizing a classic case of the baby thrown out with the bathwater, folks are rediscovering the art of cooking over slow wood fires and using black ironware in the kitchen.

As anyone who's simmered a pot of catfish stew by a riverbank can tell you, a well-seasoned iron pot or skillet is impossible to beat for creating exotic flavors in many home-cooked meals. Where other cookware strives to leave no taste in food, the iron pot when properly seasoned will instill a distinctive flavor that becomes richer as the seasoning ages over many years of use.

The trick, of course, is making certain that your iron cookware is properly seasoned. In "That Old Black Magic" in the May 1980 *Tennessee Conservationist*, Soc Clay tells how he found a mountain woman who described how to "sweeten a pot."

SMOKED SHRIMP

Clean and devein two pounds of shrimp, removing the heads but leaving the shells intact. Simmer for about three minutes or until pink in a court bouillon made by simmering one onion, one carrot, and three stalks of celery, all chopped, one bay leaf, six peppercorns, and two cloves in two quarts of water for 30 minutes. Remove and drain thoroughly, drying on absorbent paper.

Arrange the shrimp on greased racks without overlapping. When dry to touch, cold-smoke them lightly at 90 degrees Fahrenheit for 35 to 40 minutes. The smokehouse draft should be fully opened during the first 15 minutes of smoking, then half-closed, and finally three-fourths closed.

If a smokier flavor is desired, build up a dense smoke and continue the smoking at the same temperature for another 15 minutes. Cool the shrimp and wrap them in moisture-proof paper. They will keep for one week or more if stored under refrigeration.

SMOKED TURKEY

Truss a turkey as for roasting and submerge it in a brine of two cups pickling salt to three quarts water. Leave the turkey in the brine for eight hours or overnight, under refrigeration. Remove from brine and press out excess liquid gently, drying with absorbent paper. Hang the bird in a cool, drafty place to dry for several hours or until flesh is dry to touch.

Then densely smoke the turkey at 90 to 100 degrees Fahrenheit for about half as many hours as the number of pounds the turkey weighs. Raise the temperature gradually to 200 degrees and hot-smoke for the same amount of time or more, until the bird is cooked and golden red in color. Halfway through the smoking, the bird may be brushed several times with a honey glaze.

SMOKED OYSTERS

Shuck fresh oysters, drain thoroughly and dry them on absorbent paper. Place the oysters on a greased rack, without overlapping, and cold-smoke them for about an hour or until they have taken on color and their edges are curled and golden brown.

Campfire Cooking

Since campfire cooking is directly related to campfire building, most of this section is given to creating the campfire, which ensures comfort to the hungry wayfarer, as well as sustenance. Many beginners approach campfire building with the false assumption that it looks like a snap. But there are as many ways to build a campfire improperly as there are to burn or undercook your food.

Several main principles to remember are: The fire should be constructed with a good oxygen source, and it should be no bigger than necessary to do the job at hand. To make sure your food cooks evenly, let the fire burn down to graying bright coals before starting to cook. Successful campfire cooking largely depends on how hot the coals are and how closely the food is set to the fire. The food should cook slowly over the fire rather than too fast.

In "The Flavor of Fire," Nancy Coleman offers some helpful advice on campfire building in a natural setting (*South Carolina Wildlife*, May-June 1979):

Upon arrival at your campsite, the first thing to do is build a good-sized woodpile, so you won't have to search while cooking. Coniferous trees like pines, spruces and firs are the poorest to use. The best are hardwoods, especially those which shed leaves; they burn long with little smoke. Hickory is the best of all. If the wood has a tasty flavor, you can cook over a smoky fire. Otherwise, burn it to mostly black coals so all the smell is gone.

Arrange tinder, kindling and fuel separately, with fuel closest to you. Tinder is anything combustible and smaller than your little finger, such as dry grass, dry leaves, dry pine needles, twigs, shavings, bark, newspaper and even charcoal starter. Kindling ranges in size from little finger to wrist. Fuel is anything larger.

Tinder starts the fire, kindling feeds it till cooking-size, and fuel sustains it. Progress quickly from smallest tinder to about three large fuel logs. The size of the fire depends on how many logs you have; the duration depends on their size.

For serious cooking, the best fire lay is the keyhole, a combination of the tipi and the log cabin. The tipi lay, a cone-shaped stack of wood in the middle of a circle of rocks, produces a high, strong blaze. In a log cabin lay, wood is stacked at right angles in the center of a square of rocks. The log cabin burns evenly and thus is good for cooking.

The keyhole lay is a compromise. The joining together of a square and a circle of rocks with the wall between knocked out. The square end should be built toward the direction from which the wind is blowing. Build a tipi fire in the circle end for light, heat and conversation. Build a log cabin in the square for cooking. Rake coals from the tipi into the square. If you dig the keyhole shape about four inches deep, and put rocks around the edge, the fire is safer. You can save the dirt and cover it up when you leave.

COOKING IN ASHES

Potatoes: When the coals are almost burnt down, put an Irish or sweet potato in the fire itself. Put the coals on the top and leave for an hour. Then peel jacket off and eat.
Corn: Peel off a few outer skins, but keep the shuck on. Turn if you can, and if you can't, cover it with coals. Five minutes on each side.
Chestnuts: Cut a cross in them so they won't explode.
Bananas: Slit open the skins and sprinkle inside with sugar and cinnamon or chocolate chips and marshmallows.
Other things: Onions, acorn squash, apples (but don't break their skins). The good thing about corn and other things you cook with the skin on is they'll stay warm a long time after you cook them.

Buck Tyler

The high flames of the tipi fire are good for one-pot cooking and for use of the reflector oven.

As you build a log cabin lay, gradually place logs toward the center of the cabin so it takes on the appearance of a pyramid.

When using the keyhole lay, start the fire in the circle area and draw hot coals for cooking into the square area.

TILAPIA WITH PIMIENTO SAUCE

5-20-09
Darlington
News Paper.

4 6-oz. tilapia fillets
1 Tbsp. olive oil
1 small onion, cut into thin wedges
1 clove garlic, minced
1 (14-oz.) can diced tomatoes, undrained
1 cup sliced cremini or button mushrooms
3/4 cup pimiento-stuffed olives, chopped
1 Tbsp chopped fresh oregano or 1/2 teaspoon dried oregano, crushed
Salt and pepper to taste

In a large skillet, heat olive oil over medium-high heat. Add the onions and cook until tender, about 2-3 minutes. Add the garlic and cook until fragrant, about a minute more. Add tomatoes, mushrooms, olives, oregano, salt and pepper. Bring sauce to boiling.

Gently place the fish fillets in the pan and scoop some of the sauce over the fillets. Return to boiling. Reduce the heat and cover. Simmer for 8 to 10 minutes or until fish flakes easily when tested with a fork. With a wide spatula, lift fish from skillet to a serving dish. Spoon sauce over fish. Serve with rice, and/or crusty bread. Makes 4 servings.

200

Wild Food Originals

Add your favorite recipes on the following pages.

5-20-09

SESAME TILAPIA

This is a very simple dish, yet quite tasty. Serve it with black beans and rice.

2 (4 oz. each) filets tilapia
1/4 cup sesame oil
1 clove garlic, minced
1 tsp. Italian seasoning
1 tsp. sesame seeds (optional)
2 green onions, sliced
Coarse sea salt
Fresh ground black pepper to taste

Place the tilapia filets in a 1-1/2 qt. casserole dish and drizzle with the sesame oil. Season with garlic, Italian seasoning, sesame seeds, salt and pepper; sprinkle green onions on top. Cover and refrigerate at least 2 hours.

Preheat oven to 350 degrees. Bake for 30 minutes or until fish is easily flaked with a fork. Makes 2 servings.

TILAPIA WITH CRABMEAT, LEMON BUTTER SAUCE

4-6 Tilapia fillets
2 eggs, beaten
4 oz. crabmeat
1/4 cup softened butter
1 Tbsp. lemon juice
1 Tbsp. olive oil
Dash of hot pepper sauce
Pinch of salt

Add lemon juice, hot pepper sauce and salt to softened butter and whip smooth; set aside. Add olive oil to a saute pan and bring to medium-high heat. Dip each fillet in egg and sauté for 2 minutes on each side. Place fillets on plates and top with equal amounts of crabmeat. Finish with a dollop of lemon butter sauce. Place under broiler for 1 minute. Makes 4 servings.

Recipes

Recipes

Recipes

Recipes

Recipes

Recipes

Recipes

Recipes

Recipes

NUTRITIONAL VALUES IN MEAT (Based on 100 Gram Edible Portion)

Game and Domestic	% Water	Calories Food Energy	Grams Protein	Grams Fat
Beaver: cooked, roasted	56.2	248 cal.	29.2 gr.	13.7 gr.
Beef: choice grade, trimmed, raw	56.7	301 cal.	17.4 gr.	25.1 gr.
Chicken: fryers - total edible, raw	75.7	124 cal.	18.6 gr.	4.9 gr.
Duck: domestic - total edible, raw	54.3	326 cal.	16.0 gr.	28.6 gr.
Duck: wild - total edible, raw	61.1	233 cal.	21.1 gr.	15.8 gr.
Lamb: choice grade, trimmed, raw	61.0	263 cal.	16.5 gr.	21.3 gr.
Opossum: cooked, roasted	57.3	221 cal.	30.2 gr.	10.2 gr.
Pheasant: total edible, raw	69.2	151 cal.	24.3 gr.	5.2 gr.
Pork: composite of trimmed lean meat, medium fat class, raw	56.3	308 cal.	15.7 gr.	26.7 gr.
Quail: total edible, raw	56.9	168 cal.	25.0 gr.	6.8 gr.
Rabbit: raw	73.0	135 cal.	21.0 gr.	5.0 gr.
Raccoon: cooked, roasted	54.8	255 cal.	29.2 gr.	14.5 gr.
Venison: lean meat, raw	74.0	126 cal.	21.0 gr.	4.0 gr.

Source: Georgia Extension Service.

Fish and Shellfish	Calories Food Energy	Grams Protein	Grams Fat	Grams Carbohydrates
Bluefish: Baked, broiled	159	26.2	5.2	0
Cod: Cooked, broiled	170	28.5	5.3	0
Crab: Cooked, steamed	93	17.3	1.9	0.5
Croaker, Atlantic: Cooked, baked	133	24.3	3.2	0
Halibut (Similar to Flounder or Flatfish): Cooked, broiled	171	25.2	7.0	0
Lobster, Northern: Canned or cooked	95	18.7	1.5	0.3
Mackerel, Atlantic: Cooked, broiled with butter	236	21.8	15.8	0
Ocean Perch, Atlantic: Cooked, fried	227	19.0	13.3	6.0
Rockfish (Striped Bass): Cooked, oven-steamed	107	18.1	2.5	1.9
Roe: Cooked, baked, broiled	126	22.0	2.8	1.9
Salmon: Cooked, baked, broiled	182	27.0	7.4	0
Shad: Baked	201	23.2	11.3	0
Shrimp: Cooked	225	20.3	10.8	10.0
Swordfish: Cooked, broiled	174	28.0	6.0	0
Weakfish (Similar to Seatrout): Cooked, broiled	208	24.6	11.4	0

Source: U.S.Department of Agriculture

FAT CONTENT OF VARIOUS FISH

Freshwater Fish

Bass	Lean
Carp	Moderately fatty
Catfish	Moderately fatty
Crappie	Lean
Pickerel	Lean
Pike	Lean
Smelts	Fatty
Trout	Fatty
Yellow Perch	Lean
Frogs' Legs	Lean

Saltwater Fish

Bass, Black Sea	Lean
Blackfish (or Tautog)	Lean
Black Drum	Lean
Blowfish Tails	Lean
Bluefish	Fatty
Butterfish	Fatty
Crab	Lean
Crevalle (or Common Jack)	Moderately fatty
Croaker	Lean
Cod	Lean
Eel	Fatty
Winter Flounder	Lean
Fluke	Lean
Grouper	Lean
Grunt	Moderately fatty
Haddock	Lean
Hake or Whiting	Moderately fatty
Halibut	Lean
Kingfish	Moderately fatty
Lobster	Lean
Mackerel	Fatty
Monkfish	Lean
Mullet	Fatty
Ocean Perch	Lean
Pompano	Fatty
Porgy (or Scup)	Moderately fatty
Red Snapper (or Yellow Tail Snapper)	Lean
Rockfish	Lean
Roe	Moderately fatty or fatty, depending upon the fish
Salmon, Atlantic and Pacific	Fatty
Sardines (or Sea Herring)	Fatty
Scrod	Lean
Shad	Fatty
Shark	Lean
Shrimp	Lean

Skate	Lean
Smelts	Moderately fatty
Squid	Lean
Striped Bass	Moderately fatty
Swordfish	Moderately fatty
Tilefish	Lean
Tuna	Fatty
Weakfish (or Seatrout)	Moderately fatty

Key

Lean	less than 2 percent fat
Moderately fatty	2 to 6 percent fat
Fatty	over 6 percent fat

Source: U.S. Department of Agriculuture

SUBSTITUTIONS FOR A MISSING INGREDIENT

1 square *chocolate* (1 ounce) = 3 or 4 tablespoons cocoa plus ½ tablespoon fat.

1 tablespoon *cornstarch* (for thickening) = 2 tablespoons flour.

1 cup sifted *all-purpose flour* = 1 cup plus 2 tablespoons sifted cake flour.

1 cup sifted *cake flour* = 1 cup minus 2 tablespoons sifted all-purpose flour.

1 teaspoon *baking powder* = ¼ teaspoon baking soda plus ½ teaspoon cream of tartar.

1 cup *sour milk* = 1 cup sweet milk into which 1 tablespoon vinegar or lemon juice has been stirred; or 1 cup buttermilk (let stand for 5 minutes).

1 cup *sweet milk* = 1 cup sour milk or buttermilk plus ½ teaspoon baking soda.

1 cup *canned tomatoes* = about 1 1/3 cups fresh tomatoes, simmered 10 minutes.

¾ cup *cracker crumbs* = 1 cup bread crumbs

1 cup *cream, sour, heavy* = 1/3 cup butter and 2/3 cups milk in any sour milk recipe.

1 cup *cream, sour, thin* = 3 tablespoons butter and ¾ cup milk in sour milk recipe.

1 cup *molasses* = 1 cup honey.

1 teaspoon *dried herbs* = 1 tablespoon fresh herbs.

1 *whole egg* = 2 egg yolks for custards.

½ cup *evaporated milk* and ½ cup *water* or 1 cup *reconstituted nonfat dry milk* and 1 tablespoon *butter* = 1 cup whole milk.

1 package *active dry yeast* = 1 cake compressed yeast.

1 tablespoon *instant minced onion, rehydrated* = 1 small fresh onion.

1 tablespoon *prepared mustard* = 1 teaspoon dry mustard.

⅛ teaspoon *garlic powder* = 1 small pressed clove of garlic.

EQUIVALENCY TABLE

3 tsp. . . . . 1 tbsp.	2 pt. . . . . 1 qt.
2 tbsp. . . . . ⅛ c.	1 qt. . . . . 4 c.
4 tbsp. . . . . ¼ c.	⅝ c. . . . . ½ c. + 2 tbsp.
8 tbsp. . . . . ½ c.	⅞ c. . . . . ¾ c. + 2 tbsp.
16 tbsp. . . . . 1 c.	1 jigger . . . . 1½ fl. oz. (3 tbsp.)
5 tbsp. + 1 tsp. . . . . 1/3 c.	2 c. fat . . . . 1 lb.
12 tbsp. . . . . ¾ c.	1 lb. butter . . . . 2 c. or 4 sticks
4 oz. . . . . ½ c.	2 c. sugar . . . . 1 lb.
8 oz. . . . . 1 c.	2 2/3 c. powdered sugar . . . . 1 lb.
16 oz. . . . . 1 lb.	2 2/3 c. brown sugar . . . . 1 lb.
1 oz. . . . . 2 tbsp. fat or liquid	4 c. sifted flour . . . . 1 lb.
2 c. . . . . 1 pt.	4½ c. cake flour . . . . 1 lb.

3½ c. unsifted whole wheat flour . . . . 1 lb.
8 to 10 egg whites . . . . 1 c.
12 to 14 egg yolks . . . . 1 c.
1 c. unwhipped cream . . . . 2 c. whipped
1 lb. shredded American cheese . . . . 4 c.
¼ lb. crumbled blue cheese . . . . 1 c.
1 chopped med. onion . . . . ½ c. pieces
1 lemon . . . . 3 tbsp. juice
1 lemon . . . . 1 tsp. grated peel
1 orange . . . . 1/3 c. juice
1 orange . . . . about 2 tsp. grated peel
1 lb. unshelled walnuts . . . . 1½ to 1¾ c. shelled
1 lb. unshelled almonds . . . . ¾ to 1 c. shelled
4 oz. (1 to 1¼ c.) uncooked macaroni . . . . 2¼ c. cooked
7 oz. spaghetti . . . . 4 c. cooked
4 oz. (1½ to 2 c.) uncooked noodles . . . . 2 c. cooked
28 saltine crackers . . . . 1 c. crumbs
4 slices bread . . . . 1 c. crumbs
14 square graham crackers . . . . 1 c. crumbs
22 vanilla wafers . . . . 1 c. crumbs

CAN SIZE CHART

8 oz. can or jar . . . . 1 c.
10½ oz. can (picnic can) . . . . 1¼ c.
12 oz. can (vacuum) . . . . 1½ c.
14-16 oz. or No. 300 can . . . . . . 1¾ can
16-17 oz. can or jar or No. 303 can
    or jar . . . . 2 c.
1 lb. 4 oz. or 1 pt. 2 fl. oz. or No. 2 can
    or jar . . . . 2½ c.

1 lb. 13 oz. can or jar or No. 2½ can
    or jar . . . . 3½ c.
1 qt. 14 fl. oz. or 3 lb. 3 oz. or
    46 oz. can . . . . 5¾ c.
6½ to 7½ lb. or No. 10 can . . . 12-13 c.

MEAT, POULTRY, AND SEAFOOD GLOSSARY

BARBECUE . . . . To cook in a highly seasoned sauce.

BASTE . . . . To moisten meats with melted fat, meat drippings, fruit juice, or sauce during cooking to prevent drying and to add flavor.

BRAISE . . . . To cook slowly by moist heat.

BREAD . . . . To coat with crumbs.

BROIL . . . . To cook by direct heat.

BROTH . . . . A thin soup, or the liquid in which food was cooked.

CHOP . . . . To cut coarsely with a knife or cleaver.

CROQUETTE . . . . Finely chopped meat, poultry, or fish which is shaped, coated, and deep-fat fried.

CUBE . . . . To cut in small even pieces.

DEEP FRY . . . . To cook completely immersed in hot cooking oil.

DICE . . . . To cut into cubes, about ½-inch in size.

DREDGE . . . . To dip in or sprinkle with flour.

DRIPPINGS . . . . The fat or juices collected in a roasting pan or skillet.

EN BROCHETTE . . . . Food cooked on a skewer.

FILET OR FILLET . . . . . . A boneless, long-shaped piece of meat or fish.

GRILL . . . . To broil, usually on an open grating.

LARD . . . . To insert or place strips of fat on surface.

MARINATE . . . . To let stand in a highly seasoned oil-acid solution to flavor or tenderize.

PANBROIL . . . . To cook in a skillet kept dry by pouring off accumulated fat.

PANFRY . . . . To cook in a small amount of fat in a skillet.

PARBOIL . . . . To partially cook in water.

POACH . . . . To cook in water just below the boiling point.

ROAST . . . . To cook by dry heat in the oven.

SAUTÉ . . . . To cook in a small amount of fat.

SCORE . . . . To make shallow cuts in surface or edges of meat.

SEAR . . . . To brown quickly.

SIMMER . . . . To cook by moist heat at a low temperature.

SINGE . . . . To burn the hairs off poultry.

SMOKE . . . . To cook through continuous exposure to wood smoke for a long time.

STEW . . . . To cook slowly in liquid.

STOCK . . . . The liquid in which meat, fish, or poultry has been cooked.

TRUSS . . . . To fasten together with strings or skewers.

SALAD SEASONING WITH HERBS

BASIL.................Tomato and green salads, fresh tomato slices.

CARAWAY SEED.......Coleslaw, beet and potato salads.

CHIVES..............Potato, cucumber, mixed vegetable, and green salads.

DILLSEED............Coleslaw, potato and cucumber salads.

MARJORAM..........French dressing, mixed green and chicken salads.

MINT................Fruit, cabbage and celery salads, coleslaw.

MUSTARD SEED.......Potato salad, French and oil/vinegar dressing.

OREGANO...........Potato, mixed green and seafood salads, tomato aspic.

PARSLEY.............Greens, vegetables, shellfish salads, garnish for all salads.

ROSEMARY...........French dressing or mayonnaise for chicken or potato salads.

SAVORY.............Green vegetables, mixed greens, tomato and potato salads, aspic.

TARRAGON..........Chicken, seafood, vegetable and mixed green salads, oil/vinegar dressings.

THYME..............Tomato and beet salads, aspic, mayonnaise and herb dressings.

References

Joseph D. Bates, Jr., *The Outdoor Cook's Bible*, Doubleday & Company, Inc., Garden City, New York, 1963.

Vernon Bevill, William Mahan, Tommy Strange, *Game On Your Land, Part I: Small Game and Wood Duck*, S.C. Wildlife and Marine Resources Department, Columbia, South Carolina, 1978.

Jim Byford, "A Collection of Notes of a Wildlife Specialist on: Learning to Use Wild Game," Department of Foresty, Wildlife and Fisheries Agricultural Extension Service, University of Tennessee, Knoxville, Tennessee.

Soc Clay. "That Old Black Magic," *The Tennessee Conservationist*, May-June, 1980.

Nancy Coleman, "Wild Plants: Ten for the Table," *South Carolina Wildlife*, May-June 1981.

Nancy Coleman, "The Flavor of Fire," *South Carolina Wildlife*, May-June 1979.

Joe DeFalco, "Field Dressing, Skinning, Butchering and Cooking Deer," *The Complete Deer Hunt*, Manhasset, New York, 1969.

Michael and Kay Farmer, *The Farmers' Wild Food Recipe Book*, Michael H. and Kay T. Farmer, Taylors, South Carolina, 1977.

Bertha V. Fontaine, Sue Turner, and Annette Reddell, *Seafood Adventures from the Gulf and South Atlantic*, Gulf and South Atlantic Fisheries Development Foundation, Inc., Tampa, Florida.

Jocasta Innes, *Notes From a Country Kitchen*, William Morrow and Company, Inc., New York, 1979.

The Junior League of Greenville, Inc., ed., *300 Years of Carolina Cooking*, Greenville, Carolina, 1970.

Pete Laurie, "Where There's Smoke, There's Fish," *South Carolina Wildlife*, May-June 1977.

Sheryl and Mel London, *The Fish-Lovers' Cookbook*, Rodale Press, Emmaus, Pennsylvania, 1980.

Anne Moise, "A Taste of Autumn," *South Carolina Wildlife*, November-December 1972.

Ethel McCutcheon Moise, ed., *Cookbook of the Family Favorites*, Book II, Sumter Printing Co., 1977.

Charles J. Moore, Donald L. Hammond, and DeWitt O. Myatt, *A Guide to Saltwater Recreational Fisheries in South Carolina*, S.C. Wildlife and Marine Resources Department, Charleston, South Carolina, 1980.

Charles J. Moore, ed., *A Recreational Guide to Oystering, Clamming, Shrimping & Crabbing in South Carolina*, S.C. Wildlife and Marine Resources Department, Charleston, South Carolina, 1979.

Margaret Pridgen and Cassie Griffin, "Dipping, Digging & Dragging," *South Carolina Wildlife*, July-August 1977.

Blanch S. Rhett; Lettie Gay, ed.; *Two Hundred Years of Charleston Cooking*, University of South Carolina Press, Columbia, South Carolina, 1976.

Sarah Rutledge; Anne Wells Rutledge, ed.; *The Carolina Housewife*, University of South Carolina Press, Columbia, South Carolina, 1976.

Bill Sizer, *"Now That You've Got It, What're You Gonna Do With It?"*, Arizona Game and Fish Department, Pheonix, Arizona, 1961.

Jame B. Trefethan, *An American Crusade for Wildlife*, Winchester Press, New York, New York, 1975.

Jan Wongrey, *Southern Fish and Seafood Cookbook*, The Sandlapper Store, Inc., Lexington, South Carolina, 1975.

Jan Wongrey, *Southern Wildfowl and Wild Game Cookbook*, The Sandlapper Store, Inc., Lexington, South Carolina, 1976.

Jasper Guy Woodruff, *Tree Nuts: Production, Processing, Products*, 2nd ed., AVI Publishing Co. Inc., Westport, Connecticut, 1979.

Acknowledgements

South Carolina Wildlife magazine gratefully acknowledges the labors of the original editors of this cookbook, Nancy Coleman Wooten and Julie Lumpkin, and their editorial assistants Tricia Way, Holly Kyzer and Elaine Gantt. Illustrations by Diane Kennedy, and original layout and design by Meg Economy. Special thanks also to Ben McC. Moise, Jim Bishop, Maria Latto, Lin Dunbar, Derrell Shipes, Gerald Moore and Billy McTeer. Revisions and editing on this edition by Linda Renshaw.

South Carolina Wildlife magazine is published by the South Carolina Wildlife and Marine Resources Department, Conservation Education and Communications Division, Prescott S. Baines, division director, and John E. Davis, magazine editor; P.O. Box 167, Columbia, SC 29202.

Index

DRESSING GAME

Beaver 51
Deer 52-55
    Butchering Chart 55
    Care of Deer Meat 53
Fowl 11-12
    Breasting 11-12
    Dressing 11
    Trussing 12
Opossum 49
Rabbit 46
Raccoon 49
Squirrel 44

FISH 82-114

Cleaning 83
Cooking 84
Filleting 83
Selecting at Market 82
Skinning (Catfish) 98

Basic Fish Recipes 85-92

Baked Fish I 88
Baked Fish II 89
Barbecue Fish 85
Basic Baked Fish 88
Basic Broiled Fish 90
Basic Pan Fried Fish 86
Fish and Cheese Soup 92
Fish Bake 89
Fish Stew 91
Fish the Easy Way 85
Fish 'n Dressing 89
Fried Fish 87
Fried Fish (Without the Frying Pan) 87
Fried Fish Sticks 87
Grilled Fish 85
Heavenly Broiled Fish 90
Marinated Fish 86
One-Fish Fish Stew 91
Smoked Fish 86
Tempura Fish 88
Tropical Broiled Fish 90

Catfish Stews 99-103

1-2-3 Catfish Stew 100
Bo's Riverbank Catfish Stew 101
Catfish Stew I 99
Catfish Stew II 99
Catfish Stew III 101
Catfish Stew IV 102
Catfish Stew V 103
*Congaree Swamp White Catfish
    Stew* 100
D.J.'s Catfish Stew 102
Garrett's Catfish Stew 101
Laddie Boone's Catfish Stew 103
Red Catfish Stew 103
Santee Catfish Stew 100

Freshwater Fish 92-98

Baked Stuffed Rock Fish 96
Boneless Baked Shad 94
Broiled Bluegill 92
Broiled Shad 93
Campfire Trout 98
Carp in Paprika Sauce 96
Catfish Delight 98
Fancy Striped Bass Grill 95
Fried Crappie Fillets 93
*Fried Rainbow, Brown or Brook
    Trout* 98
Hickory Smoked Striped Bass 95
Pike and Wild Rice 97
Sautéed Trout with Lemon Sauce 97
Shad Fillets with Clams and Olives 93
Shad Roe 94
Special Herbed Shad Roe 94

Saltwater Fish 104-114

*Baked Sea Bass with Spinach and Bread
    Stuffing* 104
Baked Tilefish with Vegetables 113
Barbecued Swordfish Steaks 114
Bluefish Salad Supreme 112
Cayman Fish 112
Elegant Holiday Pompano 109
Flounder Casserole 107
Flounder in Wine Sauce 105

Flounder Stew 107
Flounder with Crab Stuffing 106
Fried Whiting with Vegetables 105
Heavenly Snapper 109
Marinated King Mackerel Steaks 113
Marinated Shark 113
Oriental Swordfish Steaks 114
Poached Red Snapper in Aspic 110
Porgy Stew with Bacon-Cornbread
   Dumplings 108
Porgy with Cheese Filling 108
Sea Bass Fillets 104
Shark Steaks on the Grill 114
Smothered Flounder 107
Snapper and Spaghetti Casserole 110
Tangy Bluefish Fillets 112

GAME, WILD 11-79

FOWL, WILD 11-43
Basic Fowl Recipes 12-14
Baked Ruffed Grouse, Quail or
   Pheasant 14
Old-Fashioned "Country Way" of
   Cooking Quail or Doves 13
Quail or Dove Casserole 13
Smothered Game Birds 13
Bob-white Quail 33-36
Baked Quail 34
Deep-Fried Quail 33
Fried Quail 33
McGee Barbecue Quail (or
   chicken) 33
Pan Simmered Quail 35
Quail with Mushrooms and
   Onions 35
Smothered Quail 36
Southern Fried Quail 35
Wild Quail Casserole 34
Duck 14-24
Baggy Duck 19
Baked Duck 15
Baked Duck and Vegetables 19
Barbecued Duck 20
Braised Duck 23
Braised Wild Duck 16
Chesapeake Barbecued Duck 21
Dawson's Duck 21
Duck a la Sookie 20
Duck Bog 24
Duck Breasts in Durango Sauce 22
Duck 'n Chicken 21

Duck with Dressing 23
Duck with Gravy 17
Duck with Mushroom Gravy 24
Ducks in Orange Sauce 18
Easy Roasted Wild Duck 16
Fried Duck in Gravy 22
Pan-Fried Wild Duck 22
Poacher's Stew 24
Roast Duck 15
Roasted Duck (Rare) 15
Roasted Wild Duck 14
Smoked Duck 17
Tender Wild Ducks 16
Wild Duck 17
Wild Duck 20
Wild Duck with Mushrooms 23
Wild Duck with Sausage and
   Rice 19
Wild Duck with Stuffing 18
Goose 40-41
Roast Goose 40
Roasted Goose with Wheat and
   Apricot Stuffing 41
Marsh Hen 38-40
Marsh Hen I 39
Marsh Hen II 40
Marsh Hens in Gravy 39
Smothered Marsh Hens 39
Mourning Dove 25-32
Basic Grilled Doves 26
D.J.'s Doves 29
Dove-Broccoli Casserole 31
Dove Casserole 26
Dove Jambalaya 32
Dove on the Bed 32
Dove Stew for the R., G., B.M., S.D., &
   G.R.B.A. 31
Dove Supreme 25
Doves 25
Doves in Olive Oil 29
Doves in Orange Wine Sauce 30
Doves with Grapes 25
Grilled Doves 26
Mary Draper's Doves 28
Old Maria's Doves 28
Potted Doves 29
Simmered Doves 28
Sportsman's Dove Delight 30
Wild Doves in Casserole 27
Pheasant 42-43
Pheasant in Sour Cream 42

Roasted Pheasant and Sauerkraut 43
Smothered Pheasant in Wine 42
Wild Turkey 36-38
Baked Wild Turkey I 37
Baked Wild Turkey II 38
Baked Wild Turkey III 38
Fried Wild Turkey 37
Fried Wild Turkey Breast 37
Smoked Turkey 36
Wild Turkey 37
FURBEARERS 49-52
Beaver 51-52
Barbecued Beaver in Apple Juice 52
Beaver Stew 52
Opossum; see Raccoon and Opossum
Raccoon and Opossum 49-50
Bill Harritt's Coon Stew 50
Hunter's Pilau 50
Roast Opossum 50
GAME COMBINATIONS
Carolina Version of Kentucky Burgoo 72
Hunter's Pilau 50
Poacher's Stew 24
LARGE GAME 52-79
Bear 79
Bear Paw 79
Roast Bear 79
White-tailed Deer 52-78
Bar-B-Que Venison 60
Barbecue Deer Ribs 60
Barbecued Venison 61
Billy Tolar's Deer Roast 59
Bobby Ashley's Brown Gravy Venison Stew 73
Bobby Ashley's Fried Breakfast Venison 65
Broiled Venison 56
Butterfly Venison Loin 62
Carolina Version of Kentucky Burgoo 72
Danish Deer Pate 75
Danny Ford's Grilled Venison Loin 61
Deer-Sausage Casserole 68
Deer Steak 63
Deer Tenderloin with Red Wine Sauce 62
D.J.'s Venison 71
Fried Cubed Venison 65
Hawaiian Venison Roast 56

He-Man Venison Stew 73
Kim Ashley's Venison Stew 72
Lowcountry Charcoaled Venison 60
Old Bavarian Deer Goulash 70
Owings' Venison 66
Pan Fried Venison 65
Pat's Venison Salad 75
Poppa Pierce's Venison Hash 74
Roast Deer with Gravy 56
Roast Marinade of Venison 59
Round-O-Rack (Smoked Marinated Venison) 77
Stir-Fried Venison 76
Stuffed Venison Steaks 64
Tenderloin Roast 62
Texas Venison Chili 71
Venison Casserole 68
Venison Chili Con Carne 70
Venison Chuck Roast 59
Venison Fondue 76
Venison Fried in Mustard 64
Venison Hash 75
Venison Jerky 77
Venison Meatloaf 66
Venison Party Sausage 67
Venison Pepper Steak 63
Venison Pilau I 69
Venison Pilau II 70
Venison Poupon 64
Venison Ragout 69
Venison Roast I 57
Venison Roast II 57
Venison Roast III 58
Venison Roast IV 58
Venison Roast V 58
Venison Roast VI 58
Venison Steaks 63
Venison Stefado 68
Venison Stew I 73
Venison Stew II 74
Venison Stew with Wine 74
Venison Stroganoff I 67
Venison Stroganoff II 67
West Texas Fried Venison 66
Wild Game Ragout 69
SMALL GAME 43-48
Rabbit 46-48
Grilled Rabbit or Squirrel 47
Marinated Rabbit 47
Pat Robertson's Fried Rabbit or Squirrel 47

Pat Robertson's Rabbit and/or Squirrel
   Stew 48
Rabbit Stefado 47
Rabbit Stew 48
Squirrel 43-46
Bobby Ashley's Squirrel and Pork
   Chops 45
Broiled Squirrel 44
Carolina Squirrel Stew 45
Squirrel 'n Rice Stew 46
Sweet and Sour Crock Pot Squirrel 45

MARINADES AND
SAUCES

Barbecue Sauce for Venison 61
Ben's Variation on Bernaise Sauce 145
Capers Sauce for Fish 96
Fish Marinade Sauce 92
Garlic-Dill Cream Sauce 150
Laddie Boone's Barbecue Sauce or
   "Mop" 193
Marinade for Tough Creatures 77
Marinade for Venison Steak or Roast 78
Marinade for Venison Stefado 68
Mushroom-Walnut Sauce 97
Mustard Base Barbecue Sauce for
   Chicken or Pork 193
Onion Cream Sauce 158
Tony Chachere's All-Purpose Wild
   Game Marinade 78

OUTDOOR COOKING
192-199

CAMPFIRE COOKING 197-199
Procedure 197
Cooking in Ashes 198
**GRILLING 192-194 (see also
   Game, Fish sections)**
Laddie Boone's Barbecue Sauce or
   "Mop" 193
Laddie Boone's Hash for a Large
   Crowd 193
Mustard Base Barbecue Sauce for
   Chicken or Pork 193
IRON COOKWARE 194-195
Care 195
Seasoning 195
SMOKING 195-197
Preparation 195
Hot-Smoked Catfish 196

Round-O-Rack (Smoked Marinated
   Venison) 77
Smoked Duck 17
Smoked Fish 86
Smoked Fish Spread 196
Smoked Oysters 197
Smoked Shrimp 197
Smoked Turkey 36
Smoked Turkey 197
Venison Jerky 77

PLANTS, WILD 172-190

FRUITS 181-189
Berry Cobbler 181
Camp Cobbler (with Coleman
   oven) 182
Camp Cobbler (without oven) 182
Cocoa Palm 189
Crabapple Honey 186
Crabapple Jelly 187
Deep Dish Berry Pie 181
Elderberry Jam 184
Elderberry Juice 185
Elderflower Fritters 184
Elderflower Muffins 184
Fresh Fig Preserves 187
Fresh Huckleberry Pie 182
Jellies 185
Keisler's Ice Cream Delight 183
Palm Jelly 189
Pawley's Island Blackberry Cobbler 181
Persimmon Pudding 183
Prickly Pear Jam 188
Pyracantha Jelly 186
Quince Preserves 187
Spiced Gooseberries 186
Strawberry Freezer Jam 183
Wild Grape Jelly 187
Wild Muscadine Juice 185
NUTS 189-190
Fruit Cake 190
Pecan Fudge Pie 190
VEGETABLES 172-180
Candied Petals 180
Cattail Pancakes 174
Cattails 173
Chainy-Brier 177
Common Dandelions 174
Curled Dock 176
Dandelion Greens 175

Dandy Dandelions 175
Edible Fern Tips 174
Glasswort 180
Greenbrier 177
Pokeweed 172
Poor Man's Pepper Dip 180
Rose Hip Syrup 179
Sassafras Tea 176
Sweet Goldenrod Tea 176
Violet Jelly 178
Violets 178
Wood-Sorrels 178

REFERENCES 217-218

REFERENCE TABLES 211-216

Can Size Chart 214
Equivalency Table 214
Fat Content of Various Fish 212
Meat, Poultry, and Seafood
  Glossary 215
Nutritional Values in Meat 211
Salad Seasoning with Herbs 216
Substitutions for a Missing
  Ingredient 213

SHELLFISH 115-154

Blue Crab 128-138
Preparation 128
Boiled Carolina Blue Crabs 131
Crab and Guinea Squash
  Casserole 136
Crab Casserole "To Taste" 135
Crab Dabs 134
Crab Imperial 132
Crab in Shells 134
Crab Meat Casserole 135
Crab Pizza 137
Crabmeat Dip 131
Creamy Crab Soup 130
Deviled Crab 134
Deviled Crabs 132
Dinnie Campbell's Crab
  Casserole 136
Doris's Cheesey Crab Dip 132
Fried Hard Crabs 131
Hot Crab Dip 131
Mama Ruth's Crab Casserole 136
Seafood Triangles 133

She-Crab Soup 130
Sister's Crab Meat Casserole 135
Six-Egg Crab Casserole 135
Softshells 138
Spoleto Spiral Salad 137
Calico Scallop 146-147
Charcoal Broiled Scallops 147
Scallop Kabobs 147
Scallop-Vegetable Salad 146
Eastern Oyster 142-145
Preparation 142
Alderman's Carpet Bag 145
Golden Oyster Stew 143
Oyster Pie 144
Oyster Ramekins 144
Pickled Oysters 144
Scalloped Oysters with
  Macaroni 145
Northern Clam 139-142
Preparation 139
Beach Clam 'Durves 141
Bennett's Clam Chowder 140
Campfire Clams 140
Clam Dip 142
Clamdigger Dip 142
Fried Clams 141
"Krick" Clam Delight 141
Murrells Inlet Clam Chowder 140
Steamed Clams with Broth 140
Rock Shrimp 127-128
Preparation 127
Rock Shrimp Hors D'Oeuvres 128
Seafood Combinations 148-154
Baked Seafood Salad 153
Beaufort Stew 150
Cold Day's Sea Island Chowder 152
Crab and Shrimp Pie 154
Crab Stew 151
Creole Bouillabaisse 151
Gumbo with Shrimp and Crab 149
Jambalaya 152
Kiawah Casserole 153
Lowcountry Fettucini 150
Seafood Gumbo I 148
Seafood Gumbo II 148
Seafood Quiche 154
Shrimp Puff Casserole 153

Wild food Orqinals
Tilapia p-201-200

Shrimp 115-127
Preparation 115
Alligator Pear and Shrimp
Salad 117
Beer Batter for Fried Shrimp 118
Charleston Shrimp Bake 123
Charleston Shrimp Breakfast 120
Flavorful Shrimp Salad 116
Fried Shrimp 118
Golden Shrimp Casserole 125
Lowcountry Breakfast 119
Marinated Shrimp I 117
Marinated Shrimp II 117
Shanghai Stir-Fry Vegetables with
Quick-Fry Shrimp 118
Shrimp and Rice 122
Shrimp and Wild Rice 124
Shrimp Creole I 120
Shrimp Creole II 121
Shrimp Creole III 121
Shrimp Creole IV 121
Shrimp Curry 124
Shrimp Devils 126
Shrimp Dip 127
Shrimp Fried Rice 122
Shrimp Fried Rice with Bacon 122
Shrimp in Wine Sauce 123
Shrimp Mold Spread 127
Shrimp 'n Rice 122
Shrimp Quiche 125
Shrimp Rice 123
Shrimp Salad 116
Shrimp Scampi 126
Shrimp Stew 124
Shrimp-Stuffed Potatoes 125
Shrimp with Snow Peas 119
Stuffed Shrimp Eggs 126
Stone Crab 138-139
Steamed Stone Crab Claws 139

SIDE DISHES

Giblet Gravy 41
Hog Roast Slaw 193
Hushpuppies for a Crowd 194
Mushroom Rice 27
Red Horse Bread 194

Rice for Shrimp Creole 120
Sautéed Mushrooms with
Vegetables 78
Slaw 27
Squashpuppies 87
Wild Rice 34
UNUSUAL FOODS
156-169

Bullfrog Legs 157-158
Preparation 157
Frog Legs Westfield 158
Frog's Legs 158
Frog's Legs a la Creole 158
Crawfish 159-161
Bell Peppers Stuffed with Crawfish 160
Crawfish in the Bush 159
Crawfish Jambalaya 161
Crawfish Linguine 159
Flo's Etouffee 160
Eel 161-162
Reggie's Fried Eel 162
Garfish 162
Gar Balls Toogoodoo 162
More Oddities 167-169
Albert's Barbecued Pigeons 169
Coquina Soup 168
Freshwater Mussels 168
Periwinkles 167
Prairie Oyster 169
Sautéed Mullet Gizzards 168
Sea Trout Air Bladders 168
Octopus 163
Charcoal-Broiled Octopus 163
Octopus in Tomato Wine Sauce 163
Snapping Turtle 156-157
Moise's Snapping Turtle Stew 157
Turtle Stew 156
Squid 164-165
Squid Vinaigrette 165
Stuffed Squid a la Maria 164
Whelk 165-167
Conch Stew 165
Ground Conch Seafood Cake 166
More Whelk 166
Seviche 166
Whelk Stew 167